Keyboard Shortcuts for Micro...

cut here

Command	Keyboard
Access pull-down menus	F10
Bold	Ctrl+B
Cancel	Esc
Center paragraph	Ctrl+E
Change font size	Ctrl+Shift+P
Clear	Del
Close document	Ctrl+W or Ctrl+F4
Close or Exit	Alt+F4
Copy	Ctrl+C or Ctrl+Insert
Copy format	Ctrl+Shift+C
Copy text	Shift+F2
Cut	Ctrl+X or Shift+Del
Decrease font size	Ctrl+Shift+,
Delete previous word	Ctrl+Backspace
Delete word	Ctrl+Del
Display Help	F1
Find	Ctrl+F
Find next	Shift+F4
Go To	Ctrl+G or F5
Increase font size	Ctrl+Shift+.
Insert page break	Ctrl+Enter
Italic	Ctrl+I
Justify paragraph	Ctrl+J
Left-align paragraph	Ctrl+L
New file	Ctrl+N
Next cell	Tab
Next misspelling	Alt+F7
Open document	Ctrl+O
Paste	Ctrl+V or Shift+Insert
Paste format	Ctrl+Shift+V
Previous cell	Shift+Tab
Print	Ctrl+P
Print Preview	Ctrl+F2
Proofing	F7
Repeat	F4 or Alt+Enter
Right-align paragraph	Ctrl+R
Save	Ctrl+S
Save As	F12
Select All	Ctrl+A
Style	Ctrl+Shift+S
Thesaurus	Shift+F7
Underline	Ctrl+U
Undo	Ctrl+Z

Microsoft Windows 98 Quick Reference

To Perform This Operation:	Do This:
Change your desktop settings	Right-click anywhere on the open desktop.
Connect to the Internet and check your email	Click the Outlook Express icon on the Quick Launch toolbar.
Connect to the Internet and surf the Web	Click the Internet Explorer icon on the Quick Launch toolbar.
Copy a file or folder	Pull down the Edit menu and select Copy.
Cut a file or folder	Pull down the Edit menu and select Cut.
Delete a file or folder	Pull down the Edit menu and select Delete.
Display context-sensitive pop-up menus	Right-click an object.
Display Windows Help	Click the Start button and select Help.
Find a file or folder	Click the Start button, select Find, and then select Files and Folders.
Launch Works Suite 2000	Click the Start button, select Programs, then select Microsoft Works.
Manage your files	Click the My Computer icon on your desktop.
Open the Control Panel	Click the Start button, select Settings, and then select Control Panel.
Paste a file or folder	Pull down the Edit menu and select Paste.
Reboot your computer	Press Ctrl+Alt+Del.
Rename a file or folder	Right-click the filename and select Rename.
Switch between open programs	Press Alt+Tab.
Undelete a file	Open the Recycle Bin, right-click the filename, and then select Restore.

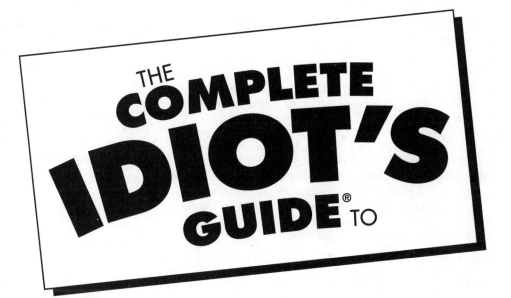

THE COMPLETE IDIOT'S GUIDE® TO

Microsoft® Works

Suite 2000

by Michael Miller

alpha
books
que®

A Division of Macmillan USA
201 W. 103rd Street, Indianapolis, IN 46290

Trademarks

Warning and Disclaimer

Associate Publisher
Greg Wiegand

Acquisitions Editor
Angelina Ward

Development Editor
Gregory Harris

Managing Editor
Thomas F. Hayes

Project Editor
Casey Kenley

Copy Editor
Kate Givens

Indexer
Sandra Henselmeier
Greg Pearson

Proofreader
Tricia Sterling

Technical Editor
Mark Hall

Illustrator
Judd Winick

Team Coordinator
Sharry Gregory

Interior Designer
Nathan Clement

Cover Designer
Michael Freeland

Copy Writer
Eric Bogert

Production
Brad Lenser

Contents at a Glance

Contents

ix

xiii

About the Author

Michael Miller is a writer, speaker, consultant, and the president/founder of The Molehill Group, a strategic consulting and authoring firm based in Carmel, Indiana. More information about the author and The Molehill Group can be found at www.molehillgroup.com, and you can email the author directly at author@molehillgroup.com.

Mr. Miller has been an important force in the book publishing business since 1987, and served for more than a decade in publishing management at Macmillan Publishing, the world's largest reference publisher. There are few who know as much about the computer industry—how it works, and why—as does Mr. Miller.

As the author of more than 30 bestselling non-fiction books, Mr. Miller writes about a variety of topics. His most recent books include *The Official PrintMaster Guide, The Complete Idiot's Guide to Fixing Your #$%@ PC, The Complete Idiot's Guide to Online Auctions, The Complete Idiot's Guide to Online Search Secrets,* and *The Complete Idiot's Guide to Surfing the Internet with WebTV.*

From his first book (*Ventura Publisher Techniques and Applications*, published in 1988) to this, his latest title, Michael Miller has established a reputation for practical advice, technical accuracy, and an unerring empathy for the needs of his readers. Many regard Mr. Miller as the consummate reporter on new technology for an everyday audience.

Dedication

To Mike and Sandy Richards, good friends for many years and in many places.

Acknowledgments

Special thanks to the usual suspects at Macmillan, including but not limited to Greg Wiegand, Angelina Ward, Gregory Harris, Kate Givens, Casey Kenley, and Mark Hall.

Tell Us What You Think!

As the reader of this book, *you* are our most important critic and commentator. We value your opinion and want to know what we're doing right, what we could do better, what areas you'd like to see us publish in, and any other words of wisdom you're willing to pass our way.

As an Associate Publisher for Alpha Books, I welcome your comments. You can fax, email, or write me directly to let me know what you did or didn't like about this book—as well as what we can do to make our books stronger.

Please note that I cannot help you with technical problems related to the topic of this book, and that due to the high volume of mail I receive, I might not be able to reply to every message.

When you write, please be sure to include this book's title and author as well as your name and phone or fax number. I will carefully review your comments and share them with the author and editors who worked on the book.

Fax: 317-581-4666

Email: consumer@mcp.com

Mail: Greg Wiegand, Associate Publisher
          Alpha Books
          201 West 103rd Street
          Indianapolis, IN 46290 USA

Introduction

If you've ever strolled through the aisles of a computer superstore, having your mind boggled by the thousands and thousands of color and confusing software boxes, you've probably wondered just *why* all these programs exist. Isn't it possible to have one single program you can use for *all* your computer-based tasks?

Well, dear reader, that program exists, and you probably already have it installed on your computer's hard disk. The program? *Microsoft Works Suite 2000.*

To be fair, Works Suite really isn't a single program—it's a *suite* of applications, tied together through a central Task Launcher. But within this suite are 12 applications that can perform just about any task you can think of, from writing letters to cataloging recipes to designing greeting cards to handling your personal finances. The programs you find on the Works Task Launcher can do all these things, and more.

But just because you have Works Suite 2000 doesn't mean you know how to use it—or use all of its components. With twelve different applications included—and a manual thin enough to count as bathroom reading—how do you learn everything you need to know to get the most out of the program?

The answer to that question is literally right in front of your face—you read this book, *The Complete Idiot's Guide to Microsoft Works Suite 2000.*

Who This Book Is For

The Complete Idiot's Guide to Microsoft Works Suite 2000 is written for anyone who is using the latest version of Microsoft Works Suite—whether you bought it in a box, upgraded from an older version, or found it preinstalled on your new PC. You don't even need to know much about computers to use this book, since I start out with "primers" on both Windows 98 and the Internet. For many users, you can use this book as your *only* book to help you use both Works Suite 2000 and your new computer.

What You'll Find in This Book

The Complete Idiot's Guide to Microsoft Works Suite 2000 is composed of 24 chapters, organized into three major sections:

➤ Part 1, "Getting Started," is your introduction to Windows 98, the Internet, and Works Suite 2000. These chapters serve as primers to get you up and running—fast—with your new PC and Works Suite 2000.

➤ Part 2, "Learn the Programs," is your guide to each of the applications that comprise Works Suite 2000. Here you'll find 12 chapters on the 12 components of Works Suite 2000: Word, Works Spreadsheet, Works Database, Works Calendar, Address Book, Money, Home Publishing, Picture It! Express, Expedia Streets & Trips, Encarta Encyclopedia, Outlook Express, and Internet Explorer.

➤ Part 3, "Get Productive," features step-by-step instructions on how to complete nine common tasks, using the appropriate Works Suite 2000 applications. Here you'll learn how to create envelopes and labels, a large merged mailing (complete with personalized form letters), a newsletter, a school report (complete with research on CD and on the Internet), a home inventory, a home budget, party invitations and favors, personalized holiday cards, and sports schedules and statistics.

At the back of the book you'll find "The Complete Idiot's Glossary of Terms," where all the fancy phrases in the book are defined, in plain English. And if you turn to the inside of the front cover, you'll see a tear-out card with the most useful commands and operations from all of the Works Suite applications.

How to Do the Things You See in This Book

To get the most out of this book, you should know how it is designed. I've tried to put things together in such a way as to make reading the book both rewarding and fun. So, here's what to do when you see any of the following:

➤ Web page addresses (URLs) are presented in a `monospace font`; you can enter the underlined text into your browser's Address box to go to that page.

➤ Anything you need to enter—into a search box, for example, or into a form—are presented in **bold text**; enter this text as-written to proceed.

➤ New terms are presented in *italicized text*; pay close attention to these terms.

Extras

To pack as much information as possible into *The Complete Idiot's Guide to Microsoft Works Suite 2000*, you are presented with additional tips and advice as you read the book. These elements enhance your knowledge, or point out important pitfalls to avoid. Along the way, you'll find the following elements:

Work Smart

These tips offer you advice on how to work more efficiently and effectively with a particular Works Suite 2000 application.

Stop Work

These warnings point out common problems and pitfalls that—with a little fore-sight—you can hopefully avoid.

Background Work

These notes reference additional information that can help you better understand the task at hand.

Get Ready to Work

Still here? It's time to get started, so turn the page and prepare to get busy—with Microsoft Works Suite 2000!

Part 1
Getting Started

New to Works Suite 2000? New to the Internet? New to computing in general? Then read these three chapters for a crash course on Windows 98, the Internet, and Works Suite—you'll learn just what you need to know, and not a byte more!

Chapter 1

Make Your Computer Work for You: A Microsoft Windows 98 Primer

In This Chapter

➤ Discover the key features of Windows 98

➤ Learn how to perform common Windows operations

➤ Find out how to cut, copy, paste, delete, and undelete files

Before you can use Works Suite 2000, you need to know how to use Windows 98, because Windows 98 essentially runs your computer for you. If you know how to use Windows 98, it will be a lot easier to learn how to use all the components in Works Suite 2000.

Windows 98 is a piece of software called an *operating system*. An operating system does what its name implies—it *operates* your computer *system*, working in the background every time you turn on your PC.

Every program that runs, every command you issue, every option that is selected has to filter through the operating system to be executed by your computer hardware. Your computer won't run without an operating system—and Windows 98 is the operating system used by almost all new personal computers sold today.

The History of Windows (*Bor-*ing!)

Microsoft Windows 98 is the friendly "face" of your computer system, the thing you see every time you power on, the system you interface with on a constant basis. Not only does it control your hardware, but it also presents a variety of functions and features you can use to ease the pain of personal computing.

The version of Windows on your personal computer (Windows 98, presumably) is not the first version of Windows ever released. There have been numerous versions of Windows released over the years, starting with version 1.0 back in the late 1980s.

95, 98... Whatever It Takes

Works Suite 2000 is compatible with either Windows 95 or Windows 98—so, unless you're using a really old version of Windows (3.0 or 3.1), you don't have to upgrade to use Works.

Before Windows, the operating system used on most PCs was the character-based MS-DOS—also published by Microsoft. In the DOS environment, users had to issue a series of obscure text commands to perform even the simplest of tasks; with Windows, these same tasks could be executed by using a mouse to click on an icon or pull down a menu.

Windows 2000?

You may have heard about another version of Windows called *Windows 2000*. This operating system (previously referred to as Windows NT 5.0) is a networked operating system that looks and feels a lot like Windows 98, but is optimized to run on large networks in a corporate environment. Windows 98, on the other hand, is a *personal* operating system, designed to run on individual computers. If you control your own PC, you should run Windows 98; if someone else (like an IT department) controls your PC, he may elect to run Windows 2000. From a user's perspective there shouldn't be much difference between the two.

Starting and Stopping Windows

Before you can use Windows 98, you have to launch it. And, after it's started, it helps to know how to stop it, as well.

Launching Windows

There is only one way to launch Windows 98: Turn on your computer!

Windows starts automatically every time you turn on your computer. Although you will see lines of text flashing onscreen during the initial startup, Windows loads automatically and goes on to display the Windows desktop.

Shutting Down Windows

When you finish running Windows applications and want to turn off the computer, you first must correctly exit Windows by using the Shut Down command—you shouldn't just turn off your computer with Windows still running (or you could damage your system!).

Shut Down Properly!

Do *not* turn your computer off without shutting down Windows. You could lose data and settings that are temporarily stored in your system's memory. Wait for the message saying it is safe to turn off your computer.

What if your computer just hangs there, without displaying the shut off message? If you've waited a few minutes without any activity on your PC (lights flashing, disk drives whirring, and so on), it's probably hung up—and you'll have to shut down your PC manually, using the on/off button. When you do this, Windows will automatically run ScanDisk (a utility that analyzes the status of your hard disk) the next time you start up, just in case any files were damaged during the emergency shutdown.

To shut down Windows, first save any documents and other data in applications that are open, and then exit all applications. Now click the Start button and select Shut Down. When the Shut Down Windows dialog box appears, select one of the following options (which may vary depending on your configuration):

➤ Stand by
➤ Shut Down

➤ Restart

➤ Restart in MS-DOS Mode

Choose Shut Down, and then click OK. If prompted as to your real intentions, choose Yes, and then turn off your computer when you see the message that says it is safe to do so. Most newer computers—including most laptops—automatically shut off your computer when the "safe to shut off" message appears, no action necessary on your part.

To restart your computer (reboot) without shutting down completely—after you install a new program, for example, or if your PC is starting to act up a little—choose the Restart option in the Shut Down Windows dialog box. To simply restart Windows without restarting your entire computer system, hold down the Shift key when you choose the Restart option, and click OK. (This performs a much faster "soft" reboot.)

Many new PCs now come withspecial "sleep" modes (also called *stand by* or *suspend* modes) that let you power down your system without shutting it off. When you select Stand By from the Shut Down Windows dialog box or the Start menu, your PC doesn't have to go through the lengthy "boot" process when you next use it, it just "wakes up" instead.

To Sleep, Perchance to Dream

When your PC is in sleep mode, it looks like it's completely shut down. The difference is that "awakening" from sleep mode takes much less time than fully booting up your PC from a complete shutdown. Note, however, that going into sleep mode does not reboot your machine, so if you need to turn your computer on and off for any reason (to recover "lost" memory, or refresh your system in the wake of a program crash), sleep mode won't do the job. Also note that your computer will go into sleep mode after a preset time of inactivity—and that means inactivity from you, the user. Activation of a screen saver will not affect the timing of sleep mode activation.

Understanding the Windows Desktop

The Windows 98 desktop includes a number of shortcut icons, a taskbar, and other recognizable elements. However, if you elect to activate Windows 98's *single-click mode*, the desktop changes a bit—you still have all the old elements, but now they behave like hyperlinks on a Web page; you highlight icons by hovering over them, and you launch applications by single-clicking icons. (*Without* single-click mode activated, you single-click to highlight and double-click to launch.)

Activating Single-Click Mode—and Learning How to Hover

To make your Windows 98 desktop work like a Web page (single-clicking instead of double-clicking), click the Start button, select Settings, and then select Folder Options. When the Folder Options dialog box appears, select Web Style, and then click OK. (To return to the traditional double-click mode, select Classic Style from the Folder Options dialog box.)

By the way, if you activate single-click mode, you have to learn a new way to highlight items. This new technique is called *hovering*, which involves placing the cursor over an item without clicking your mouse. When an object is hovered over, it is automatically highlighted, and the cursor turns from an arrow into a hand shape.

Select this icon to display a list of drives, folders, and files on your system.

Open application window

Figure 1.1

The Windows 98 desktop—click any item to make something happen!

Desktop

Minimized application—click to maximize the application.

Drag files here to delete them from your system.

Click here to display the Start menu.

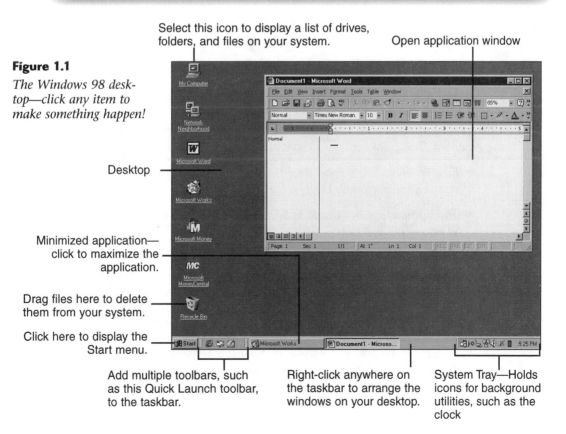

Add multiple toolbars, such as this Quick Launch toolbar, to the taskbar.

Right-click anywhere on the taskbar to arrange the windows on your desktop.

System Tray—Holds icons for background utilities, such as the clock

The major parts of the Windows desktop are

➤ **Start button.** Opens the Start menu, which has submenus leading to many other folders and applications.

➤ **Taskbar.** Displays buttons for your open applications and windows, as well as different toolbars for different tasks.

➤ **Toolbar.** A separate button bar that can be attached to the main taskbar, specific to Windows 98. Windows 98 includes toolbars for Web Addresses, links to favorite Web sites, Desktop icons, and Quick Launch of Web utilities; in addition, you can create your own personalized toolbars.

➤ **System Tray.** The part of the taskbar that holds the clock, volume control, and icons for other utilities that run in the background of your system.

➤ **Shortcut icons.** Allow you to launch applications and load documents with a single click of the mouse.

➤ **Windows.** When open on the desktop, can be moved around and resized.

Background Work

Learn More About Windows 98

This book is only so big; there isn't enough space here to deal with everything you want to know about Works Suite 2000 *and* Windows basics, too. So if you're a complete Windows novice, I recommend that you examine one of the following excellent Que books to learn more about the subject at hand:

➤ *Easy Windows 98*, a good step-by-step, full-color, visually oriented introduction for beginning users.

➤ *The Complete Idiot's Guide to Windows 98*, an unintimidating overview of Windows ins and outs.

➤ *Special Edition Using Windows 98*, a comprehensive reference that tells you everything you could ever want to xknow about Windows.

If you're having *problems* with Windows 98 or your personal computer, you also might want to check out a book that I authored, *The Complete Idiot's Guide to Fixing Your #$%@! PC*. This books is a well-written (well, I certainly think so!), user-friendly guide for troubleshooting all sorts of PC-related problems.

Important Windows Operations

Now, to use Windows 98 efficiently you need to master a few simple operations—such as pointing and clicking.

Left Is Right

For the purposes of discussion, I'll assume that you're right-handed, and therefore using the left mouse button as your main mouse button and the right mouse button as your secondary mouse button. If, however, you're a southpaw, you can select the Mouse icon in the Windows Control Panel to reconfigure Windows so that your mouse operates backwards—that is, so the right mouse button is your main mouse button and the left mouse button is your secondary mouse button. So if you're left-handed, when I refer to the right mouse button, you need to transpose that to mean the left mouse button, and vice versa. Right?

Pointing and Clicking

The most common mouse operation is *pointing and clicking*. Simply move the mouse so that the pointer is pointing to the object you want to select, and then click the left mouse button once. Pointing and clicking is an effective way to select menu items, directories, and files.

Right Is Right

Windows and many Windows applications use the right mouse button to display a pop-up menu containing commands that directly relate to the selected object. Refer to your individual programs to see if and how they use the right mouse button.

Double-Clicking

If you're using the double-click mode of Windows 98, you'll need to *double-click* on an item to activate an operation. This involves pointing at something onscreen with the pointer, and then clicking the left mouse button twice in rapid succession. For example, to open program groups or launch individual programs, simply double-click on a specific icon. (With Windows 98's single-click mode activated, you just single click to perform the same operations.)

Dragging and Dropping

Dragging is a variation of clicking. To drag an object, point at it with the pointer, and then press and hold down the left mouse button. Move the mouse without releasing the mouse button, and drag the object to a new location. When you're done moving the object, release the mouse button to drop it onto the new location.

Launching Applications

The easiest way to launch an application is to either click (in single-click mode) or double-click (in double-click mode) its desktop icon or Start menu item. There are several other ways you can start a program, however.

If you know the path and name of the program you want to launch, you can click the Start button and select Run. When the Run dialog box appears, type the program path and name into the Open box and click the OK button; the program launches automatically.

If you don't know the name of the program, you can still launch it via My Computer or Windows Explorer. Simply scroll through the folders and files until you find the file you want, and then click or double-click on the filename, and the program launches. It's as simple as that.

Using Dialog Boxes, Tabs, and Buttons

When Windows or an application requires a complex set of inputs, you are often presented with a *dialog box*. A dialog box is like a form where you can input various parameters and make various choices—and then register those inputs and choices when you click the OK button.

There are various types of dialog boxes, each one customized to the task at hand. However, most dialog boxes share a set of common features, including

> ➤ **Buttons.** Most buttons either register your inputs or open an auxiliary dialog box. The most common buttons are OK (to register your inputs and close the dialog box), Cancel (to close the dialog box without registering your inputs), and Apply (to register your inputs without closing the dialog box). Click a button once to activate it.

➤ **Tabs.** These allow a single dialog box to display multiple "pages" of information. Think of each tab, arranged across the top of the dialog box, as a "thumbtab" to the individual page in the dialog box below it. Click a tab to change to that particular page of information.

➤ **Text boxes.** These are empty boxes where you type in a response. Position your cursor over the empty input box, click your left mouse button, and begin typing.

➤ **Lists.** These are lists of available choices; lists can either scroll or drop down from what looks like an input box. Select an item from the list with your mouse; you can select multiple items in some lists by holding down the Ctrl key while you click with your mouse.

➤ **Check boxes.** These are boxes that let you select (or deselect) various stand-alone options.

➤ **Option buttons.** These are the round "boxes" that you check to select an option; typically, selecting one option *deselects* all other options.

➤ **Sliders.** These are sliding bars that let you select increments between two extremes—like a sliding volume control on an audio system.

➤ **Spinner arrows.** These are controls that let you "spin" through a number of selections by clicking the up or down arrow buttons.

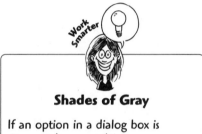

Shades of Gray

If an option in a dialog box is dimmed (or grayed), that means it isn't available for the current task.

Below is a common dialog box—the Display Properties dialog box. (To display this dialog box, right-click an empty part of the desktop, and then select Properties from the pop-up menu.) As you can see, this dialog box includes buttons, tabs, lists, and check boxes —everything *except* a text box and a slider.

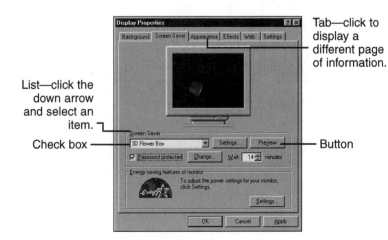

Tab—click to display a different page of information.

List—click the down arrow and select an item.

Check box

Button

Figure 1.2

In the Display Properties dialog box, you can set all sorts of parameters for your desktop and display.

Fiddling with Files

All of the information on your computer is stored in *files*. A file is nothing more than a collection of data of some sort. Everything on your computer's hard drive is a separate file, with its own name, location, and properties. The data (information) in a file can be a document from an application (such as a Works worksheet or a Word document), or it can be the executable code for the application itself.

Every file has its own unique name. A defined structure exists for naming files, and its conventions must be followed for Windows to understand exactly what file you want when you try to access one. Each filename must consist of three parts, as described in Table 1.1.

Table 1.1   Parts of a Filename

Filename Part	Description
Name	The first part of the filename, which can include either letters or numbers.
Period	The period following the file's name acts as a divider between the name and the extension.
Extension	This last part of the name, used to denote various types of files.

Putting it all together, you get filenames that appear onscreen something like this: FILENAME.EXT.

Background Work

Naming Files

In the "old days" of personal computing (pre-Windows 95), filenames had to conform to what was called the "eight dot three" (8.3) convention—eight characters for the name, a period, and then a three-character extension. In Windows 95 and Windows 98, the filename can now contain up to 256 characters, in any combination (including multiple periods—and spaces!). This ability is called *long file naming*.

Windows stores files in folders. A *folder* is like a master file; each folder can contain both files and additional folders. The exact location of a file is called its *path* and contains all the folders leading to the file. For example, a file named FILENAME.DOC that exists in the SYSTEM folder that is itself contained in the WINDOWS folder on your C:\ drive has a path that looks like this: C:\WINDOWS\SYSTEM\ FILENAME.DOC.

Mastering files and folders is a key aspect of using your computer. You may need to copy files from one folder to another, or from your hard disk to a floppy disk. To do this, you use one of Windows' two file-management tools—My Computer or Windows Explorer.

Using My Computer and Windows Explorer to Manage Your Files

My Computer is a file-management tool that lets you manage your hard drive(s), mapped network drives, peripheral drives, folders, and files. My Computer is extremely versatile; in Windows 98 you can use My Computer to view the contents of the Control Panel and Printers folders, as well as to browse pages on the World Wide Web. To open My Computer, just select the My Computer icon on your desktop.

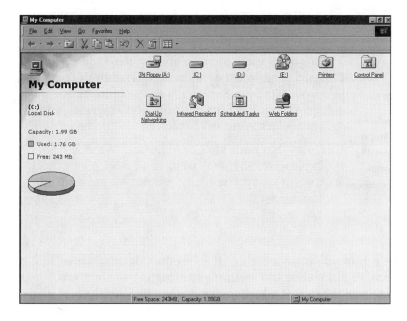

Figure 1.3

To manage your files, use My Computer...

Figure 1.4

...or use Windows Explorer; they both perform the same file-management tasks.

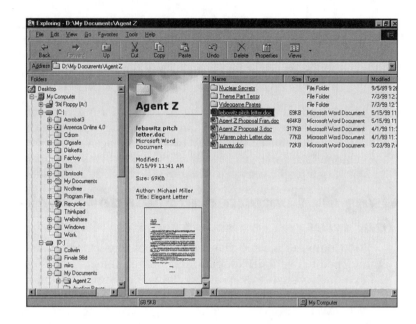

Too Many Explorers

Don't confuse Windows Explorer—which you use to view and manipulate folders and files—with Internet Explorer, Microsoft's Web browser.

Windows Explorer is another Windows file-management tool, similar to My Computer. It differs from My Computer in that it displays two different *panes* of information; the left pane contains a directory tree of all the folders on your system, and the contents for selected items are displayed in the right pane. Windows Explorer is a little more difficult to open; click the Start button, select Programs, and then select Windows Explorer.

Know that both My Computer and Windows Explorer do the same things and work pretty much the same way. Use whichever one you're most comfortable with.

Copy Files

Copying a file or folder is how you place a copy of it at another location (either in another folder or on another disk) while still retaining the original where it was. Copying is different from moving in that when you copy an item, the original remains; when you move an item, the original is no longer present in the original location.

18

There are nine different ways you can copy a file in Windows:

➤ **The toolbar method.** From My Computer or Windows Explorer, highlight the file to copy and click the Copy button on the toolbar; paste the copy into a new folder by navigating to the folder and then clicking the Paste button on the toolbar.

➤ **The pull-down menu method.** Select the file to copy and then pull down the Edit menu and select Copy; paste the copy into a new folder by pulling down the Edit menu and selecting Paste.

➤ **The pop-up menu method.** Right-click the file to copy and select Copy from the pop-up menu; paste the file into a new folder by right-clicking anywhere in the new folder and selecting Paste from the pop-up menu.

➤ **The Send To method.** To copy a file to another disk drive, right-click the file to copy, select Send To, and then select the drive (typically A or B) from the pop-up menu. (This method copies files into the root folder of the destination drive; you can't select a different destination folder.)

➤ **The drag-and-drop method.** Select the file to copy, and then hold down the Ctrl key while you drag it to the new location; release the mouse button and the Ctrl key to drop the copy. (If you drag and drop a file onto a *different drive*— from C to A, say—the file is automatically copied without need to hold down the Ctrl key during the operation.)

➤ **The right-drag method.** Select the file to copy, and then *right-drag* the file to the new location. (Right-dragging is dragging while holding down the *right* mouse button.) When you release the mouse button, you'll be presented with a pop-up menu; select Copy Here.

➤ **The shortcut key method #1.** Select the file to copy, and then press Ctrl+Insert; press Shift+Insert to paste the copied file.

➤ **The shortcut key method #2.** Select the file to copy, and then press Ctrl+C; press Ctrl+V to paste the copied file.

➤ **The DOS method.** Finally, for anyone who was using a PC back in the 1980s, you can open a DOS window and type the following at the DOS Prompt: `copy filename.ext c:\newlocation\`, where *filename.ext* is the name of the file to copy, and *newlocation* is the folder you want to copy to.

Refreshing!

If you have moved, copied, or deleted some files and folders but don't see the changes, update your display by pulling down the View menu and selecting Refresh—or just press the F5 key.

Moving Files

Moving a file or folder is different from copying a file or folder. Moving deletes the item from its previous location and places it in a new location; copying leaves the original item where it was *and* creates a copy of the item elsewhere. In Windows there are seven different ways to move a file:

➤ **The toolbar method.** From My Computer or Windows Explorer, highlight the file to move and click the Cut button on the toolbar; paste the file into a new folder by clicking the Paste button on the toolbar.

➤ **The pull-down menu method.** Select the file to move, pull down the Edit menu, and then select Cut; paste the copy into a new folder by pulling down the Edit menu and selecting Paste.

➤ **The pop-up menu method.** Right-click the file to move and select Cut from the pop-up menu; paste the file into a new folder by right-clicking anywhere in the new folder and selecting Paste from the pop-up menu.

➤ **The drag-and-drop method.** Select the file to move, and then drag it to the new location; release the mouse button to drop the file into a new folder. (Note that this procedure, if used to drag files to a different drive, actually *copies* the file, rather than moving it; this method only works when moving a file to a different directory on the same drive.)

➤ **The right-drag method.** Select the file to move, and then *right-drag* the file to the new location. When you release the mouse button, you'll be presented with a pop-up menu; select Move Here.

➤ **The shortcut key method.** Select the file to move, and then press Ctrl+X; press Ctrl+V to paste the file into a new folder.

➤ **The DOS method.** Another option for old-timers—open a DOS window and type the following at the DOS Prompt: `move filename.ext x:\newlocation\`, where *x* is the destination drive and *newlocation* is the destination folder.

Deleting Files

Because disk space is a resource you don't want to waste, you should delete files and folders you no longer need. Note that deleting a file is different from cutting a file. When you cut a file (in preparation for a move), you keep it in memory for pasting; when you delete a file, you send it to the Recycle Bin.

There are eight different ways to delete a file in Windows:

➤ **The delete key method.** Highlight the file and press the Del key on your keyboard.

➤ **The *permanent* delete key method.** Highlight the file and press Shift+Del; this will bypass the Recycle Bin and permanently delete the file, with no restoration possible.

➤ **The toolbar method.** From My Computer or Windows Explorer, highlight the file to move and click the Delete button on the toolbar.

➤ **The pull-down menu method.** Select the file to move, pull down the File menu, and then select Delete.

➤ **The pop-up menu method.** Right-click the file to move and select Delete from the pop-up menu.

➤ **The drag-and-trash method.** Select the file to move, and then drag it to the Recycle Bin.

➤ **The drag-and-*permanently*-trash method.** Select the file to move, hold down the Shift key, and drag it to the Recycle Bin; this will bypass the Recycle Bin and permanently delete the file, with no restoration possible. (Note, however, that because you can also use the Shift key to select multiple files, you may want to start the drag maneuver before you press the Shift key for permanent deletion.)

➤ **The DOS method.** Yet another option for mouse-haters from the ancient days of personal computing; open a DOS window and type the following at the DOS Prompt: `del filename.ext` where *filename.ext* is the file you want to delete.

Undeleting Files

If you delete a file and later decide you made a mistake, you're in luck. Windows stores deleted files in the Recycle Bin for a period of time—if you have deleted the file recently, it should still be in the Recycle Bin.

As long as a deleted file is still in the Recycle Bin, you can easily restore it to its previous location. Start by opening the Recycle Bin by selecting its icon on the desktop. When the Recycle Bin opens, locate the file or folder you want to restore. Right-click the item's icon and choose Restore from the pop-up menu.

If you open the Recycle Bin and you can't find the file you're looking for, you're out of luck—you waited too long, and the file has been permanently deleted from your hard disk.

Deleting Files—*Permanently*

If you want to free up some extra disk space, you can manually empty the Recycle Bin. Doing so permanently removes deleted files from your hard disk. Just right-click the Recycle Bin icon and, when the pop-up menu appears, select Empty Recycle Bin. When the Confirm File Delete dialog box appears, click Yes to completely erase the files, or click No to continue storing the files in the Recycle Bin.

In addition, if you use Shift+Del to delete a file (or hold down the Shift key while dragging a file to the Recycle Bin), the file will be permanently deleted without being stored first in the Recycle Bin.

Files do not stay in the Recycle Bin indefinitely. By default, the deleted files in the Recycle Bin can occupy 10 percent of your hard disk space. (You can change this setting by right-clicking the Recycle Bin icon, selecting Properties from the pop-up menu, and adjusting the slider in the Recycle Bin Properties dialog box.) When you have enough deleted files to exceed 10 percent of your disk space, the oldest files in the Recycle Bin are completely deleted from your hard disk.

Recycling Is for Hard Disks Only

The Recycle Bin only holds files deleted from your hard disk. Files deleted from other drives—disk drives and Zip drives, for example—do *not* get placed in the Recycle Bin. When you delete files from non-hard disk drives, they're really deleted—*permanently!*

Finding Files

Locating a specific file can sometimes be difficult, especially if you have a large drive or
several drives to search. Fortunately, Windows
includes a Find utility to search through a
drive for you.

Click the Start button, select Find, and then
select Files or Folders. When the Find dialog
box appears, select the drive you want to
search or the drive and folder you want to
search. Enter the name of the file or folder
you want and click the Find Now button.
When the search is complete, the dialog box
expands to display any matching files or folders. You can open, move, copy, or delete any
files listed.

Go Wild

You can use *wildcard* characters
when performing searches with the
Find utility. For example, if you use
* in place of multiple characters,
searching for **FILE*** will find **FILE-
NAME**, **FILETYPE**, and **FILES**. If
you use **?** in place of a single character, searching for **FILE?** will find
only **FILES**.

Renaming Files and Folders

File and folder names should ideally describe the contents of the file or folder.
Sometimes, however, the contents may change or the file or folder may contain a
revision number that needs updating. If you have a file or folder with a name that
just isn't right, you can rename it.

Just locate the file or folder you want to rename. Right-click the file or folder icon,
and choose Rename from the pop-up menu; the filename is now highlighted. Type a
new name for your folder (which overwrites the current name) and press Enter.

When you rename a file, however, avoid changing its extension—you could mess up
the file's association and perhaps make it unreadable by some applications.

Working with File Types

As you use My Computer and Windows Explorer to browse files and folders, you'll
notice that some files have specific icons. These icons let you know what *type* the
file is.

The file type determines more than just the icon, however; it also determines the
description you see if you look at the file's details and the application that will be
used to open the file. (This is called the *file association*.) Windows also uses the characters in the extension of a filename (the characters to the right of the period in the
filename) to determine a file's type.

Note that, depending on how you have Windows configured, file extensions might not be visible when you look at files with My Computer or Windows Explorer. To display all file extensions, click the Start button, select Settings, and then select Folder options. When the Folder Options dialog box appears, select the View tab and uncheck Hide File Extensions for Known File Types. Click OK to register this new setting.

Table 1.2 shows you some of the icons you'll encounter when you open My Computer or Windows Explorer, and their corresponding file types and typical extensions.

Table 1.2   Icons and File Types

Icon	File Type and Typical Extensiion
	System file (.SYS)
	Configuration settings file (.INI)
	Text file (.TXT)
	Microsoft Word document file (.DOC)
	Microsoft Works spreadsheet file (.WKS)
	Microsoft Works database file (.WDB)
	Microsoft Home Publishing file (.PHP)
	Microsoft Picture It! file (.MIX)
	Microsoft Excel worksheet file (.XLS)
	Web page file (.HTM or .HTML)
	Sound file (.WAV)
	MIDI music file (.MID)
	Bitmap image file (.BMP)
	TrueType font file (.TTF)
	Help file (.HLP)
	Application (.EXE)
	Unknown file type (or has no extension)

The Least You Need to Know

➤ Windows is an operating system with a graphical user interface.

➤ The latest version of Windows is Windows 98.

➤ Most of the important parts of Windows are easily accessed from either the desktop or the Start menu.

➤ You manage all the files on your hard disk using either My Computer or Windows Explorer; you can copy, move, delete, and rename your files.

➤ Files you delete from your hard drive are temporarily stored in Windows' Recycle Bin; you can *undelete* files as long as they're still in the Recycle Bin.

Chapter 2

Make the Internet Work for You: An Online Primer

In This Chapter

➤ Find out what the Internet is—and what it isn't

➤ Learn how to establish a connection to the Internet

➤ Discover the different activities available on the Internet—including email, chat, newsgroups, and the World Wide Web

It used to be that most people bought personal computers to do work—word processing, spreadsheets, databases, the sort of programs that still make up the core of Works Suite 2000. But today, a large number of people also buy PCs to access the Internet—to send and receive email, surf the Web, and chat with other users.

If you're not yet on the Internet, you will be, soon—and you'll need to know how to get connected, and what to do when you get there. So let's take a quick trip around the Internet and see what it takes to get connected—and *stay* connected!

What the Internet Is—and What It Isn't

If you're new to the Net, keep one thing in mind—the Internet isn't a thing. You can't touch it, see it, or smell it; you can't put it in a box and buy it. The Internet is like the huge power grid that provides electricity to homes across the country—it exists in-between the points that matter.

Get Networked

A network is a group of two or more computers or electronic devices connected together. A *local-area network* (LAN) is a network of computers that are geographically close together; a *wide-area network* (WAN) is a network with computers not all in the same place. The Internet is the widest-area network today, connecting computers and computer networks from all around the world.

America Online—It's Not the Internet, Although It's Connected to It

You probably know someone who is connected to America Online—or you may be an AOL subscriber yourself. America Online is a *commercial online service*, in that it exists independent to the Internet, with its own distinct connections and its own proprietary software, content, and interface. However, AOL also functions as a *gateway* to the Internet, so that AOL users can connect to the Internet through the AOL service. So if you're on AOL, you can access the Internet—even if the AOL service itself can't be accessed by non-AOL users.

So if the Internet isn't a physical thing, what is it? It's really more simple than you might think; the Internet is nothing more than a really big computer network. In fact, it's a computer network that connects other computer networks—what some would call a "network of networks." Computers connect to the Internet (typically through larger networks, most often supplied by an *Internet service provider*), and thus have access to other computers and devices that are also connected to the Internet. After you're connected, you can access anything or anybody else also connected to the Internet, seamlessly and practically invisibly. With a single click, you connect through the Internet to a computer down the street or half-way around the world; on the Internet, distance doesn't matter.

By my estimate, there were more than 150 million users connected to the Internet at the beginning of 1999. According to the Computer Industry Almanac, that number is expected to grow to 320 million by the end of 2000, and to 720 million by 2003.

Just being connected to the Internet, however, really doesn't accomplish anything. It's much the same as having electricity run to your home—that wall outlet doesn't do anything until you plug something into it. The same thing with the Internet; the Internet itself just kind of sits there until you plug something into it that takes advantage of it.

There are many activities that are plugged into—or sit on top of—the Internet, including email, Usenet newsgroups, and the World Wide Web. The Internet itself doesn't perform any of these activities, of course—but it does *enable* these activities to happen. And when you connect to the Internet through your personal computer, you have access to all these activities and more.

How an Internet Connection Works

All Internet connections work pretty much the same way. First, your personal computer connects to an

Internet service provider (ISP) via standard telephone lines. (If you use your computer at work to connect to the Internet, you actually go through your company's local area network to a dedicated line to the Internet, bypassing conventional phone lines.) Your computer uses a piece of hardware called a *modem* to translate the signals from your keyboard to signals that can be sent over standard phone lines; your ISP has a modem on the other end of the line that converts the signals back into digital format for transmission over the Internet.

An Internet service provider is a company that does nothing more than connect individual users to the Internet. Some ISPs (such as America Online) are also commercial online services, and provide their users with an easy-to-use onscreen interface and proprietary content and navigation. But these commercial online services also function as traditional ISPs, consolidating thousands of incoming telephone lines into a single gateway to the Internet for their users.

So you connect to an ISP with your phone line, and your ISP then plugs you into the Internet. After you're on the Internet, you're on your own, free to use (or not to use) individual Internet services, to visit (or not to visit) individual sites and servers connected to the Internet, and to communicate (or not) with individual users who are also plugged into the Internet. After you disconnect from your ISP (that is, hang up your phone line), you're no longer connected to the Internet, and you can't access any Internet services or contact any other users—and they can't contact you, either—until you connect again.

Talk or Surf—Your Call

While you're connected to your ISP, your phone line *is* busy—which means that you can't place or receive normal telephone calls while you're surfing the Internet. If you use the Internet a lot, you may want to invest in a second phone line just for your modem.

Getting Connected

Before you can explore the wonders of the Internet, you first have to find and subscribe to an Internet service provider, and then configure Windows for your new Internet connection.

Creating a New Connection

If you don't yet have an account with an ISP, you need to establish one. The easiest way to both choose an ISP and create a new Internet connection is to use the Internet Connection Wizard found in Works Suite 2000. Just follow these steps to get set up:

1. Launch Works Suite 2000 by clicking the Windows Start button, selecting Programs, and then selecting Microsoft Works.

2. Works now displays the Task Launcher screen; select the Programs tab at the top of the screen.

3. Select Internet Explorer from the Programs list.

4. Select New Internet Connection from the task list, and then click Start.

5. When the Internet Connection Wizard appears, select the first option (I Want to Sign Up for a New Internet Account) and click Next.

6. The wizard now connects to the Microsoft Internet Referral Service and retrieves a list of ISPs in your area. Follow the onscreen instructions to select an ISP and create a new Internet connection in Windows.

Figure 2.1

Use the Internet Connection Wizard to find an ISP and connect to the Internet.

Other ISPs

There are thousands of ISPs in America alone, some of them large and national in scope, many of them smaller and local. You can find ISPs listed in your local yellow pages, in local computer magazines and newspapers, and at various online sites.

For a comprehensive listing of both local and national ISPs, go to CNET's Ultimate ISP Guide (www.cnet.com/Content/Reviews/Compare/ISP) which lists more than 4,000 ISPs, or to The List (thelist.internet.com) which ranks more than 7,000 ISPs.

If You Already Have an ISP

If you already have an Internet service provider and want to set up a new connection to that account on this PC, select the second option (I Want to Transfer My Existing Account to This Computer) on the wizard's opening screen. Follow the onscreen instructions to create a new Internet connection using your existing ISP account.

If you have the right information at your fingertips, you can select the *third* option (I Want to Set Up My Internet Connection Manually) on the wizard's opening screen—which is actually the fastest way to set up a connection. You'll need to know the following information (typically supplied by your ISP):

➤ The area code and telephone number of your ISP (its dial-up number, *not* its voice number!)

➤ Your username and password as assigned by your ISP

➤ Your email address (in the form of *xxx@xxx.xxx*) as assigned by your ISP

➤ The names of your ISP's incoming and outgoing email servers (with some ISPs, the incoming and outgoing servers may be the same)

➤ Your email POP account name and password as assigned by your ISP

➤ The name of your ISP's news server

➤ Whether your ISP offers LDAP "white pages" service (not all do), the name of your ISP's LDAP server

We should define what LDAP stands for. MhNote that, for most ISPs, your username, email name, and POP account name will be the same name. It's also likely that your login password and POP password will also be the same.

Alphabet Soup

Don't get confused by all the initials in the preceding list. *POP* stands for *Post Office Protocol*, which is how your ISP's email server is identified on the Internet. *LDAP* stands for *Lightweight Directory Access Protocol*, which is a way to access directory services on the Internet.

Connecting to the Internet

After you've created the Internet connection for your ISP account, you connect to the Internet by following these steps:

1. From within the Works Suite 2000 Task Launcher, select the Programs tab.

2. From the Programs list, select Internet Explorer.

3. Select WWW New Internet Connection from the task list, and then click Start.

4. Internet Explorer is now automatically launched and a Dial-Up Connection dialog box appears. Make sure all the information is correct, and then click Connect.

Other Ways to Start

You can also connect to the Internet by starting Outlook Express. From the Task Launcher, select Outlook Express, select Check E-mail Messages, and then click Start. In addition, all of the tasks in Task Launcher's MSN section (and any other task indicated by the MSN logo) automatically launch Internet Explorer and connect you to your ISP.

Connect Without a Prompt

If you check the Connect Automatically option on the Dial-Up Connection dialog box, all future connections will be established without showing this dialog box.

5. Windows now dials into and establishes a connection with your ISP, and Internet Explorer takes you to your designated start page.

After you're connected, you can launch any other Internet application and get down to business. In fact, you can run multiple Internet applications at one time—so you can surf the Web while checking your email, or instant message another user while posting an article in a Usenet newsgroup.

The Most Important Parts of the Internet

When you're connected to the Internet, there are a variety of different services you can use. These include messaging services (email and chat), community services (Usenet newsgroups), and interactive/informational services (the World Wide Web). What follows is a little background on each of these popular services.

Email—The Most-Used Service on the Internet

Electronic mail (*email*) is a means of communicating with other Internet users through letters, written and delivered electronically over the Internet. Although email messages look a lot like traditional letters, email itself is a lot different from the so-called "snail mail" delivered by the United States Postal Service.

There's More to Learn

To learn more about using Outlook Express for Internet email, see Chapter 14, "Send and Receive Email with Outlook Express."

When you send an electronic letter to another Internet user, that letter travels from your computer to your recipient's computer (through the Internet) almost *instantly*. Your messages travel at the speed of electrons over a number of phone lines and Internet connections, automatically routed to the right place just about as fast as you can click the Send button. That's a *lot* different from using the U.S. Postal Service, which can take days to deliver a similar message.

You compose an email message just as you would a letter, except you use your computer keyboard and monitor (and an email program, such as Outlook Express). You then send the message to the recipient, by specifying the recipient's unique email address. Your message, after sent, is stored in your recipient's electronic mailbox (which resides on a separate email *server* at your recipient's ISP), until the recipient fetches and reads it.

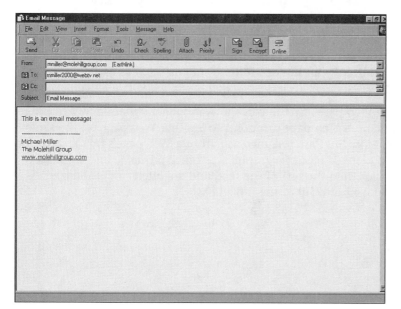

Figure 2.2

Sending Internet email with Outlook Express.

To make sure your message goes to the right recipient, you have to use your recipient's email *address*. Every Internet user has a unique email address, composed of three parts:

➤ The user's login name

➤ The @ sign

➤ The user's domain name (usually the name of their Internet service provider)

As an example, if you used the Microsoft Network as your Internet provider (with the domain name of `msn.com`) and your login name was `worksuser`, your email address would be `worksuser@msn.com`.

In addition to standard ISP server-based email, you can also send and receive email from special Web-based email services. These services, such as the ever-popular Hotmail (`www.hotmail.com`), let you access your email from *any* computer, using any Web browser; if you use a PC at work or on the road, this is a convenient way to check your email at any time of day, no matter where you are. Second, you can use this auxiliary email account as a second Internet identity, distinct from your normal email address; some users use their Web-based email to access the Internet under an assumed name, for privacy purposes. Third, these Web-based email accounts are free—which is reason enough for some people.

The World Wide Web—Colorful, Graphic, and Interactive

The World Wide Web is the showiest part of the Internet, the place where information of all types is presented in a highly visual, often multimedia, format.

Information on the World Wide Web is presented in pages. A *Web page* is like a page in a book, made up of text and pictures (also called *graphics*). A Web page differs from a book page, however, in that it can include other elements, such as audio and video, and *links* to other Web pages.

It's this linking to other Web pages that makes the Web such a dynamic way to present information. A link on a Web page can point to another Web page on the same site, or to another site. Most links are included as part of a Web page's text and are called *hypertext links*. (If a link is part of a graphic, it's called a *graphic link*.) Links are usually in a different color than the rest of the text, and are often underlined; when you click a link, you're taken directly to the linked page.

Getting Rid of the Junk

If you've been using the Internet for any time at all, you've probably started to receive unwanted emails—and lots of them. These junk emails—referred to as *spam*—eat up telephone time while they download, clog up your inbox, and generally just annoy the heck out of you.

Although the easiest way to deal with a spam message is to simply delete it, there are a few things you can do to reduce the number of spam messages you receive.

First, realize that any time you put your email address on the Internet, you have potentially supplied your address to a spammer. So the first step in fighting spam is to limit the number of places where you post your email address.

Another spam-fighting technique is to use a phony email address. Whenever possible, *don't* leave your real email address; enter something else instead—as long as you don't want to receive replies!—to throw off the spammers.

You can also alter your email address when you post to newsgroups or mailing lists, using something called a *spamblock*. Because most spammers use software programs (called *spambots*) to automate the name-retrieval process, manually adding NOSPAM (the spamblock) to your address will throw off the spambots, yet still be manageable for any human beings who want to respond to your message. Just write your address like this: myname@domain.NOSPAM.com; real users will see to take out the spamblock in their reply, whereas the so-called *spambots* will be totally thrown off.

The bottom line, however, is that it's very difficult— if not impossible—to stop all junk emails, just as it's difficult to stop postal junk mail. The best thing to do is limit the exposure of your email address, and learn to ignore the spam.

Figure 2.3

A Web page viewed with Internet Explorer.

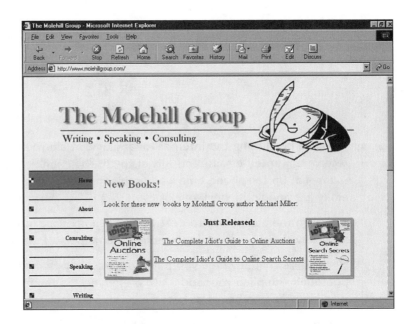

Know the Code

A Web page is created using a special code, kind of a low-level programming language. This code, called HTML (for HyperText Markup Language), describes what each element on the Web page looks like, and how it behaves. Users never see the HTML code; it operates in the background. Instead, you see the result of the code—the Web page itself.

Web pages reside at a Web *site*. A Web site is nothing more than a collection of Web pages (each in its own individual computer file) residing on a host computer. The host computer is connected full-time to the Internet so that you can access the site—and its Web pages—anytime you access the Internet. The main page at a Web site is usually called a *home page*, and it often serves as an opening screen that provides a brief overview and a sort of menu of everything you can find at that site. The address of a Web page is called a *URL*, which stands for Uniform Resource Locator.

You view a Web page with a Web *browser*. The two most popular browsers today are Microsoft's Internet Explorer (included with Works Suite 2000) and Netscape Navigator (part of the Netscape Communicator suite). Both of these browsers work pretty much the same way, and have pretty much the same features.

There's More to Learn

To learn more about using Internet Explorer, see Chapter 15, "Surf the Web with Internet Explorer."

Web pages and Web sites can contain just about any type of information you can imagine. Some Web sites contain static or historical information; others contain up-to-the-minute news, weather, and other current information. Some Web sites are created by individuals and hobbyists; others are run by large commercial businesses. Some Web sites are strictly informative, where others try to sell you things (and let you input your personal information and credit card numbers). With literally hundreds of millions of pages currently existing, just about anything you can think of is available somewhere on the Web.

I find that cruising the Web is like browsing through an encyclopedia. Invariably when I'm reading one article in an encyclopedia, I find a reference to a related article that interests me. When I turn to the new article, I find a reference to another article, which references another article—and, before I know it, I have all twenty-four volumes open in front of me. When you're on the Web, it's the same sort of experience. In the course of a single session, it's not unusual to discover that you've visited more than a dozen different sites—and still have lots of interesting places to go!

Be the Duke of URL

A Web address—otherwise known as a URL—precisely points to a single Web page, through the use of addressing standards. The first part of the URL is the `http://`, which tells Web browsers that what follows is a Web page. (There are other prefixes for other types of Internet sites—`ftp://` for FTP sites, for example.)

Following the prefix, in most instances, is the site address, in the form of `www.site.com`. This is *not* a standard, however; site addresses can start with something other than `www.` and end with something other than `.com`. (For example, sites for non-profit organizations often end in `.org`, educational sites end in `.edu`, government sites end in `.gov`, and sites from other countries end in specific country codes—such as `.uk` for the United Kingdom.)

When you enter a site address, you'll automatically be taken to the home page of that site. In most cases, the home page has an address that looks like this: `www.site.com/index.html`. You don't have to enter the `index.html` because your Web browser automatically looks for and loads the `index.html` page when you just enter a site address.

If a site has a lot of pages, the pages might be organized into *directories* or "child sites," with each directory representing a specific topic. Each directory will be preceded by the "backslash" symbol, and the directory's contents (including any subdirectories within the directory) will follow a backslash. So, if the `bob.html` page was found in the `frank` directory on our hypothetical site, its address would be `www.site.com/frank/bob.html`.

Usenet Newsgroups—A Kind of Community, Online

Usenet is a network that operates within the overall confines of the Internet. Its purpose is to provide a group of online communities—called *newsgroups*—for users with similar interests. You use a *newsreader* program to access these newsgroups; many email programs (including Outlook Express) double as newsreaders.

A newsgroup is kind of like an electronic bulletin board. Within a newsgroup users post messages (called *articles*); other users read these articles and, when so disposed, respond. The result is a kind of on-going, freeform discussion, in which dozens—or hundreds—of users might participate.

In many ways, a newsgroup is like an old-fashioned town meeting. Anyone can attend, and anyone can speak his or her mind. At times things can get a bit disorganized, and it's not uncommon for several people to talk about different things at the same time. But, all in all, a lot of interesting opinions are expressed, for all to hear.

Search through all 25,000+ newsgroups to find one that focuses on a topic you're interested in, and then *subscribe* to the newsgroup to access it daily. It's fun to follow the conversation *threads* between newsgroup members—you'll want to join in and add your two cents' worth!

Other Parts of the Internet

Email, newsgroups, and the Web are the three most popular parts of the Internet—but not the *only* parts. Here are some of the other activities you can engage in while online:

➤ **Internet Relay Chat (IRC).** A series of servers and chat *channels* where groups of Internet users "talk" to each other in real-time.

➤ **Instant Messaging (IM).** A method for real-time one-on-one conversations between two Internet users.

➤ **Internet Radio.** Where Web-based radio stations "broadcast" in real-time over the Internet.

➤ **MP3.** A method to download and record near-CD quality music from the Internet.

➤ **FTP (File Transfer Protocol).** A method for downloading computer files from dedicated servers.

➤ **Gopher.** An older service for storing files and information. (Gopher was widely used at many universities in the early and mid-1990s; because it's text-based, it isn't used much at all anymore.)

Install the Software

As I wrote at the beginning of this chapter, just connecting to the Internet doesn't get you much. To do anything on the Internet, you have to install the proper software. Table 2.1 details different Internet activities, and their corresponding software.

Table 2.1   Internet Activities and Software

Internet Activity	Software
Chat	mIRC (www.mirc.com) PIRCH (www.pirchat.com)
Email	Eudora (www.eudora.com) Microsoft Outlook Express (www.microsoft.com/ windows/oe/—and included with Works Suite 2000) Netscape Messenger (home.netscape.com/computing/download/)
FTP (file downloading)	BulletProof FTP (www.bpftp.com) WS_FTP (www.csra.net/junodj/ws_ftp32.htm)
Instant Messaging	ICQ (www.icq.com) AOL Netscape Instant Messenger (www.newaol.com/aim/netscape/adb00.html)
Usenet Newsgroups	Free Agent (www.forteinc.com/agent/freagent.htm) Microsoft Outlook Express (www.microsoft.com/ windows/oe/—and included with Works Suite 2000) Netscape Messenger (home.netscape.com/computing/download/)
World Wide Web	Microsoft Internet Explorer (www.microsoft.com/ windows/ie/—and included with Works Suite 2000) Netscape Navigator (home.netscape.com/computing/download/)

Software for Free

You can find the software (generally for free) at the Web sites listed in the table, or at most general Internet software repository sites, such as Download.com (www.download.com) or Tucows (www.tucows.com). Many of these programs are also available (not for free) at your local computer retailer. You don't have to install every type of program, just those necessary for the activities you want to participate in.

Works Suite 2000 includes two programs that can perform the majority of your Internet-related tasks: Internet Explorer and Outlook Express. Internet Explorer is Microsoft's Web browser, whereas Outlook Express is both an email program and a newsreader for Usenet newsgroups. See chapters 14 and 15 to learn more about these two programs.

Learn More About the Internet

There's a lot more to learn about the Internet than I can discuss in this single chapter. If you want to learn more about the Internet (and all the things you can do online), you might want to check out some or all of these excellent Que books, available wherever computer books are sold:

> ➤ *Easy Internet,* a terrific step-by-step, full-color, visually oriented introduction for beginning users.

> ➤ *The Complete Idiot's Guide to the Internet,* an unintimidating overview of Internet ins and outs.

> ➤ *The Complete Idiot's Guide to Online Search Secrets,* a really good guide to finding all sorts of stuff on the Internet (and written by me, to boot!)

> ➤ *The Complete Idiot's Guide to Online Auctions,* another one of many books I've written recently, all about buying and selling things via eBay and other online auction sites.

> ➤ *The Complete Idiot's Guide to Online Shopping,* not written by me, but a great book nonetheless, essential for anyone doing their shopping over the Internet.

> ➤ *The Complete Idiot's Guide to Online Investing,* one of the few computer books that show you how to *make* money (instead of spend it!) online.

The Least You Need to Know

➤ You configure your system's modem to connect to an Internet service provider (ISP), which then connects you to the Internet.

➤ Your ISP will provide you with your own unique email address and account.

➤ After you're connected to the Internet, you have access to different activities—including email, Web pages, Usenet newsgroups, and chat.

➤ You use different software programs to perform different Internet-related activities.

➤ Two of the more popular Internet programs are included with Works Suite 2000—Internet Explorer (for surfing the Web) and Outlook Express (for email and newsgroups).

I'LL HAVE MY PEOPLE CALL YOUR PEOPLE...

Chapter 3

Make Works Work for You: A Microsoft Works Suite 2000 Primer

In This Chapter

➤ Learn all about Microsoft Works Suite 2000—and its component applications

➤ Discover how to create new tasks and open Works Suite applications from the Works Task Launcher

➤ Find out what most of Works' applications have in common

So you're the proud owner of a brand-new copy of Microsoft Works Suite 2000. What do you do now?

Just What Is Works?

Microsoft Works Suite 2000 isn't a single software program—it's a collection of 12 different programs (or program components) that combine to handle just about any task you can think of performing on your personal computer. With all the parts of Works Suite 2000 installed, you can now write letters and memos, perform spreadsheet calculations, store all sorts of data, manage your schedules and contacts, manage your checkbook and bank online, create cards and crafts, work with digital photographs, look up facts and figures, plan your next road trip, send and receive email, and surf the Internet—all from a single Task Launcher "shell" program.

Works Suite 2000 is one of the most popular pieces of computer software in use today, in part because some or all of it is installed on many new PC systems. Chances are *you* just purchased a new PC, with Works Suite 2000 already installed.

There are actually three different versions of Microsoft Works, of which Works Suite 2000 is the most versatile, and the most popular. The basic Microsoft Works 2000 program contains a basic word processor, the Works Spreadsheet, Works Database, Works Calendar, and Address Book programs—as well as Microsoft Internet Explorer and Outlook Express, to help you get productive on the Internet.

Microsoft Works Suite Basic 2000 takes Works 2000 and adds two more programs: Microsoft Money 2000 Standard and Microsoft Encarta Encyclopedia 2000. Microsoft Works Suite 2000 adds to all this with Microsoft Home Publishing 2000, Microsoft Picture It! Express, and Microsoft Expedia Streets & Trips 2000—and replaces the basic Works word processor with the powerful and popular Microsoft Word 2000 software.

This Book Is About Works Suite 2000

Because Works Suite 2000 includes all the components that are in all the other versions of Works—except Works Word Processor—I've written this book about the "superset" version of the program. If you have plain old Works 2000 or Works Suite Basic 2000, you can still use this book; just ignore those chapters on applications you don't have in your installation.

Table 3.1 details the programs included in each version of Works 2000.

Table 3.1   Works 2000 Versions

Program	Works 2000	WorksSuite Basic 2000	WorksSuite 2000
Works Spreadsheet	Yes	Yes	Yes
Works Database	Yes	Yes	Yes
Works Calendar	Yes	Yes	Yes
Address Book	Yes	Yes	Yes
Internet Explorer 5	Yes	Yes	Yes

Program	Works 2000	WorksSuite Basic 2000	WorksSuite 2000
Outlook Express	Yes	Yes	Yes
Money 2000 Standard	No	Yes	Yes
Encarta Encyclopedia 2000	No	Yes	Yes
Word 2000	No	No	Yes
Home Publishing 2000	No	No	Yes
Picture It! Express	No	No	Yes
Expedia Streets & Trips 2000	No	No	Yes

Different PC manufacturers install different versions of Works on their PCs. You might find that some *components* of Works Suite 2000 are installed, while others aren't—even though they may be available for installation from the accompanying CD-ROMs. Check with your PC's documentation to determine which components are preinstalled on your system—and which components are available for installation.

Installing Works Suite 2000 Components

If you need to install—or reinstall—any of the individual programs that make up Works Suite 2000, all you need to do is insert Disc 1 from the Works Suite 2000 installation CDs. When you insert this CD, the Works Suite 2000 Setup program should launch automatically; follow the onscreen instructions to add new components to your system.

If the Setup program *doesn't* start automatically, click the Windows Start button and select Run. When the Run dialog box appears, enter **x:\setup.exe** (where *x* is the letter of your CD-ROM drive) in the Open box, and then click OK; this will start the Setup program manually.

What's in Works

If you have all of Works Suite 2000 installed, you now have a dozen different programs—or program components—installed on your personal computer. Let's take a quick look at each of these programs. (All 12 of these programs are covered in more depth in Part 2, "Learn the Programs," later in this book.)

Microsoft Works 2000—Including Works Spreadsheet, Works Database, Works Calendar, and Address Book

Microsoft Works 2000 is the core of Works Suite 2000. Works is centered around the Task Launcher (discussed later in this chapter), and includes four different pieces of component software.

Take the Fifth

The version of Works included with the Microsoft Works 2000 and Microsoft Works Suite Basic 2000 programs includes a fifth component—the Works Word Processor. The version of Works included with Works Suite 2000 *doesn't* incorporate this word processor; instead, Microsoft Word 2000—a more full-featured word processing program—has been added to the suite of products.

Works Spreadsheet is a simple spreadsheet program, kind of like an easier-to-use version of Microsoft Excel. Works Spreadsheet lets you enter rows and columns of numbers and other data, and then perform basic calculations and analysis on those numbers. You can sort and graph your data, and use the program to create all sorts of lists and logs.

Learn more about Works Spreadsheet in Chapter 5, "Crunch Your Numbers with Works Spreadsheet."

Works Database is a simple database program that functions more-or-less like a giant electronic filing cabinet. You create the database files (the "drawers" in the filing cabinet), and then manage individual records (the "index cards" in each "drawer") within each file. You can use Works Database to keep track of all sorts of household records—from your favorite recipes to the names on your Christmas card list.

Learn more about Works Database in Chapter 6, "Organize Your Stuff with Works Database."

Works Calendar is a schedule management program. You see a simple calendar onscreen, and to that calendar you add your appointments and other important dates. Works Calendar then alerts you to important meetings and events.

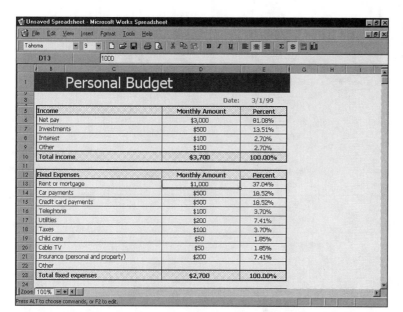

Figure 3.1

Crunch your numbers with Works Spreadsheet.

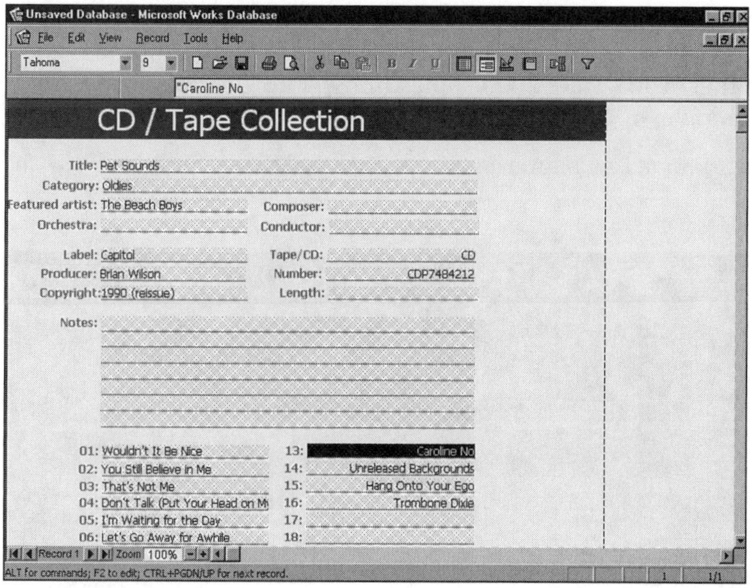

Figure 3.2

Organize your stuff with Works Database.

Learn more about Works Calendar in Chapter 7, "Manage Your Schedule with Works Calendar."

Figure 3.3

Manage your schedule with Works Calendar.

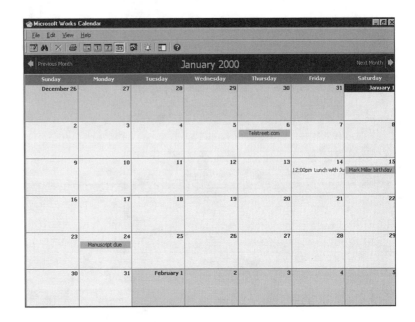

Address Book is an all-purpose contact manager. You store names, addresses, phone numbers, email addresses, and other information in the Address Book, and then import that data into other Works Suite 2000 applications—into Outlook Express for email addressing, for example, or into Word 2000 for merged mailings.

Learn more about Address Book in Chapter 8, "Keep Track of Friends and Family with Address Book."

Figure 3.4

Keep track of friends and family with Address Book.

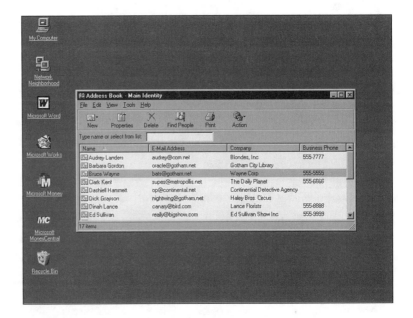

Internet Explorer

Internet Explorer 5 (otherwise known as IE5) is the latest version of Microsoft's Web browser. With IE5—and a connection to the Internet—you can quickly and easily surf, search, and shop the Web. In addition, many Works Suite 2000 tasks automatically launch IE5 to access special Microsoft topic-specific Web sites—making Works Suite 2000 as up-to-date as the Web itself!

Learn more about Internet Explorer in Chapter 15, "Surf the Web with Internet Explorer."

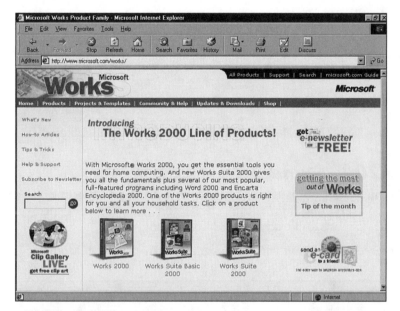

Figure 3.5

Surf the Web with Internet Explorer.

Outlook Express

Outlook Express is a companion program to Internet Explorer. You use Outlook Express to compose, send, and receive email messages—and as a newsreader for Usenet newsgroups. Outlook Express can send and receive messages in HTML format, and can access email from any ISP's email server.

Learn more about Outlook Express in Chapter 14, "Send and Receive Email with Outlook Express."

Figure 3.6

Send and receive email with Outlook Express.

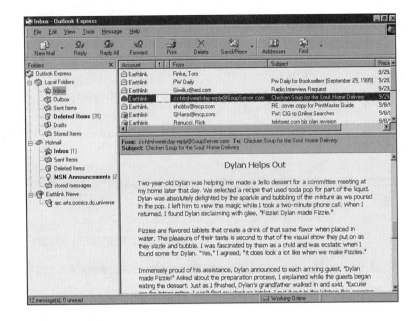

Microsoft Money 2000 Standard

When you want to computerize your personal finances, turn to Microsoft Money. This program lets you do everything from writing checks and balancing your checkbook to creating financial reports and tracking your investments online.

Learn more about Money 2000 in Chapter 9, "Manage Your Finances with Money."

Figure 3.7

Manage your finances with Microsoft Money.

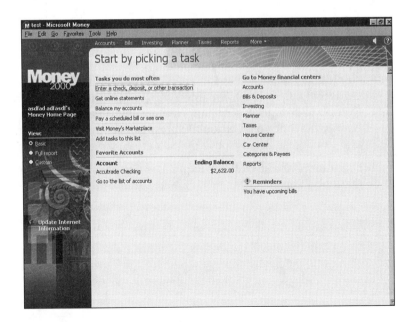

Microsoft Encarta Encyclopedia 2000

Encarta is an electronicversion of a traditional encyclopedia—with the added benefit of multimedia audio and video! If you have children, this application will get a lot of use—it's great for researching homework and reports, or just answering all your kids' questions.

Learn more about Encarta in Chapter 13, "Look Up Almost Anything with Encarta Encyclopedia."

Figure 3.8

Look up almost any-thing with Encarta Encyclopedia.

Microsoft Word 2000

Microsoft Word is the most popular word processing program in the world—and the most powerful. With Word you can create anything from simple memos and letters to complex newsletters and reports. Word even integrates with other Works Suite programs to create merged mailings and sophisticated documents. If you're like most users, you'll find that you use Word almost every day—it's that essential!

Learn more about Word 2000 in Chapter 4, "Write Letters and Other Documents with Microsoft Word."

Figure 3.9

Write letters and other documents with Microsoft Word.

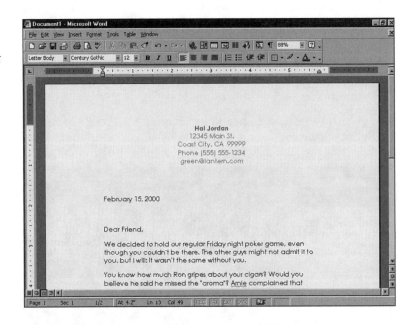

Microsoft Home Publishing 2000

Just to show that Works isn't all work, Microsoft has included Home Publishing 2000. Home Publishing is an easy-to-use program that lets you create cards, banners, posters, and other crafts. Home Publishing projects look particularly good when printed out on a good four-color printer—and they're really fun to make!

Learn more about Home Publishing in Chapter 10, "Make Fun and Useful Projects with Home Publishing."

Microsoft Picture It! Express

If you're getting into digital photography—or just want to put some pictures on your Web site, or send them via email—then you need the simple picture editing tools of Picture It! Express. This program lets you import pictures from digital cameras and scanners, take the red(eye) out, crop out unwanted parts of your pictures, and organize your pictures into collages, calendars, and photo albums. (Plus, you can take the pictures you edit with Picture It! Express and import them into other Works Suite 2000 applications!)

Learn more about Picture It! Express in Chapter 11, "Fix Your Photos with Picture It! Express."

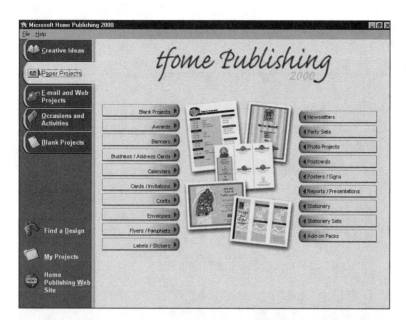

Figure 3.10

Make fun and useful projects with Home Publishing.

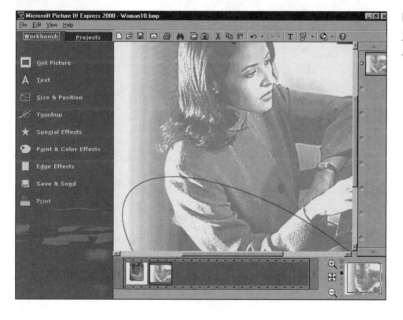

Figure 3.11

Fix your photos with Picture It! Express.

Microsoft Expedia Streets & Trips 2000

Never get lost again with the detailed driving directions generated by Microsoft Expedia Streets & Trips. Find addresses, print out maps, and generate turn-by-turn driving directions—all from your own computer!

Learn more about Microsoft Expedia in Chapter 12, "Get Driving Directions with Expedia Streets & Trips."

Figure 3.12

Get driving directions with Expedia Streets & Trips.

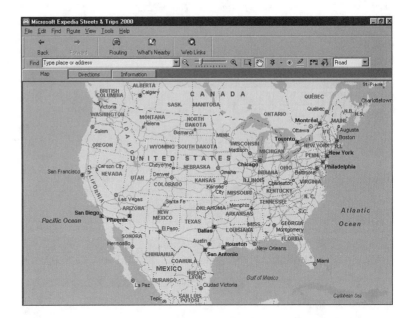

The Thirteenth Application

There is actually a thirteenth "application" on the Task Launcher's Programs tab, labeled MSN. This isn't really an application at all, but rather a collection of links to Microsoft's topic-oriented Web sites. When you click a "task" on the MSN tab, Task Launcher launches Internet Explorer, connects to the Internet, and takes you to the MSN site corresponding to the "task" you selected.

Working Works

You start MicrosoftWorks Suite 2000 by clicking the Windows Start button, selecting Programs, and then selecting Microsoft Works. This launches the Works Task Launcher, which is the "home base" for all your Works applications and tasks.

You can start the individual Works Suite applications either from within Works (using the Task Launcher, discussed next) or from the Windows Start menu.

There's More to Do from the Task Launcher

With most Works Suite applications, you have more options available when you launch the program from the Works Suite Task Launcher. For example, starting Word from the Task Launcher displays a huge number of task-based templates and wizards—many of which are *not* available from within the Word program itself!

Finding Your Way Around the Task Launcher

When you launch Works Suite, the Works Task Launcher appears onscreen. The Task Launcher has three tabs along the top; each tab represents a different way to enter a program or document.

Here are the three tabs you see in the Task Launcher:

➤ **Tasks.** Use the Tasks tab to identify a certain task you want to perform—select the task, and the Task Launcher will launch the appropriate program, with the appropriate template or wizard already loaded.

➤ **Programs.** Use the Programs tab to launch a specific Works Suite 2000 program—then select the task you want that program to perform.

➤ **History.** Use the History tab to reload any document you've recently edited with any Works Suite application.

When Task Launcher is launched, select a tab, select a program or task, and then you're ready to work!

Launching a Program

You use the Program tab to launch individual Works Suite 2000 applications. Just follow these steps:

1. From the Works Task Launcher, select the Programs tab.
2. From the Programs list, select a program.
3. From the tasks list for that program, select a task.
4. Click Start.

The Task Launcher now launches the program you selected, with the appropriate task-based template or wizard loaded.

Figure 3.13

Click the Programs tab to launch a specific Works Suite 2000 program.

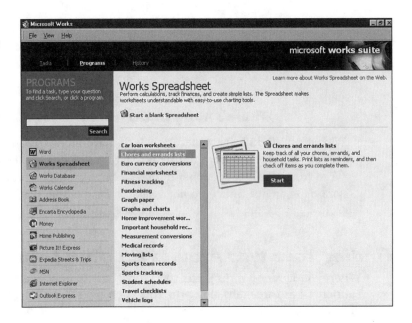

Search for a Task

If you're not sure what program to open for a specific task, you can use the Search command (located on both the Programs and Tasks tabs) to find that task for you. Just enter the name of the task in the Search box, and then click Search; Task Launcher displays all tasks that match your query. Just select a task from the Search Results list, and the right program will be loaded for the task you selected.

Launching a New Task

To start a specific task—and have Works load the right program for that task, automatically—you use the Tasks tab in the Task Launcher. Just follow these steps:

1. From the Works Task Launcher, select the Tasks tab.

2. From the Tasks list, select a task category.

3. From the tasks list for that category, select a specific task.

4. Click Start.

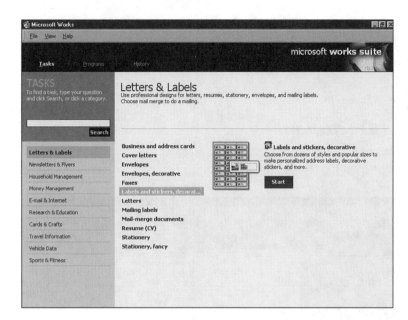

Figure 3.14

Click the Tasks tab to get started with a specific task—and let Works Suite 2000 figure out which program to launch!

The Task Launcher now launches the appropriate program for your selected task—and, in most cases, presents you with a task-based template or wizard for getting started automatically.

Here are the task categories you'll find on the Tasks tab:

➤ **Letters & Labels.** Includes business letters, envelopes, mailing labels, résumés, faxes, mail-merge documents, and stationery.

➤ **Newsletters & Flyers.** Includes brochures, flyers, pamphlets, and newsletters.

➤ **Household Management.** Includes appointments, lists for chores and errands, grocery lists, home inventory worksheets, journals, medical records, menus, and recipe books.

➤ **Money Management.** Includes balancing your accounts, calculating your debt, financial worksheets, monthly financial reports, bill payments and deposits, portfolio status, savings calculator, and stock research.

➤ **E-Mail & Internet.** Includes email, Web surfing, shopping, playing online games, and Web searching.

➤ **Research & Education.** Includes browsing and searching the encyclopedia, creating school reports and schedules, and making notes and outlines.

➤ **Cards & Crafts.** Includes awards, banners, calendars, cards, certificates, crafts, invitations, photo albums and collages, and posters.

➤ **Travel Information.** Includes address finder, car rental, currency converter, driving directions, flight reservations, room reservations, and travel journals.

➤ **Vehicle Data.** Includes car loan worksheets, vehicle comparisons and reviews, vehicle logs, and new car price quotes.

➤ **Sports & Fitness.** Includes fitness tracking, sports team records, and sports statistics.

Launching an Old Document

You use the Tasks tab to create brand-new documents; you use the History tab to reopen documents you previously created.

Figure 3.15

Click the History tab to view a list of recent files—click a column header to sort items by that column.

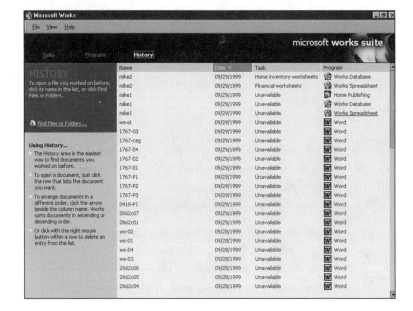

The History tab lists all your recently used files, in reverse chronological order. (That's newest files first, for those of you who are vocabulary impaired.) For each file, the Task Launcher includes the file Name, the Date it was last worked on, the type of Task it was (when this is knowable), and the Program associated with that file. You can resort the list of files by any column by clicking on the column header. For example, if you wanted to sort files by name, you'd click on the Name header; click a second time to sort in the reverse order.

To open a file listed in the History pane, just click its name. Task Launcher will launch the program associated with that file, and then load the selected file into the program.

If the file you want isn't listed on the History tab, Task Launcher lets you search for that file. When you click the Find Files or Folders link (in the top-left corner of the screen), Task Launcher displays the Find: All Files dialog box, shown below.

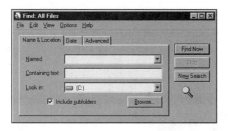

Figure 3.16

Search for files with the Find: All Files dialog box.

This neat little tool lets you search your entire system for specific files. By selecting different tabs in this dialog box, you can search by:

➤ **Name & Location.** Enter a full or partial filename in the Named box, or enter some of the text of the document in the Containing Text box. Pull down the Look In list to select *where* to look (which hard drive, which folder, and so on), and check the Include Subfolders option if you want to look in all folders *below* the selected drive or folders. (To select a specific folder, click the Browse button to display the Browse for Folder dialog box.)

➤ **Date.** You can elect to search for All Files, or to Find All Files Modified, Created, or Last Accessed either Between two dates or During the Previous selected number of Months or Days.

➤ **Advanced.** Pull down the Of Type list to select specific types of files to look for. You can also select files where the Size Is At Least or At Most a selected number of kilobytes (KB).

You can select options on any or *all* of these three tabs. The more specific your query, the fewer matching files you're likely to find; the fewer criteria you select, the more files that will be matched. Click the Find Now button to start your search.

The results of your search will be displayed at the bottom of this dialog box. Click aspecific file to open it (and its associated program).

Working on Your Works Skills

Most—but not all—Works Suite 2000 applications share a common look and feel and common operating procedures. In particular, you'll find that all applications *except* Encarta, Home Publishing, and Money use a similar interface that incorporates a series of toolbars, pull-down menus, and pop-up menus (displayed when you right-click particular items).

Getting Started with Templates and Wizards

When you launch most Works Suite 2000 tasks, you're presented with either a *template* or a *wizard*.

A template is a preformatted document specific to your task; you add text and objects to this template to create your final document. A wizard is a series of screens that lead you step-by-step through the creation of a specific document—you enter the requested information, and the document is created for you.

Figure 3.17

Answer the questions in this wizard to create various sports tracking tasks.

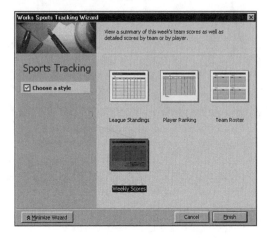

Get used to seeing these templates and wizards—they're the way Works works to make sure you successfully complete the tasks you've selected!

Using Works' Pull-Down and Pop-Up Menus

Pop-Up Menus Are Efficient!

A good rule of thumb is if you need to perform a task, right-click your mouse. Chances are you'll see a pop-up menu that contains that one command you need to use.

The menus in the Works Suite 2000 applications function just like the menus in most other Windows applications. Click on the title of the menu with your mouse, and the menu pulls down to reveal all the associated commands and operations. Most of the applications share a similar menu system, including menus for File, Edit, Tools, and Help operations.

In addition to the normal pull-down menus, most Works Suite 2000 applications also include context-sensitive pop-up menus. These menus contain commands specific to a particular task, object, or area of the program, and are displayed when you right-click your mouse.

Getting Help

At any time during your Works session, you can open the built-in Help system for your specific application. All you have to do is press the F1 key—or pull down the Help menu and make a selection.

Although the Help system differs somewhat from application to application, in most cases the Help window appears in a pane on the right side of the workplace. You can make a selection from the initial Help page, or enter a specific question in the Answer Wizard box. (If this box isn't visible, click the Answer Wizard button on the Help toolbar.) When you click the Search button, Works displays the Help topic that best answers your question.

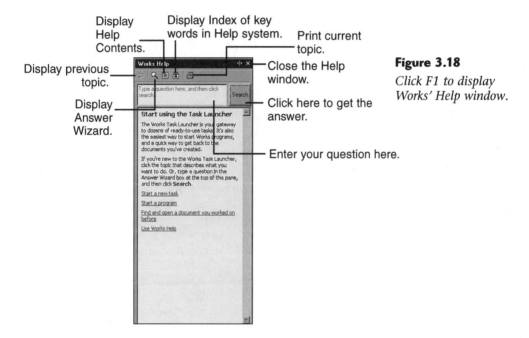

Display Help Contents.

Display Index of key words in Help system.

Print current topic.

Display previous topic.

Close the Help window.

Display Answer Wizard.

Click here to get the answer.

Enter your question here.

Figure 3.18

Click F1 to display Works' Help window.

You can also click the Contents button on the Help toolbar to display all the Help topics for this particular application, or click the Index button to display an index of all key words contained in the Help system.

To close the Help window (and give you back that valuable screen space!), click the X in the top-right corner of the Help window.

The Least You Need to Know

➤ Microsoft Works Suite 2000 is a collection of a dozen different applications and components.

➤ You launch applications and create new tasks from the Works Task Launcher.

➤ Create new tasks—and launch the associated application—from Task Launcher's Task tab; launch Works Suite 2000's applications directly from the Programs tab; or open a previously created file from the History tab.

➤ Most—but not all—Works Suite 2000 applications share the same interface, menu structure, and context-sensitive pop-up menus.

Part 2
Learn the Programs

Works Suite 2000 includes a dozen different programs, each designed to help you perform specific types of tasks. In this section you'll learn how to work all 12 Works programs—Word, Works Spreadsheet, Works Database, Works Calendar, Address Book, Money, Home Publishing, Picture It! Express, Expedia Streets & Trips, Encarta Encyclopedia, Outlook Express, and Internet Explorer. (Think about it—this section is kind of like getting a dozen books for the price of one!)

Chapter 4

Write Letters and Other Documents with Microsoft Word

In This Chapter

➤ Discover how Word 2000 works

➤ Learn how to create and save simple documents

➤ Find out how to format your documents—and add graphics and other objects

Microsoft Word 2000 is the full-featured word processing program included with both Microsoft Works Suite 2000 and Microsoft Office 2000. (Regular Works 2000 and Works Suite Basic 2000 include a very basic Works-based word processor.) Word is a terrific tool for all your writing needs—from basic letters to fancy newsletters, and everything in-between. And when you use Word in conjunction with the other components of Works Suite 2000, you can create some very sophisticated output—including personalized mailings and graphics-heavy reports.

Opening—and Closing—Word

You can start Word either from Windows or from the Works Suite 2000 Task Launcher.

Starting from Works

To launch Word from the Works Suite 2000 Task Launcher, follow these steps:

1. Select the Programs tab.
2. Select Word from the Programs list.
3. To start Word with a blank document, select Start a Blank Word Document. To select Word with a specific task loaded, select the task from the task list and click Start.

Word now launches, with whatever document you selected open in the workspace.

Starting from Windows

Works doesn't have to be running for you to use Microsoft Word. To launch Word outside of Works, follow these steps:

1. Click the Windows Start button.
2. Select Programs
3. Select Microsoft Word.

Word now launches, with a blank document loaded.

Closing the Program

When you're done using Word, you close the program by pulling down the File menu and selecting Exit. (If you have any unsaved documents open, Word will prompt you to save them first, and then close.)

There's More in the Store

Word 2000 is definitely a program that you could read a whole book about. If you *want* to read a whole about Word 2000, take a look at some of the best:

➤ *The Complete Idiot's Guide to Microsoft Works 2000*, a kind-of companion book to the one you're currently reading

➤ *Easy Microsoft Word 2000*, an easy-to-use four-color visual guide to Word basics

➤ *Special Edition Using Microsoft Word 2000*, a comprehensive guide that covers virtually every aspect of the program—written by the pros for heavy-duty Word users

All these books are available wherever computer books are sold—or go to www.mcp.com for more information.

Working Your Way Around the Word Workspace

Before we get started, let's take a quick tour of the Word 2000 workspace—so you know what's what and what's where.

Word in Works Is Different from Word in Office—Slightly

If you're used to using Word 2000 as part of the Microsoft Office 2000 suite, you'll find that a few menu items are a tad different in the Works Suite 2000 version of Word. This difference is because Works adds some ease-of-use features to Word—mainly in the form of additional Wizards and templates—that require some very slight interface changes. Not to worry—the basic Word is the same, even if a few menu items are shuffled around a little.

What's Where in Word

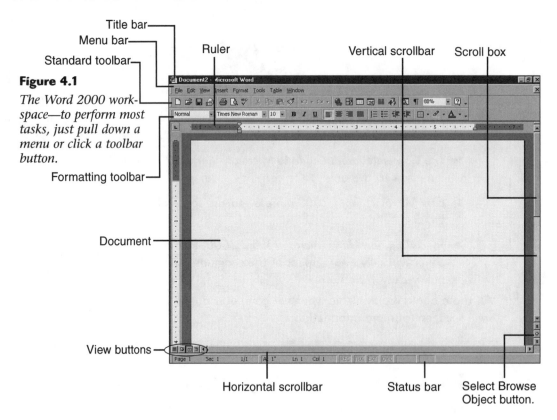

Figure 4.1

The Word 2000 work-space—to perform most tasks, just pull down a menu or click a toolbar button.

The Word workspace, shown above, is divided into seven main parts:

➤ **Title bar.** This is where you find the filename of the current document, as well as buttons to minimize, maximize, and close the window for the current Word document.

➤ **Menu bar.** This collection of pull-down menus—actually a kind of text-based toolbar—contains virtually all of Word's commands. Use your mouse to click a menu item, and then the menu pulls down to display a full range of commands and options.

➤ **Toolbars.** By default, two toolbars—Standard and Formatting—are docked at the top of the workspace, just underneath the menu bar. Word 2000 includes 16 different toolbars that you can display anywhere in the Word workspace. Click a button on any toolbar to initiate the associated command or operation.

Display a Tip

If you're not sure just what button on which toolbar does what, you're not alone—those little graphics are sometimes hard to decipher. To display the name of any specific button, just hover your cursor over the button until the descriptive *ScreenTip* appears.

➤ **Ruler.** This allows you to measure the width of a document—and set tabs and margins.

➤ **Document.** This main space displays your current Word document.

➤ **View buttons, scrollbars, and the Select Browse Object control.** The View buttons let you switch between different document views. The scroll bar at the bottom of the page lets you scroll left and right through the current page; the scroll bar along the side of the workspace lets you scroll through a document from top to bottom. At the bottom of the vertical scroll bar is the Select Browse Object control, which lets you jump to any particular point in your document.

➤ **Status bar.** This provides information about your current document—including what page you're on.

Viewing a Word Document—in Different Ways

Word can display your document in one of four different editing *views*. Each view is a particular way of looking at your document:

➤ **Normal View.** This is primarily a text-based view, because certain types of graphic objects—backgrounds, headers and footers, and some pictures—aren't displayed. *Not* a good view for laying out the elements on your page.

➤ **Web Layout View.** This is the view you use when you're creating a document to be displayed on the Web. In this view all the elements in your document (including graphics and backgrounds) are displayed pretty much as they would be if viewed by a Web browser.

➤ **Print Layout View.** This is the view you use to layout the pages of your document—with *all* elements visible, including graphics and backgrounds.

➤ **Outline View.** This is a great view for looking at the structure of your document, presenting your text (but *not* graphics!) in classic outline fashion. In this view you can collapse an outlined document to see only the main headings, or expand a document to show all (or selected) headings and body text.

In addition to these four editing Views, Word 2000 also includes two *preview* views and a special Document Map view. Print Preview displays your current document exactly as it will appear on the printed page; in this view you can choose to display the full page, a zoomed view of the page, or multiple pages on a single screen. Web Page Preview opens your Web browser and displays your current document as a Web page. You access both these views from Word's View menu.

➤ **Document Map View.** This isn't a standard view (and doesn't have a View button assigned to it), but can be accessed by pulling down the View menu and selecting Document Map (or by clicking the Document Map button on Word's Standard toolbar). In Document Map view, an outline of your document appears in a separate left pane, while the document itself (in whatever view you select) is displayed in the right pane. Although you can't edit the outline in the Document Map pane, you *can* click on a heading in the Document Map to jump directly to that part of your document in the right pane.

See It All

You can also choose to display your document across your entire computer screen, with all menus and toolbars hidden. Just pull down the View menu and select Full Screen; to return to normal viewing, click the Close Full Screen button in the floating toolbar.

Zooming to View

With Word 2000, it's easy to change the size of the document displayed in the Word workspace. The Standard toolbar includes a pull-down Zoom list, from which you can select a pre-set zoom level (from 10% to 500%). You can also choose to have your document automatically fill up the entire width of your screen by selecting the Page Width option.

Another way to change the onscreen size of your document is to pull down the View menu and select Zoom to display the Zoom dialog box. This dialog box lets you choose from both preselected and custom zoom levels—and previews your selected zoom level.

Choosing Between Full and Personalized Menus

In an attempt to simplify what is actually a quite complex program, Word 2000 incorporates *personalized* menus that (by default) only show those commands that you've recently used. (These menus are sometimes called *short* menus because they don't include all the commands found on the long menus.) So if you never use a particular command, you won't see it cluttering up things when you pull down that menu.

The only problem with this feature is that it makes it a tad difficult to find those menu items that you *don't* frequently use. (If you don't use it, it doesn't show up anywhere—and you don't know where to look for it!) Fortunately, you can easily display items otherwise "hidden" on a particular menu by clicking on the down arrow at the bottom of the menu. This expands the menu to show all items, recently used and otherwise.

If you'd prefer to turn off the personalized menu feature to display every single command available in Word, pull down the Tools menu and select Customize. When the Customize dialog box appears, select the Options tab, uncheck the Menus Show Recently Used Commands First option, and then click OK.

Push-Button Operation with Word's Toolbars

Word 2000 contains 16 built-in toolbars, only two of which (Standard and Formatting) appear in the workspace when you first launch Word. Other toolbars can be displayed as needed, and you can move any toolbar to any part of your screen. You can even create your own custom toolbars for your own specific Word needs.

To select which toolbars you see, pull down the View menu and select Toolbars. (You can also right-click on any toolbar to display this same list as a pop-up menu.) When the list of toolbars appears, check those toolbars you want to display, and uncheck those you want to hide.

You can move any toolbar to any area of the Word workspace screen by grabbing the thick handle on the far left of the toolbar with your mouse and dragging the toolbar to a new position. If you drag a toolbar to any side of the screen (top, bottom, left, or right) the toolbar automatically docks to that side. If you drop the toolbar in the middle of the screen, it remains there in a floating window.

If two toolbars docked side-by-side are longer than the available space, buttons at the end of one or both of the toolbars will not be displayed. Instead, you'll see a More Buttons arrow; click this double-arrow to display a submenu of the leftover buttons.

At the far right of every toolbar is a down arrow. When you click this arrow, a submenu appears listing extra buttons that can be added to that current toolbar. Check those buttons you want to add, and uncheck those you want to hide—and click the Customize option to select from even more buttons. (You can also pull down the Tools menu and select Customize to display the Customize dialog box; select the Toolbars tab to choose which toolbars to display, or the Commands tab to add new buttons to your toolbars.)

Changing the Way Word Works

Most of Word 2000's customization settings are located in two dialog boxes—the Customize dialog box and the Options dialog box. The *Customize* dialog box is where you customize Word 2000's toolbars, menus, andkeyboard shortcuts. You access the Customize dialog box by pulling down the Tools menu and selecting Customize. The *Options* dialog box is where you configure most of Word 2000's operating and display options. You access the Options dialog box by pulling down the Tools menu and selecting Options.

Make It and Save It

After Word is launched, you can either create a new document or open and edit an existing one. (And remember to save your work when you're done!)

Creating a New Document

Any new Word document you create is based on what Word calls a template. A *template* combines selected styles and document settings—and, in some cases, pre-written text or calculated fields—to create the building blocks for a specific type of document. You can create new documents—based on specific templates—from within Word, or from the Works Suite Task Launcher.

To create a new Word document from within Word, follow these steps:

1. Pull down the File menu and select New. You now have three options on the resulting submenu: Blank Document (to open a blank, unformatted document); Works Task Launcher (to return to Task Launcher, where you can choose from Works Suite 2000 templates); or More Word Templates (which opens the New dialog box).
2. Select More Word Templates.
3. When the New dialog box appears, select the template tab that contains the type of document you want to create.

4. Select the document template you want to use.
5. Click OK.

To create a new document from the Works Suite 2000 Task Launcher, follow these steps:

1. Select the Programs tab.
2. Select Word from the Programs list.
3. Select a specific template from the tasks list.
4. Click Start.

Note that the templates in the Task Launcher are arranged alphabetically, whereas the templates in Word's New dialog box are arranged by document type.

Make a New Document— Fast!

You can quickly create a generic Word document—based on the Normal template—by clicking the New button on Word's Standard toolbar.

Opening an Existing Document

After you've created and saved a document, it's easy to reopen that document for further editing.

To open an existing document from within Word, follow these steps:

1. Pull down the File menu and select Open (or click the Open Document button on Word's Standard toolbar).
2. From the Open dialog box, navigate through your folders and select the file you want to open.
3. Click Open.

To open an existing Word document from the Works Suite Task Launcher, select the History tab, and then select a file from the documents list.

Saving Your Documents

Every document you make—that you want to keep—must be saved to a file. To save a new file, follow these steps:

1. Pull down the File menu and select Save As.
2. When the Save As dialog box appears, select a location for the file and enter a new filename.
3. Click Save.

After you've saved a file once, you don't need to go through the whole Save As routine any more—the file already has a name and location, after all. To "fast save" an existing file, all you have to do is click the Save button on Word's Standard toolbar (or pull down the File menu and select Save).

What's Up, Doc?

Files created by Microsoft Word are automatically assigned the .DOC extension. For example, if you name a file MYFILE, Word saves it as MYFILE.DOC.

Finding Your Way from Here to There

Navigating with Word is relatively easy. Beyond using your keyboard's arrow keys or clicking the scroll bars with your mouse, Word offers a few other tools to help you find your way around your documents.

Going Places

The fastest way to go to a specific point in your document is by using Word's Go To command (found on the Go To tab of the Find and Replace dialog box, shown below). Access Go To by pulling down the Edit menu and selecting Go To—or by pressing either F5 or Ctrl+G.

Figure 4.2

Go anyplace—fast—with the Go To command.

Select what you want to go to.

Select where you want to go.

Click to go there.

To go directly to any specific page or element within your text, select what type of element you want to go to from the Go To What list, and then enter the specific element you want to go into the Enter box. (This box varies dependent on the type of element selected.) Click the Go To button to go to the selected location.

Browse from the Scrollbar

Word's Select Browse Object tool—actually three buttons at the bottom of the vertical scrollbar—lets you jump quickly between different types of document elements. You select what document element you want to browse by clicking the Select Browse Object button. This displays a pop-up menu of 10 different element types, including section, page, and heading. After you select which type of element you want to browse, click the Previous or the Next button to jump to the next instance of that element within your document.

Finding—and Replacing—Just About Anything

It's really simple. The Find command finds locations and items and text in your document; the Replace command lets you replace what you found with something different.

Here's how you use the Find command:

1. Pull down the Edit menu and select Find (or press Ctrl+F).
2. From the Find tab (of the Find and Replace dialog box), click the More button (to display all search options).

3. Enter the text (or other element) you want to find in the Find What box.

4. Select any additional options for your search.

5. Click the Find Next button to find what you're looking for (or to find the next appearance of what you're looking for).

After you've entered your search criteria, you can press Shift+F4 to find the next instance of the item without displaying the Find and Replace dialog box. When Word reaches the end of the document, it asks if you want to continue your search at the beginning; answer Yes to search from the top.

Finding More Than Words

In addition to searching for words or phrases in your documents, you can click the Format button to search for specific formatting within your document, or click the Special button to search for special characters in your text.

To access Word's Replace command, press Ctrl+H—or pull down the Edit menu and select Replace. Replace works just like Find, except you have the added option of replacing the item you found with something different.

You can choose to replace the current instance of whatever you're looking for (click the Replace button), or to automatically search your document and replace all instances of what you've found. If you choose to replace one instance at a time (which lets you confirm or cancel each potential replacement), you can either click the Find Next button or press Shift+F4 to find the next instance of the item.

Working with Word

After you have a document open in the Word workspace, it's time to get down to the real work—entering and editing your text. (It isn't that hard, really—kind of like typing, but on steroids.)

Entering Text

You enter text in a Word document at the *insertion point*, which appears onscreen as a blinking cursor. When you start typing on your keyboard, the new text is added at the insertion point.

You move the insertion point with your mouse by clicking on a new position in your text. You move the insertion point with your keyboard by using your keyboard's arrow keys.

Entering Text *Anywhere* with Click and Type

Where the normal Word insertion point is always "in line" with your text, Word 2000's *Click and Type* feature lets you add new text *anywhere* in your document—even outside the normal lines and paragraphs.

To insert text using Click and Type, position your cursor over a blank area of your document. When the cursor changes shape, double-click. When the insertion point starts blinking, start typing. The text you enter with Click and Type will be automatically aligned according to its position on the page—which is indicated by the shape of the Click and Type cursor.

You can use Click and Type in either Print Layout or Web Layout views—but *not* in Normal or Outline views.

Entering AutoText

Word 2000's AutoText feature lets you automate the entering of dozens of pre-written words and phrases. There are two ways to insert an AutoText entry into your text. First, you can pull down the Insert menu and select AutoText, and then select a category and entry from the resulting submenu. Alternatively, you can display the AutoText toolbar, and then click the All Entries button and select a category and entry from the resulting list. When you select an AutoText entry, the AutoText text is inserted into your document at the current insertion point.

You can quickly and easily create your own AutoText entries for text that you find yourself entering on a frequent basis. Just follow these steps:

1. Enter the text for your AutoText entry somewhere in your current document, and then select the text.
2. Click the New button on the AutoText toolbar. (Alternatively, you can pull down the Insert menu and select AutoText, and then select New—or press F3.)
3. When the Create AutoText dialog box appears, enter a name for the new entry, and then click OK.

Editing Your Text

After you've entered your text, it's time to edit. With Word you can delete, cut, copy, and paste text—or graphics—to and from anywhere in your document, or between documents.

Before you can edit text, you first have to *select* the text to edit. The easiest way to select text is with your mouse—just hold down your mouse button and drag the cursor over the text you want to select. You can also select text using your keyboard. In general, you use the Shift key—in combination with other keys[mg]to highlight blocks of text. For example, Shift+Left Arrow selects one character to the left; Shift+PgDn selects all text to the end of your document.

Any text you select will appear as white text against a black highlight. After you've selected a block of text, you can then edit it in a number of ways, as detailed in Table 4.1.

Table 4.1   Word 2000 Editing Operations

Operation	Key Function	Menu Function
Delete	Del	Pull down the Edit menu and select Clear.
Copy	Ctrl+Insert	Pull down the Edit menu and select Copy.
Cut	Shift+Del or Ctrl+X	Pull down the Edit menu and select Cut.
Paste	Shift+Ins	Pull down the Edit menu and select Paste.

Use the Mouse for Drag and Drop Editing

You can also use Windows' Drag and Drop operation to copy or move text using your mouse. Begin by using your mouse to select the text you want to copy, and then hold down the *right* mouse button and drag the text to the new location. When you release the mouse button, Word displays a pop-up menu. Select from any operation on this menu (move, copy, link, or create hyperlink) to apply the operation to the drag-and-dropped text.

Cut Once, Cut Twice—and Paste 'Em All!

Word 2000 enhances the standard Cut/Copy/Paste function with *Collect and Paste*, which enables you to store up to twelve different cut or copied items in the Clipboard, and then select which of the multiple items you want to paste into your document.

To best use Collect and Paste, you should have the Clipboard toolbar displayed on your desktop. After you've cut or copied several elements, go to the Clipboard toolbar and click the button for the item you want to paste. (If you have the Clipboard menu docked, you'll need to pull down the Items menu to display the Clipboard items.) The item you selected will then be pasted into your document.

Paste—In a Different Format

You can cut or copy text and graphics from *any* Windows program and paste it into a Word document. However, if you use the standard Paste command, the item will be inserted in its native format, with its original formatting. While this may work in some instances, more often than not you'll want to paste the item into your document in a more "Word-friendly" format.

To change the way Word pastes text or graphics into your document, pull down the Edit menu and select Paste Special. When the Paste Special dialog box appears, select from one of the available formats, and then click OK.

Undoing—and Un-Undoing—Your Editing

What if you make a mistake while editing your Word document? Is there any way to "take back" that one operation you performed in error?

The answer—fortunately for all us ham-handed typists—is *yes*. When you click the Undo button on Word's Standard toolbar (or pull down the Edit menu and select Undo), your last action will be reversed. If you click Undo again, the action before that will be reversed. In fact, virtually all your actions during an editing section are capable of being reversed, if you click Undo enough times. (Click the down arrow on the Undo button to see a list of all actions that can be undone.)

What if you make a mistake while undoing another mistake? To undo any actions you've undone, click the Redo button (next to the Undo button on Word's Standard toolbar). Like the Redo button, you can click the button to redo one action at a time, or click the down arrow on the button to display a list of all actions that can be redone.

Making Things Look Better

After your text is entered and edited, you can use Word's numerous formatting options to add some pizzazz to your document. Just activate the Print Layout view and follow the instructions in the next few sections—and before long, you'll have a professional-looking document on your hands!

Formatting Fancy Fonts

Formatting text is easy—and most achievable from Word's Formatting toolbar, shown below.

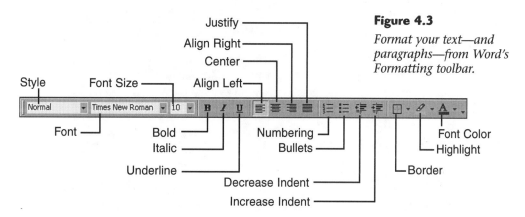

Figure 4.3

Format your text—and paragraphs—from Word's Formatting toolbar.

To format a block of text, highlight the text and then click the desired format button. You can turn on formatting for all text at the insertion point by clicking the format button and then typing at the insertion point.

Table 4.2 shows some of the text formatting you can apply in Word 2000; in most cases, you can apply multiple formatting to any selected text.

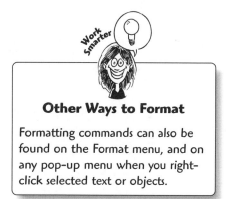

Other Ways to Format

Formatting commands can also be found on the Format menu, and on any pop-up menu when you right-click selected text or objects.

Table 4.2 Word 2000 Text Format Operations

Operation	Format Button	Keyboard Shortcut
Bold	Bold	Ctrl+B
Italicize	Italic	Ctrl+I
Underline	Underline	Ctrl+U
Change font	Font	Ctrl+Shift+F
Change font size	Font Size	Ctrl+Shift+P
Change font color	Font Color	None

There are lots more text formatting options available in the Font dialog box, shown below. To display this dialog box, pull down the Format menu and select Font.

Figure 4.4

Find even more font formatting options in the Font dialog box.

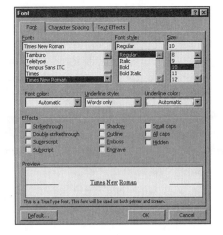

From here you can format the standard stuff (such as font, font style, font color, and so on) and lots of non-standard stuff—strikethrough, superscript, subscript, shadow, outline, emboss, engrave, character spacing, and text animation. Just choose the formatting you want and click OK.

Producing Pretty Paragraphs

Text (or font) formatting lets you format one character at a time; paragraph formatting affects how an entire paragraph looks.

Table 4.3 shows some of the paragraph formatting you can apply in Word 2000; in most cases, you can apply multiple formatting to any selected paragraph.

Table 4.3   Word 2000 Paragraph Format Operations

Operation	Format Button	Keyboard Shortcut
Create a numbered list	Numbering	None
Create a bulleted list	Bullets	None
Left align paragraph	Align Left	Ctrl+L
Right align paragraph	Align Right	Ctrl+R
Center paragraph	Center	Ctrl+E
Justify paragraph	Justify	Ctrl+J
Increase paragraph indent	Increase Indent	Tab
Decrease paragraph indent	Decrease Indent	Backspace
Add border to paragraph	Border	None

Additional paragraph formatting options are found in the Paragraph dialog box, accessible when you pull down the Format menu and select Paragraph. From here you can precisely adjust indentation, line spacing, and widow/orphan control.

Setting Up Snazzy Styles

If you have a preferred paragraph formatting that you use over and over and over, you don't have to format each paragraph individually—you can assign all your formatting to a paragraph *style*, and then assign that style to paragraphs in your document. Most templates come with a selection of predesigned styles; you can modify these built-in styles, or create your own custom styles.

Styles include formatting for the following elements:

➤ Font

➤ Paragraph

➤ Tabs

➤ Border

➤ Language

➤ Frame

➤ Numbering

To apply a style to a paragraph, position the insertion point anywhere in the paragraph, and then pull down the Style list and select a style. (You can also access this pull-down list by pressing Ctrl+Shift+S.)

To modify a style, follow these steps:

1. Pull down the Format menu and select Style.
2. When the Style dialog box appears, select the style you want to edit.

81

Figure 4.5

Modify or create para-graph styles in the Style dialog box.

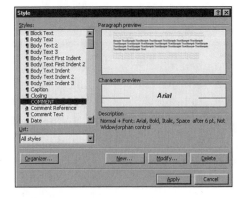

3. Click the Modify button.

4. When the Modify dialog box appears, click the Format button.

5. When the pull-down list appears, select the style property you want to edit.

6. When the selected property dialog box appears, make your changes and click OK.

7. From the Modify dialog box, click Shortcut Key to assign this style to a keyboard shortcut.

8. From the Modify dialog box, click OK to return to the Style dialog box.

9. Click Apply to apply this style to the current paragraph and close the dialog box, or click Cancel to close the dialog box without applying the style.

Cancel Doesn't Really Cancel

Note that when you click Cancel in the Style dialog box, you don't cancel the modifications made to the selected style—those modifications were saved when you clicked OK in the Modify dialog box. (If you really wanted to cancel your modifications, you should have clicked Cancel back in the Modify dialog box.)

If you click the New button in the Style dialog box, you create a new style based on the current style. Make whatever changes you want, and then save the new style under a new name.

Adding Pictures—and Other Things—to Your Documents

Although memos and letters might look fine if they contain nothing but text, other types of documents—newsletters, reports, and so on—can be jazzed up with the inclusion of pictures and other graphic elements. Word makes it easy to insert all sorts of these types of objects—including items you create with other Works Suite 2000 components.

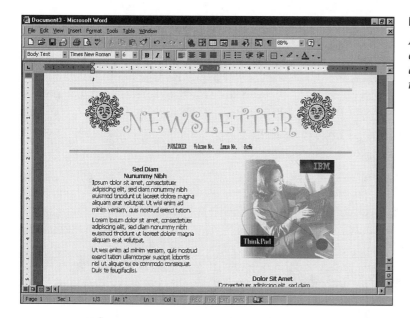

Figure 4.6

Add visual interest to your documents with pictures and other non-text elements.

Inserting Pictures and Objects into Your Text

Whether you're adding clip art, a picture from a file, a pie chart, or a Works spreadsheet to your Word document, you follow pretty much the same procedure:

1. Position the insertion point where you want to insert the object.
2. Pull down the Insert menu and select the type of item you want to insert. For example, you might select Picture, and then select From File.
3. You'll now get the opportunity to choose the individual item you want to insert. Follow the specific instructions to find and insert that item.

Here are just some of the non-text items you can add to your documents:

➤ Autoshapes
➤ Charts

➤ Clip art

➤ Drawing objects

➤ Files

➤ Objects from other Windows programs

➤ Pictures

➤ Text boxes

➤ WordArt

Editing and Formatting Your Objects

After you've inserted an object, you may need to format it for your document. When you double-click most objects you display a Format dialog box. (If double-clicking doesn't display the dialog box, try right-clicking and selecting Format from the pop-up menu.) From here you can typically format the following properties:

➤ Colors and lines (fill and line styles and colors)

➤ Size (sizing and scaling)

➤ Layout (text wrapping)

➤ Picture (brightness, contrast, and cropping for pictures)

➤ Text box (internal margins for text boxes)

➤ Web (alternative text if used on a Web page)

In most cases you can move and resize the object with your mouse, by dragging the entire object (to move) or by dragging a selection handle (to resize). To maintain the original shape/dimensions when resizing, hold down the Shift key.

Working with Tables

A table is another useful object to add to your text. Word makes it very easy to create the rows and columns necessary to hold your tabular data.

Just follow these steps:

1. Position the insertion point where you want to insert the table.

2. Click the Insert Table button on Word's Standard toolbar.

3. When the pull-down menu appears, select the number of rows and columns you want your table to contain.

4. Your table will now appear on your desktop, ready for data input or formatting.

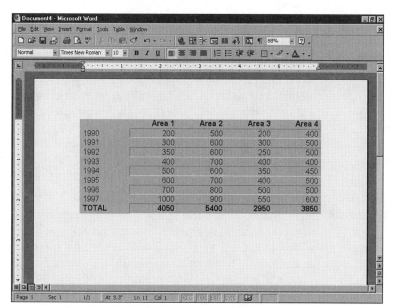

Figure 4.7

Use tables to display numbers and other columnar data.

You can resize the columns in your table by positioning your cursor on any column divider and moving it left or right with your mouse. You add new columns or rows to your table by pulling down the Table menu and selecting Insert, and then choosing what you want to insert (and where). You delete rows and columns by pulling down the Table menu and selecting Delete, and then choosing what you want to delete.

To add or modify the borders in your table, click the Borders button on Word's Formatting toolbar and select a border style. You can format your entire table by pulling down the Table menu and selecting Table Properties; make your selections from the Table Properties dialog box.

Format Faster

Choose from dozens of preselected table formats by pulling down the Table menu and selecting Table AutoFormat. When the Table AutoFormat dialog box appears, choose from the list of formats, select what elements of the style you want to apply, and then click OK.

Proofing Your Documents

After you've created your document and entered and edited your text, it's time to proof your document for errors. Word includes several different proofing tools—including a spell checker, grammar checker, and thesaurus—that make it easy to fix any mistakes in your document.

Spell It Write

Onscreen Proofing Only

The red wavy underline Word adds to misspelled words only appears on screen; these proofing marks do *not* appear in your printed documents.

Word's Automatic Spell Checking checks the spelling of each and every word your type. Any word not found in the spelling dictionary is assumed to be misspelled, and flagged with a wavy red underline. When you right-click a potentially misspelled word, Word displays a pop-up menu containing suggested corrections, as well as a command to Ignore All instances of this word (useful if the word isn't actually misspelled) or to Add this word to Word's spelling dictionary.

You can also check the spelling of your entire document in a single operation. You start a document-wide spell check by pulling down the Tools menu and selecting Spelling and Grammar, or by pressing F7 (or selecting the Spelling and Grammar button on Word's Standard toolbar). When Word's spell checker finds a word it doesn't recognize, it displays the Spelling dialog box. The word in question is listed in the Not in Dictionary box, and suggested spellings are listed in the Suggestions list. After you change or ignore a misspelling, Word's spell checker moves to the next potentially misspelled word in your document.

Say It Right

Word 2000 incorporates a state-of-the-art grammar checker to analyze your documents for grammatical correctness—and offer suggestions on how to improve your writing. With Automatic Grammar Checking is enabled, Word checks your grammar as you type; any grammatically questionable phrases are flagged with a wavy green underline.

To examine (and possibly fix) a flagged phrase, right-click anywhere within the underlined phrase. Word displays a pop-up menu that contains a brief explanation of why the phrase was flagged. From here, you can select to Ignore the advice, or you can go back into your document to edit the phrase to be more grammatically correct.

You can also check your grammar at the same time you do a document-wide spell check. Just make sure the Check Grammar with Spelling option is checked in the Spelling & Grammar tab of the Options dialog box.

Say It Differently

Beyond spelling and grammar checking, Word 2000 also includes a thesaurus—so you can find synonyms for selected words in your documents. To use the thesaurus, position the insertion point anywhere in the word you want to look up, and then press

Shift+F7 (or pull down the Tools menu and select Language, and then Thesaurus). This opens the Thesaurus dialog box, where you select the proper definition from the Meanings list, select a synonym from the Replace with Synonym list, and then click Insert.

Printing Your Documents

When your document is done—really and truly done—you're ready to print it out.

Preview Before You Print

Unless you own stock in a paper company, it's a good idea to preview your documents onscreen *before* you print them—so you can minimize the wasted paper caused by unexpected print format glitches. To view your document with Word's Print Preview, do one of the following:

Look Up Synonyms—Quickly (or Fast or Rapidly or Expediently)

Word 2000 offers the option of displaying a short list of synonyms directly from a pop-up menu. Just right-click on any word and select Synonyms from the pop-up menu. You can then select any of the listed synonyms, or select Thesaurus to display the more fully featured Thesaurus dialog box.

➤ Click the Print Preview button on Word's Standard toolbar

➤ Pull down the File menu and select Print Preview

➤ Press Ctrl+F2.

To zoom in or out of the preview document, click the Magnifier button and then click the magnifier cursor anywhere on your document. When you're done previewing your document, click the Close button.

Print It Fast

The fastest way to print a document is with Word's fast print option—activated when you click the Print button on Word's Standard toolbar. When you initiate a fast print of your document, you send your document directly to your default printer—bypassing the Print dialog box and all other configuration options.

Print It However You Want It

Of course, there are times when fast printing isn't an option—if you need to print multiple copies, for example, or if you want to print to a different (non-default) printer. For these instances, you need to use Word's Print dialog box to initiate printing.

You open the Print dialog box, shown below, by pulling down the File menu and selecting Print—or by pressing Ctrl+P.

Select your printer.

Figure 4.8

Print your document—with options.

Click to configure printer properties.

Select what part(s) of your document to print.

Select how many copies to print.

Select other items to print.

Select special print scaling and zooming.

Click for more print options.

Click to print.

After you have the Print dialog box displayed, you can configure any one of a number of options specific to this particular print job. After you've made your choices, click the OK button to start printing.

Background Work

Learn How to Make Different Documents

To learn how to create specific types of documents using Word 2000 and other Works Suite 2000 programs, turn to these chapters later in this book:

➤ Chapter 16, "Create Envelopes and Labels"

➤ Chapter 17, "Create a Large Mailing"

➤ Chapter 18, "Create a Newsletter"

➤ Chapter 19, "Create a School Report"

The Least You Need to Know

➤ To get a head start on your writing, create a new Word document based on a specific *template*.

➤ Use Word's Normal view to enter mass quantities of text; use the Print Layout view to lay out pages of text and graphics.

➤ Use the buttons on the Format toolbar to apply formatting to your text and paragraphs.

➤ Use paragraph *styles* to apply formatting document-wide.

➤ Spell check, grammar check, and preview your document before you print— then configure your printing options in the Print dialog box.

Chapter 5

Crunch Your Numbers with Works Spreadsheet

In This Chapter

➤ Discover what a spreadsheet is, what it does, and how it works

➤ Learn how to enter, edit, and format spreadsheet data

➤ Find out how to use formulas and functions to make calculations within your spreadsheet

➤ Learn how to turn your numerical data into a pie, line, or bar chart

Think of a spreadsheet as a giant list. Your list can contain just about any type of data you can think of—text, numbers, even dates. You can take any of the numbers on your list and use them to calculate new numbers—you can add them together, subtract one from another, even perform relatively complex mathematical operations to come up with new values. You can sort the items on your list, and pretty them up and print up the important points in a report. You can even graph your numbers in a color pie, line, or bar chart!

In a spreadsheet, all your data—all the items and information on your list—are stored in *cells*. Your spreadsheet is divided up into hundreds or thousands of these cells, each located in a specific location on a giant grid made of *rows* and *columns*. Each single cell represents the intersection of a particular row and column. Any given cell can contain a piece of text, a date, a number, or a *formula*. Formulas can be internal to a particular cell, or reference other cells. (As an example, you can create a formula to add the values of two different cells; the result of that formula—the sum of the two other cells—is then displayed in the cell containing the formula.)

The Works Spreadsheet makes it easy to create lists, calculations, and charts. Many common spreadsheet-oriented tasks are available as wizards or templates from the Works Task Launcher; other tasks are almost as easy to create from scratch. Read on to learn how to use Works Spreadsheet for your own number and list-related tasks!

Opening—and Closing—Works Spreadsheet

As with most Works Suite 2000 applications, you can start Works Spreadsheet either from Windows or from the Works Task Launcher.

To launch Works Spreadsheet from the Works Task Launcher, select the Programs tab and select Works Spreadsheet from the Programs list. If you want to start with a blank spreadsheet, select Start a Blank Spreadsheet; if you want to start with a specific task loaded, select the task from the task list and click Start.

Of course, Works Suite 2000 doesn't have to be running for you to use Works Spreadsheet. To launch Works Spreadsheet without using the Task Launcher, just click the Windows Start button, select Programs, select the Microsoft Works folder (*not* the Microsoft Works program icon!), and then select Microsoft Works Spreadsheet.

When you're done using Works Spreadsheet, you close the program by pulling down the File menu and selecting Exit. (If you have any unsaved spreadsheets open, Works Spreadsheet will prompt you to save them first, and then close.)

Navigating the Spreadsheet Workspace

Before we get started, let's take a quick look at the Works Spreadsheet workspace in Figure 5.1—so you can know what's what and what's where.

What's Where

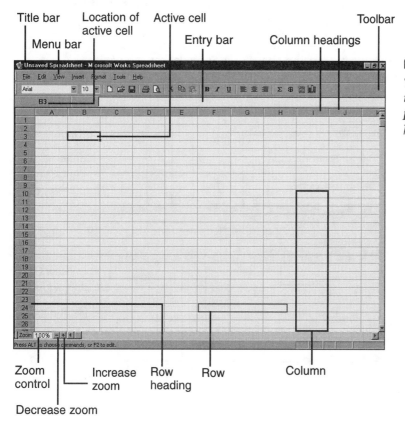

Title bar   Location of   Active cell   Toolbar
             active cell
                           Entry bar   Column headings
Menu bar

Figure 5.1

The Works Spreadsheet—use the toolbar and the pull-down menus to perform most tasks.

Zoom   Increase   Row   Row   Column
control   zoom   heading

Decrease zoom

Each column has an alphabetic label (A, B, C, and so on). Each row has a numeric label (1, 2, 3, and so on). The location of each cell is the combination of its column and row location. For example, the cell in the top-left corner of the spreadsheet is in column A and row 1; its location is signified as A1, the cell to the right of it is B1, and the cell below A1 is A2.

You use the vertical and horizontal scrollbars to scroll through a spreadsheet, as you would scroll through any Windows-based application. You use your keyboard's arrow keys to move from cell to cell, or use the PgUp and PgDn keys to move up or down your spreadsheet one screen at a time.

The Entry bar at the top of the workspace echoes the contents of the selected, or *active*, cell. You can type data directly into the active cell, or into the Entry bar.

Using the Toolbar

The most common spreadsheet commands and operations are located on the toolbar; *all* commands and operations are accessible from the pull-down menus on the menu bar.

Figure 5.2 shows the default buttons on the Works Spreadsheet toolbar.

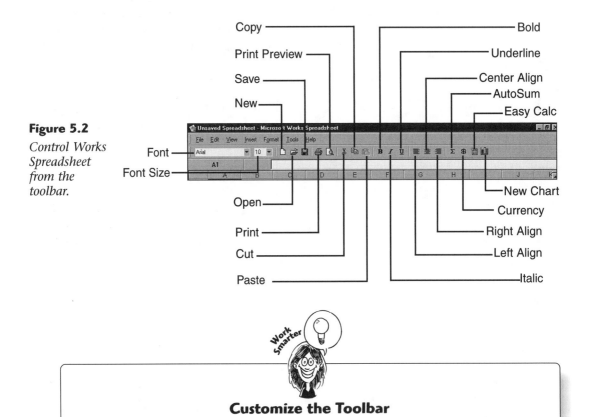

Figure 5.2

Control Works Spreadsheet from the toolbar.

Customize the Toolbar

Works Spreadsheet lets you add new buttons to—or delete buttons from—the toolbar. Just pull down the Tools menu and select Customize Toolbar. When the Customize Works Toolbar dialog box appears, select the Category containing the button you want to add, and then select a button and drag it to the toolbar. (To see a description of a button's operation, click the button before you drag it.) To delete a button from the toolbar, open the Customize Works Toolbar, and then drag the button off the toolbar and drop it anywhere—it will disappear automatically. Click OK to close the dialog box when you're done.

Zooming to View

By default, your spreadsheet is displayed full size (otherwise known as *100% zoom*). To change the size of the spreadsheet onscreen, use the Zoom controls at the bottom left of the spreadsheet workspace.

To increase the zoom (make it larger) in 50% intervals, click the + button. To decrease the zoom (make it smaller) in 50% intervals, click the – button. To select a different zoom value, click the Zoom button and select a new zoom value from the pop-up menu. If you select Custom from this menu, the Zoom dialog box appears; enter a specific value in the Custom box and click OK.

Make It and Save It

After the Works Spreadsheet is up and running, you can either create a new spreadsheet or open and edit an existing one. (Always remember to save your work when you're done!)

Creating a New Blank Spreadsheet

To open a blank spreadsheet in the Works Spreadsheet workspace—with no template or task applied—all you have to do is click the New button on the toolbar. A blank spreadsheet is now loaded into the workspace, ready to accept any text or numbers you want to enter.

Creating a Task-Based Spreadsheet

To use a template or wizard to create a spreadsheet for a specific task, pull down the File menu and select New. When the Works Task Launcher appears, make sure you're on the Programs tab with Works Spreadsheet selected, select a task from the Tasks list, and then click Start.

When you start most tasks, a spreadsheet template is loaded into the workspace. This template, like the Home Improvement Budget shown in Figure 5.3, has been preformatted for the task at hand—all you have to do is edit your own personal data, and everything else is calculated automatically.

Off to See the Wizard

Some tasks are launched via a step-by-step wizard. Answer the questions and fill in the blanks, and your spreadsheet will be completed automatically.

Figure 5.3

Use a preformatted spreadsheet template to automate many common tasks.

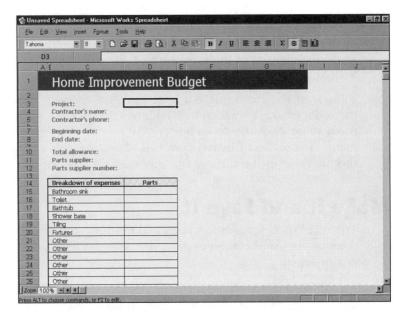

Opening an Existing Spreadsheet

After you've created and saved a spreadsheet, it's easy to reopen that spreadsheet for further editing.

To open an existing document from within Works Spreadsheet, pull down the File menu and select Open (or click the Open button on the toolbar). When the Open dialog box appears, navigate through your folders, select the file you want to open, and then click Open.

To open an existing spreadsheet from the Works Task Launcher, select the History tab, and then select a file from the documents list.

Here's How It WKS

Spreadsheet files created by Works Spreadsheet are automatically assigned the .WKS extension. For example, if you name a file MYFILE, it is saved as MYFILE.WKS.

Saving Your Spreadsheet

Every time you create a new spreadsheet, you need to save it to a file. You save a new spreadsheet file as you'd save any new Windows file—by pulling down the File menu and selecting Save As. When the Save As dialog box appears, select a location for the file, enter a new filename, and click Save.

After you've saved a spreadsheet, you don't need to go through the whole Save As routine to resave the spreadsheet—the file already has a name and location. To "fast save" an existing spreadsheet, all you have to do is click the Save button on the toolbar (or pull down the File menu and select Save).

Fill It Up

After you've opened a blank spreadsheet, it's time to fill it up—with numbers, text, and dates.

Selecting Cells and Things

Before you fill up individual cells or groups of cells, it helps to know how to *select* the cells in which you want to enter data. After the cell or *range* of cells is selected, you then can enter data into the cell(s).

Table 5.1 shows you how to select various parts of your spreadsheet.

Table 5.1   How to Select Parts of a Spreadsheet

Part	Operation
Single cell	Click the cell.
Group of cells	Click the first cell and drag your mouse across the other cells, or hold down the Shift key while you move from cell to cell with one of the arrow keys.
Column	Click the column heading.
Row	Click the row heading.
Multiple columns	Click the first column heading and drag your mouse across the other column headings.
Multiple rows	Click the first row heading and drag your mouse pointer the other row headings.
Entire spreadsheet	Click the box in the top-left corner of the spreadsheet, between the column and row headings.

Entering and Editing Data

Entering text or numbers is easy. Just remember that data is entered into each cell individually—you can fill up a spreadsheet with hundreds or thousands of cells filled with their own individual data!

To enter data into a specific cell, follow these steps:

1. Select the cell into which you want to enter data.

2. Type your text or numbers into the cell; what you type will be echoed in the Entry bar at the top of the screen.

3. When you're done typing data into the cell, press Enter.

Stop Work

Undo What You Just Did

If you want to undo your last cell entry, pull down the Edit menu and select Undo Entry.

When you press Enter, you enter the cell's contents into your spreadsheet, and move the active cell down one row.

Entering Repeating Data

If you're entering a series of data—like a list of consecutive numbers, or the months of the year—you don't have to enter each cell separately. If you enter enough information so that Works Spreadsheet can figure out the rest of your series, you can have Works Spreadsheet fill in the rest of the series for you.

Here's how it works:

1. Enter the first few cells of your series. For example, if you're entering a numbered series, you would enter **1** in the first cell and **2** in the second.

Works Knows Dates

If you're entering months—either as January or January 1999—you only have to enter the first cell for Works to autofill the rest of the series. If you're entering a specific date, Works will autofill *days* if you only enter the first cell.

2. Select the cells into which you just entered data.

3. Move your cursor to the lower-right corner of the cell range; the cursor changes to a FILL icon.

4. Grab this corner and drag it either right or down to fill out the balance of your row or column.

5. Release the mouse button; Works automatically completes the series for the number of cells you selected.

As an example, let's say you want the columns of your spreadsheet to represent the years 1990–2000. You'd enter **1990** in cell B1 and **1991** in cell B2, and then select both cells and drag the Fill handle over the next nine cells to the right. Works' autofill automatically enters **1992, 1993,** and so on into the other cells, saving you the trouble of manually doing so.

This autofill feature is a *great* way to automate the tedious task of labeling rows and columns in your spreadsheet!

It's Only So Smart...

For autofill to work, it has to be able to figure out your intended data series. It can guess that if you enter **January** you want to create a series of months, but if you enter **1**, it can't figure out what the rest of the series should be. That's why you have to enter a *second* cell (**2**, for example, if you want a simple numbered list, or **3** if you want an odd-numbered list) so autofill can know what kind of series to create.

Applying Date and Number Formats

When you enter a number into a cell, Works applies what it calls a "general" format to the number—it just displays the number, right-aligned, with no commas or dollar signs. You can, however, select a specific number format to apply to any cells in your spreadsheet that contain numbers.

Table 5.2 lists the different number formats available in Works Spreadsheet.

Table 5.2 Works Spreadsheet Number Formats

Format	Description	Example
General	Displays exactly as entered	1234.5
Fixed	Displays a selected number of decimal places	1234.50
Currency	Displays dollar sign and two decimal places	$1234.50
Comma	Displays "thousands" commas	1,234.5
Percent	Displays number as a percent	1234.5%
Exponential	Displays number in scientific notation	1.23E+02
Leading Zeros	Displays a selected number of leading zeroes	001234.5
Fraction	Displays decimal numbers as fractions	1234 1/2

continues

Table 5.2   Continued

Format	Description	Example
True/False	Zero values display FALSE, nonzero values display TRUE	TRUE
Date	Select from a variety of day, month, and year formats	2/14/00
Time	Select from a variety of hour, minute, and second formats	2:48 PM
Text	Formats cell contents (even numbers) as text (which can't be calculated)	1234.5

Follow these steps to apply a number format to selected cells:

1. Select the cell or cells.
2. Pull down the Format menu and select Number.
3. When the Format Cells dialog box appears, make sure the Number tab is selected.
4. Check one of the options in the Format list.
5. If the format has additional options (such as decimal points, or various date or time formats), configure these as desired.
6. Click OK.

As an example, if you entered **1-2000** in a cell but wanted to "spell out" the date, you'd select the Date option and then select October 1999 from the Date Options list; when you click OK, your date would be displayed as **January 2000**.

Quick Cash

You can quickly apply Works' Currency format by selecting the cell(s) and then clicking the Currency button on the toolbar.

Turning Numbers into Text

One number format deserves a special mention. The *text* format is useful not only for non-number text (although, Works can kind of figure out that you've entered text, and format things accordingly), but also when you enter a number that you want to treat as text—that is, a number that you don't want to add or subtract or otherwise calculate. As an example, if you enter a phone number (such as 555-1234), you don't want Works to treat it as a number that can be formatted (with strange results!) or calculated. In essence, you want Works to leave it alone—and the best way to do that is to format it as text.

A quick way to indicate text formatting is to enter a quotation mark (") before you enter the text in the cell. So, using our phone number example, you'd enter **"555-1224"**, and Works would know to apply the text format to that cell.

Shooting Blanks

If you have a blank cell in a row or column of numbers, that cell will display a zero (0). If you'd rather display an empty cell instead of a zero, you have two options.

First, you could simply enter **"** into the cell. The quotation mark forces text formatting; because nothing follows the **"**, a big fat space is displayed.

The other option is to format that cell to hide all zero values. Select the cell, pull down the Tools menu, and then select Options. When the Options dialog box appears, select the Data Entry tab, check the Hide Zero Values option, and then click OK.

Work with What You Got: Name, Search, and Sort

When it comes to manipulating your spreadsheet data, Works Spreadsheet provides lots of options. You can select specific cells in your spreadsheet, assign them a name, search for and replace information within specific cells, and even sort your data in different ways. Read on to learn more about naming, searching, and sorting with Works Spreadsheet.

Home on the Range

A range is a series of cells all in a row. For example, cells A1 through A4 constitute a range. You denote a range by using the first and last cells in the range, separated by a colon (:). For example, the range of cells from A1 through A4 is denoted A1:A4.

Note that cell ranges aren't limited to a single column or row. As an example, the range A1:C5 references the range of cells that starts at A1 (in the top-left corner) and ends at C5 (in the bottom-right corner). This includes cells from three columns and five rows, all of which are adjacent to each other.

Naming Cells and Ranges

Using a range of reference is less cumbersome than naming all the cells in the range individually, but there's an even easier way to refer to specific cells or groups of cells. Works Spreadsheets lets you assign a *name* to any cell or range; you can then reference that name in any formulas you create.

To name a cell or range, follow these steps:

1. Select the cell or range of cells you want to name.
2. Pull down the Insert menu and select Range Name.
3. When the Range Name dialog box appears, enter a name in the name box.
4. Click OK.

As an example, if you named a range of cells "Bob," you could use the following function to sum all the cells in the range: **=sum(Bob)**. (Functions are discussed a little later in this chapter; feel free to read ahead if you like.)

Jump to a Cell

To jump to an unnamed cell in your spreadsheet, press Ctrl+G to open the Go To dialog box, enter the cell location (A1 or C10 or whatever) in the Go To box, and then click OK.

Jumping to a Named Cell or Range

After you've assigned cell or range names, you can use Works' Go To command to jump to a specific range. Follow these steps:

1. Pull down the Edit menu and select Go To, or press Ctrl+G.
2. When the Go To dialog box appears, select a name from the Range Name list.
3. Click OK to jump to that range.

Searching for Specific Stuff

If you have a big spreadsheet chock full of data, how do you find the one cell that contains a specific piece of information? It's easy—when you use Works' Find command.

With Works' Find command, you can choose to look in either rows or columns. You can also choose to look in the formulas contained in the spreadsheet cells, or in the *values* created by the formulas.

Here's how you search the cells of your spreadsheet:

1. Pull down the Edit menu and select Find (or press Ctrl+F).
2. When the Find dialog box appears, enter what you're looking for in the Find What box.
3. Select whether you want to search By Rows or By Columns.
4. Select whether you want to look in Formulas or Values.
5. Click OK to start the search.

Works will now highlight the first cell that matches your query. Press Ctrl+F to redisplay the Find dialog box and continue searching.

Replacing Cell Contents

Works' Replace command works similarly to the Find command. You specify the contents you're searching for, and what you want to replace them with, and let Works find them and replace them for you. Follow these steps:

1. Pull down the Edit menu and select Replace (or press Ctrl+H).
2. When the Replace dialog box appears, enter what you're looking for in the Find What box, and what you want to replace it with in the Replace With box.
3. Select whether you want to search By Rows or By Columns.
4. To find each instance of the original data (and prompt you manually to replace), click the Find Next button.
5. To replace all instances of the first data with the second, click the Replace All button.

Sorting Your Data

If you have a list of either text or numbers, you may want to reorder the list for a different purpose. For example, if you have columns representing accounts, balances, and due dates, you may want to list the data alphabetically by account, or in descending order of dollar balances, or by chronological due date. When it comes time to rearrange your lists, you need to use Works' Sort command.

Works lets you sort your data by any column, in either ascending or descending order. Here's what to do:

1. Select the cells that you want to sort.

2. Pull down the Tools menu and select Sort.

3. A dialog box appears asking if you want to sort the highlighted information or if you want to sort *all* the information in your spreadsheet. Check the Sort Only the Highlighted Information option and click OK.

4. When the Sort dialog box appears, select whether your list does or doesn't have a header row, as shown in Figure 5.4.

Figure 5.4

Sort your list by any col-umn, in any order.

5. Pull down the Sort By list and select which column you want to sort by.

6. Select whether you want to sort in Ascending or Descending order.

7. Click Sort to sort the data.

Bad Sort!

If you made a mistake when sorting —such as not selecting the entire range of cells you really wanted to sort—you need to undo the sort *immediately*, before you make any other edits on your data. To undo a sort, pull down the Edit menu and select Undo Sort.

If you want to sort the information in your list by more than one column, you have to click the Advanced button in the Sort dialog box. When the advanced Sort dialog box appears, you now have *three* different ways to sort, in a "nested" fashion.

Works sorts by the first column first, then by the second column, then by the third. So if you chose to search by due date first and account name second, your list would be ordered by due date, but within each due date, all accounts would be alphabetized.

Crunch the Numbers

If all you want to do with Works Spreadsheet is create a pretty list, you've read all you need to read of this chapter. If, on the other hand, you want to take some of the numbers in your list and *do something with them*, this section is for you!

Adding, Subtracting, Multiplying, and Dividing—with Formulas

Works lets you enter just about any type of algebraic formula into any cell. You can add, subtract, multiply, divide—and perform any nested combination of those operations. Best of all, you can instruct Works to perform these operations using data contained in other cells in your spreadsheet.

When you enter an equal sign (=) into any cell, Works knows you're starting a formula. You start your formula with the equal sign, and enter your operations *after* the equal sign.

For example, if you wanted to add 1 plus 2, you'd enter this formula in a cell: **=1+2**. When you press Enter, the formula disappears from the cell—and the result, or *value*, is displayed.

Use the Entry Bar

Although the value is always displayed in the cell, the formula is always displayed in the Entry bar at the top of the workspace. You can use the Formula bar to edit existing formulas; select a cell with a formula, move your cursor to the Entry bar, and edit away!

Table 5.3 shows the algebraic operators you can use in Works Spreadsheet formulas.

Table 5.3   Works Spreadsheet Operators

Operation	Operator
Add	+
Subtract	-
Multiply	*
Divide	/

To perform calculations using values from cells in your spreadsheet, you enter the cell location into the formula. For example, if you want to add cells A1 and A2, you'd enter this formula: **=A1+A2**.

An even easier way to perform operations involving spreadsheet cells is to select them with your mouse while you're entering the formula. To do this, follow these steps:

1. Select the cell to contain the formula.
2. Enter **=**.
3. Click on the first cell you want to include in your formula; that cell location is automatically entered in your formula.
4. Enter an algebraic operator.
5. Click on the second cell you want to include in your formula.
6. Repeat steps 3–5 to add additional cells to your formula.
7. Press Enter when your formula is complete.

Let's revisit the example of adding cells A1 and A2. Using this method, you type **=**, use your mouse to click on cell A1, type **+**, use your mouse to click on cell A2, and then press Enter. The resulting formula (**=A1+A2**) has been automatically entered by Works.

Using Built-In Functions

In addition to the basic algebraic operators (+, -, *, and /), Works Spreadsheet also includes a variety of *functions* that replace the complex steps present in many complex formulas. For example, if you wanted to total all the cells in column A, you could enter the formula **=A1+A2+A3+A4**—or you could use the *SUM* function, which lets you sum a column or row of numbers without having to type every cell into the formula. In short, a function is a type of prebuilt formula.

You enter a function in the following format: **=*function*(*argument*)**, where *function* is the name of the function, and *argument* is the range of cells or other data you want to calculate. In the example presented in the previous paragraph, to sum cells A1 through A4, you'd use the following function-based formula: **=sum(A1:A4)**.

Works Spreadsheet includes over 100 different functions. You can access and insert any of Works' functions by following these steps:

1. Select the cell where you want to insert the function.
2. Pull down the Insert menu and select Function.
3. When the Insert Function dialog box (shown in Figure 5.5) appears, select a function category, and then select a function.

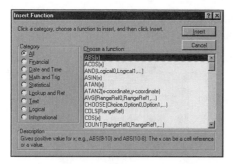

Figure 5.5

Choose from over a hundred different functions in the Insert Function dialog box.

4. Click the Insert button.

This operation inserts the function in your cell, waiting to accept your manual entry of the function's argument.

Although you can enter any function manually, an easier method is to use Works' Easy Calc feature—which helps you create function-based formulas in a step-by-step fashion.

The Easiest Function: AutoSum

The most-used function in any spreadsheet is the Sum function—used for totaling rows or columns of numbers. For that reason, Works Spreadsheet has an AutoSum button on its toolbar. When you select the cell at the end of a row or column of numbers and click AutoSum, Works automatically sums all the preceding numbers—and places the total in the selected cell.

Making Complex Formulas Easy—with Easy Calc

Works Spreadsheet features *Easy Calc*, a type of wizard that leads you through the creation of complex formulas with just a few clicks of your mouse button. With Easy Calc you don't have to remember all of Works' functions or know how to construct complex algebraic expressions—Easy Calc does all that work for you!

Here's how you use Easy Calc to create a formula:

1. Select the cell to contain the formula.
2. Click the Easy Calc button on the toolbar.

3. When the Easy Calc Wizard (shown in Figure 5.6) appears, click the button for the type of calculation you want to perform.

Figure 5.6

Use Easy Calc to create complex calculations with the click of a button.

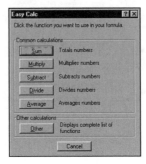

4. Follow the onscreen instructions specific to your selection.

The Hard Stuff's Under "Other"

Works Spreadsheet's two most common functions (Sum and Average) have dedicated buttons on Easy Calc's main screen. The other hundred or so functions—which, though used less frequently, can be quite powerful—are accessed by clicking the Other button.

Let's work through a quick example. Let's say you wanted to average the values in cells A1 through A4. From Easy Calc, you click the Average button. The next screen asks for the *range* of cells you want to average. You can either enter A1:A4, or use your mouse to highlight cells A1 through A4. When you click the Next button, Easy Calc asks where you want to display the result; you can keep the current cell, or enter a new cell. When you click Finish, the average of cells A1 through A4 is displayed in the cell you selected.

Make It Pretty

After you've entered data into your spreadsheet, it's time to make it look better than just boring rows and columns of text and numbers. (If you're an accountant, feel free to skip this section—I've found that, for some unknown reason, most financial folks actually *prefer* plain, unformatted columns of numbers!)

Inserting and Deleting Rows and Columns

No matter how carefully you plan, there will come a time when you discover that need to insert an additional row or column of information into your spreadsheet. Don't panic—it's easy to do! Just follow these steps:

1. Click the row or column header *after* where you want to make the insertion.
2. Pull down the Insert menu and select either Insert Row or Insert Column.

Works now inserts a new row or column either above or to the left of the row or column you selected.

Deleting a row or column is just as easy. Follow these steps:

1. Click the row or column header for the row or column you want to delete.
2. Pull down the Insert menu and select either Delete Row or Delete Column.

The row or column you selected will be deleted, and all other rows/columns moved up or over to fill the space.

Hiding What You Don't Want to See

What if you have a row or column that contains data you needed for calculations, but that you don't want to show on your final report? If you delete the row/column, you'll lose the important data and mess up all your calculations. Well, instead of deleting the row/column, you can choose to *hide* it from your final printout.

To hide a selection, follow these steps:

1. Click the row or column header for the row or column you want to hide.
2. Pull down the Format menu and select either Row Height or Column Width.
3. When the Row Height or Column Width dialog box appears, enter **0** as the value, and then click OK.

This procedure hides the selected row or column by reducing its height or width to zero.

To unhide a hidden row or column, follow these steps:

1. Pull down the Edit menu and select Go To.
2. When the Go To dialog box appears, enter one of the cells in the hidden row/column into the Go To box, and then click OK. (For example, if column D is hidden, enter D1.)
3. The cursor now appears in the margin between two visible rows or columns. (The cell you went to is still hidden, remember?)
4. Pull down the Format menu and select either Row Height (if the row is hidden) or Column Width (if the column is hidden).
5. Click the Best Fit button.
6. Click OK.

109

Your previously hidden row or column will now reappear, sized to the largest cell within the range.

Formatting Cell Contents

You can apply a variety of formatting options to the contents of your cells. You can make your text bold or italic, or change the font type or size, or even add shading or borders to selected cells. As an example of how you can make your spreadsheet appear, look at the fully formatted spreadsheet shown in Figure 5.7.

Figure 5.7

A plain-Jane spreadsheet spruced up with a variety of cell formatting.

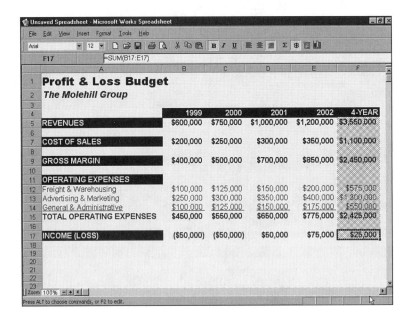

All or Nothing

Works lets you format the entire cell at once—but doesn't let you format individual words or numbers within a cell. That means you can make all the contents of a cell bold, for example, but you can't boldface selected words within a cell.

To format a cell (or range of cells), all you have to do is select the cell (or range) and then apply the formatting from either the toolbar or the Format menu. Table 5.4 lists some of the cell formatting that you can apply.

Table 5.4   Works Spreadsheet Number Formats

Format	Instructions
Change text font	Pull down the Font Name list and select a new font.
Change text size	Pull down the Font Size list and select a new size.
Bold text	Click the Bold button (or press Ctrl+B).
Italic text	Click the Italic button (or press Ctrl+I).
Underline text	Click the Underline button (or press Ctrl+U).
Change text color	Pull down the Format menu and select Font and Style; when the Format Cells dialog box appears, select the Font tab and select a new option from the Color list, and then click OK.
Left-align text in cell	Click the Left Align button.
Center text in cell	Click the Center Align button.
Right-align text in cell	Click the Right Align button.
Add background shading	Pull down the Format menu and select Shading; when the Format Cells dialog box appears, select the Shading tab and select a Shading Pattern, Foreground Color, and Background Color, and then click OK.
Add border around cell or range	Pull down the Format menu and select Border; or when the Format Cells dialog box appears, select the Border tab and select where you want the border to appear (Outline, Top, Bottom, Left, or Right), the Line Style, and the Color, and then click OK.

Work Smarter

Format Fast with AutoFormat

You don't have to format each cell individually if you don't want to. Works' AutoFormat command lets you apply preselected formatting to your entire spreadsheet. Just pull down the Format menu and select AutoFormat; when the AutoFormat dialog box appears, choose from one of more than a dozen different formats, and then click OK. (If the last row or column of your spreadsheet contains "total" data, make sure you check the Format Last Row and/or Column as Total option.)

Turn Numbers into Pictures

Numbers are fine, but sometimes the story behind the numbers can be told better through a picture—and the way you take a picture of numbers is with a *chart*.

Works Spreadsheet lets you create the following types of charts:

➤ Area

➤ 3-D Area

➤ Bar

➤ 3-D Bar

➤ Line

➤ 3-D Line

➤ Stacked Line

➤ Pie

➤ 3-D Pie

➤ X-Y Scatter

➤ Radar (also known as a "spider" chart)

➤ Combination (combines a line and a bar chart on different axis)

Create a Chart

Here's how you create a chart from data entered into the cells of your spreadsheet:

1. Select the range of cells you want to include in your chart. If the range has a header row or column, include that row or column when selecting the cells.

2. Click the New Chart button.

3. When the New Chart dialog box appears as shown in Figure 5.8, select the Basic Options tab.

Figure 5.8

Create one of a dozen different types of charts to visually represent your data.

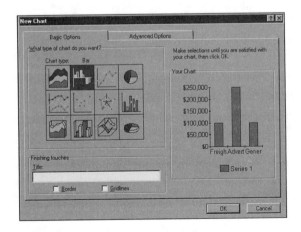

4. Select a chart type; a preview of the chart of your data appears in the Your Chart section.

5. If you want your chart to have a title, enter the title in the Title box.

6. To display a border around your chart, check the Border option.

7. If you want to show gridlines within your chart, check the Gridlines option.

8. Click OK.

Your chart now appears in a new, separate, unnamed, and unsaved spreadsheet, as shown in Figure 5.9. You should pull down the File menu, select Save As, and save this chart file now.

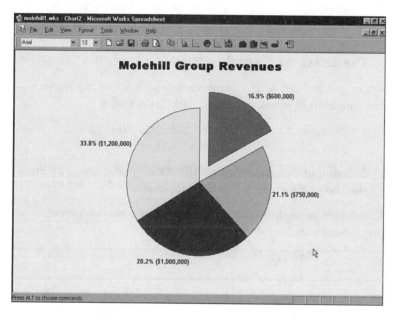

Figure 5.9

A newly created chart, in its own spreadsheet file.

Change the Chart Type

You can accept the chart as-is, or you can tweak the chart type to some degree.

To change the chart type completely, click a new chart type button on the chart toolbar. When the Chart Type dialog box appears, select the Basic Types tab, select a new type, and then click OK.

There's a second tab on the Chart Type dialog box—the Variations tab. This tab contains a number of popular variations on the selected basic chart type. For example, if you select Pie as your basic chart type and then click the Variations tab, you see six different types of pie charts—with labels, without labels, with values, without values, with exploded slices, and without exploded slices. Select the variation you want, and then click OK.

113

Pretty It Up

A variety of chart formatting options can be found when you pull down the Format menu. Select the item you want to format, make your changes, and click okay.

The Least You Need to Know

➤ You can open Works Spreadsheet with a blank spreadsheet, or with a preformatted task-based spreadsheet (from the Works Task Launcher).

➤ Spreadsheet data is entered into cells, which are ordered into rows and columns.

➤ Use formulas to perform specific operations on the data in your spreadsheet; use functions to take the place of overly complex formulas.

➤ Click the New Chart button on the Spreadsheet toolbar to create a chart from selected spreadsheet data.

Chapter 6

Organize Your Stuff with Works Database

In This Chapter

➤ Discover what a database is, what it does, and how it works

➤ Learn how to enter, edit, and format database data

➤ Find out how to output and summarize your data with reports

---

If a spreadsheet is a giant list, a database is a giant file cabinet. Each "file cabinet" is actually a separate database file; each filing cabinet includes individual index cards (called *records*) filled with specific information (arranged in *fields*). You use the Works Database application both to create these database files and records and to organize them into something useful.

You can use Works Database to create and store anything that includes a large amount of data. For example, you can create a database that contains all your favorite recipes, or the contents of your CD or video collections.

Opening the Program—and Creating a New Database

When you launch Works Database, you not only start the program, you also create a new database—from scratch!

Launching the Program

You launch Works Database the same way you launch most other Works Suite 2000 applications, from either the Windows Start menu or the Works Task Launcher.

To launch Works Database from the Works Task Launcher, select the Programs tab and select Works Database from the Programs list. If you want to start with a blank database, select Start a Blank Database; if you want to start with a specific task loaded, select the task from the task list and click Start.

It's also easy to start the Works Database if Works Suite 2000 isn't running. Just click the Windows Start button, select Programs, select the Microsoft Works folder (*not* the Microsoft Works program icon!), and then select Microsoft Works Database.

Close It Up

When you're done using Works Database, you close the program by pulling down the File menu and selecting Exit. (If you have any unsaved databases open, Works Database will prompt you to save them first, and then close.)

Creating a New Database

When you launch Works Database to start a blank database, you're presented with the Create Database dialog box. Now you're faced with some immediate choices. (Don't worry—if you don't like the choices you make, you can always go back and change them at any time.)

First, you need to decide how many *fields* to include in your database. In general, you should create one field for each type of information you want to store. If you're creating a database for your movie collection, for example, you might create fields for Title, Lead Actor, Lead Actress, Director, Running Time, and Year.

Each field you add is assigned a specific *format*. You can choose from the following formats:

➤ **General.** Use when you aren't sure what will be entered into the field.

➤ **Number.** Choose from a list of preselected number formats.

➤ **Date.** Choose from a list of preselected date formats.

➤ **Time.** Choose from a list of preselected time formats.

➤ **Text.** Use when a field will contain text entries—or numbers that won't be sorted or calculated.

➤ **Fraction.** Choose from a list of preselected fraction formats.

➤ **Serialized.** Use to add a unique and consecutive number to your record.

When you see the Create Database dialog box, shown in Figure 6.1, follow these steps:

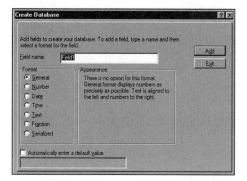

Figure 6.1

Launch the program, create a database, and add fields via the Create Database dialog box.

1. Enter a name for the first field in the Field Name box.
2. Select a format for this field from the Format list; select any specific options for this format type.
3. Click Add to add the field to your database.
4. To add additional fields to your database, repeat steps 1–3.
5. When your database construction is completed, click Done.

Navigating the Database Workspace

After your database is created, it is displayed in the database workspace in the *List view*, shown in Figure 6.2. At this point the database is empty; we'll add data in just a few minutes.

The List view (selectable by clicking the List View button on the toolbar) displays your database kind of like a spreadsheet. The fields of your database are displayed as columns, whereas the individual records are displayed as rows.

You can also switch views to display each record in your database one at a time. When you click the Form View button, you see the contents of the first record in your database, as shown in Figure 6.3. Click the record navigation arrows (at the bottom left of the database workspace) or the Ctrl+PgUp and Ctrl+PgDn keys to move from one record to another.

Figure 6.2

Display your database like a spreadsheet using List view.

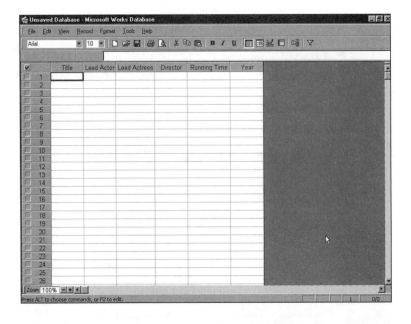

Figure 6.3

Use the Form view to look at one record at a time.

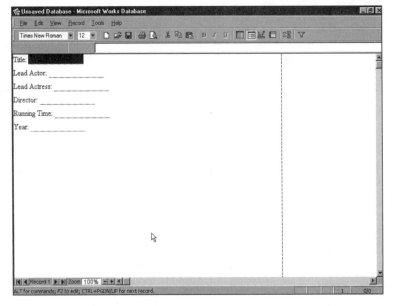

Working with a New Database

So, what do you do with this empty database? Fill it up, of course!

Entering Data

No matter which view you're using, it's easy to add data to your database.

If you're in List view, you add data to your database as you'd add data to a spreadsheet. Move your cursor to any particular field (what you'd call a *cell* in a spreadsheet) and type your data. Use the Tab key to move to the next field in a record; use the Enter key to move to the next record.

You may prefer to add data one record at a time, as you'd enter data on an individual card in a file cabinet. Switch to Form view and enter all the data for the fields in the current record. Use the Tab key to move from field to field; when you reach the end of one record, pressing Tab moves you to the first field of the next record.

Creating New Fields

After you get going in a database, you may discover that you want to include more information for each record. Going back to our movie database example, you might decide that you want to add a field for Category/Genre. Fortunately, it's easy to add new fields to existing databases; just follow these steps:

1. Click the List View button to switch to List view.
2. Position your cursor anywhere in the field before where you want to insert the new field.
3. Pull down the Record menu, select Insert Field, and then select After.
4. When the Insert Field dialog box appears, enter a name and format for the new field, and then click Add.
5. To add another field, repeat step 4.
6. When you're done inserting fields, click Done.

Works now adds the new field(s) to every record in your database. This field will be blank, of course, so you'll have to go back through your existing records and fill it in, as appropriate.

Adding New Records

If you're in List view, adding a new record is as simple as starting to type in the first empty record row. If you're in Form view, just click the Insert Record button; a new blank record appears in the workspace.

Making It Look Pretty

You can format either the List view or the forms displayed in the Form view.

Formatting the List

You format the Works Database List view in the same way you formatted a spreadsheet in Works Spreadsheet—except that any formatting you apply to a field applies to that field across all records. All you have to do is select the field you want to format, and then use the formatting buttons (Bold, Italic, or Underline) on the toolbar, or pull down the Format menu to select either the Alignment, Font and Style, Border, or Shading options.

Formatting the Form

If you use Form view to enter your data, you might want to create a better-looking form than the default Works form. To do this, switch to Form view and then click the Form Design button. This switches you to a special Form Design mode.

In this mode you can move and resize any and all fields in your form. Just use your mouse to move a field to a new position anywhere onscreen, or to resize the field entry box.

While you're in the Form Design mode, you can also add other objects to your form. Pull down the Insert menu and select one of the following items:

➤ **Label.** Adds random text (unassociated with any field) to your form.

➤ **Rectangle.** Use to "border" specific areas of your form.

➤ **ClipArt.** Adds pictures and graphics.

➤ **WordArt.** Adds specially formatted text.

➤ **Note-It.** Adds pop-up "post-it" type comments.

➤ **Drawing.** Adds freeform drawings.

➤ **Object.** Embeds other Windows objects, such as maps and charts.

After you select an item, you "draw" it onscreen with your mouse. You exit the Form Design mode by clicking on the Form view button.

You can get really fancy when designing forms; see the form in Figure 6.4 for an example.

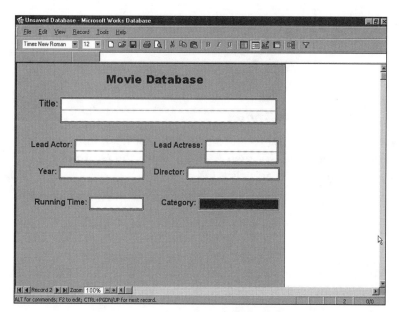

Figure 6.4

Make inputting data more enjoyable with a fancy form.

Making Meaningless Data Meaningful

So far we've focused on inputting data. Now let's learn how to work with the data you've inputted.

Finding—and Replacing

When you have a large number of records in a database, finding any particular record gets increasingly difficult. The best way to find a record is to use Works Database's Find command.

Follow these steps:

1. Pull down the Edit menu and select Find (or press Ctrl+F).
2. When the Find dialog box appears, enter what you're looking for in the Find What box, and then check the Next Record option.
3. Click OK.

Works now displays the first record that matches your query. Press Ctrl+F to continue searching.

You can also use the Replace command to replace any specific data you find. This command works pretty much like the Find command (with the added option of entering replacement data); pull down the Edit menu and select Replace (or press Ctrl+H) to display the Replace dialog box and start the operation.

Get Going

You can use the Works Go To command to go to any particular field. Just pull down the Edit menu and select Go To (or press Ctrl+G). When the Go To dialog box appears, select a field from the list and click OK.

Sorting

When you're in List view, by default the records are listed in order entered. This typically isn't very useful. Still using the movie database as an example, you may want to list your movies by category, or by year produced. To do this, you want to *sort* the database.

To sort your database, follow these steps:

1. From the List view, pull down the Records menu and select Sort Records.

Sort Your Forms

You can also sort from Form view, but why would you want to? (You're still looking at one form at a time, after all...)

2. When the Sort Records dialog box appears, select the first field you want to sort by from the Sort By list, and select whether you want to sort in Ascending or Descending order.

3. If you want to sort the results *within* the initial sort, select a second field from the first Then By list, and select either Ascending or Descending.

4. If you want to perform a third subsort, select a field from the second Then By list, and select either Ascending or Descending.

5. Click OK to sort your database.

Works now sorts your database as directed.

Filtering

Another option you have in Works Database is to display only those records that match a specific criteria. (For example, in your movie database you may want to display only Humphrey Bogart movies.) This is called *filtering* the database, and it's easy to do. Just follow these steps:

1. Click the Filters button on the toolbar.

2. When the Filter Name dialog box appears, enter a name for the filter, and then click OK.

3. When the Filter dialog box appears, as shown in Figure 6.5, pull down the first Field Name box and select the first field you want to filter.

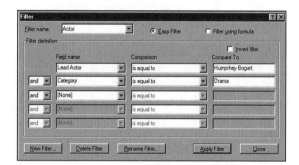

Figure 6.5

Filtering your data to display only selected records.

4. Pull down the first Comparison list and select a criteria (is equal to, does not contain, and so on) for the filter.

5. In the first Compare To box, enter the value for the selected criteria.

6. Repeat steps 3–5 if you want to further restrict what is displayed.

7. Click Apply Filter to turn on the filter and limit your display.

Using our movie database example, if you wanted to display only Humphrey Bogart movies, you'd select **Lead Actor** as the Field Name, pull down the Comparison list and select **Contains**, and then enter **Humphrey Bogart** in the **Compare To** box. Works Database will look for those records where the Lead Actor field contains Humphrey Bogart, and display only those records.

Reporting

Probably the most useful thing you can do with your database is to analyze and summarize its contents with a *report*. Works Database includes a special ReportCreator tool that makes creating custom reports a snap.

Print the List

You don't have to create a report to print your data. You can print the contents of your current List view, or you can print the current record in Form view by enabling the view and then clicking the Print button on the toolbar.

To create a report, follow these steps:

1. Click the Report View button on the toolbar.

2. When the Report Name dialog box appears, enter a name for your report and click OK.

3. When the Report Creator dialog box appears, as shown in Figure 6.6, select the Title tab. Enter or edit the report title, select an orientation and font, and then click Next.

Figure 6.6

Use the ReportCreator to create custom reports.

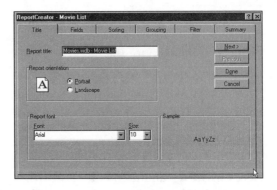

4. From the Fields tab, select those fields you want to include in your report, and then click Add. If you want to display the field names at the top of your page, check the Show Field Names at the Top of Each Page option; if you want to summarize the data in your fields, check the Show Summary Information Only option. Click Next to proceed.

5. From the Sorting tab, select which fields you want to sort by, in either Ascending or Descending order, and then click Next.

6. From the Grouping tab, select any fields you want to group or subtotal, and how you want them grouped. (Note: Only sorted fields are available for grouping.) Click Next to proceed.

124

7. From the Filter tab, select any previously created filter from the Select a Filter list, or click the Create New Filter button to create and apply a new filter. Click Next to proceed.

8. From the Summary tab, select any fields you want to summarize, how you want to summarize (sum, average, count, and so on), and where you want to display the summaries (under each column, at the end of the report, and so on). Click Done.

9. You're now asked if you want to preview or modify the report. Click Preview.

Your report is now displayed onscreen in Preview mode, as shown in Figure 6.7. If you like what you see, click Print. If you don't, click Cancel and edit your report parameters using the report commands on the Tools menu.

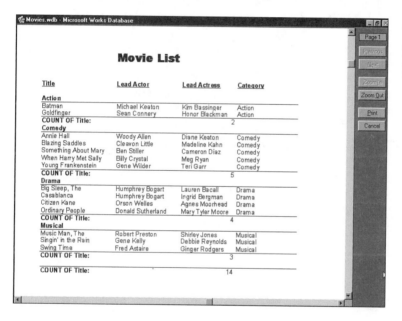

Figure 6.7

Summarize and analyze your database with custom-created reports.

Start from Scratch

You can start a new report at any time by pulling down the Tools menu and selecting ReportCreator.

125

The Least You Need to Know

➤ A database is comprised of multiple records, each containing data entered into fields.

➤ You can view and edit your Works databases in either List or Form views.

➤ Works' Form view can be formatted similarly to the way you'd format a spreadsheet; the Form view can be formatted in the special form design mode.

➤ You create reports based on your data by using the ReportCreator wizard.

Chapter 7

Manage Your Schedule with Works Calendar

In This Chapter

➤ Learn how to use Works Calendar to schedule appointments and events

➤ Discover how to add information from your Address Book to your calendar

➤ Find out how to print out various types of appointment calendars

---

In addition to the heavy hitters (the word processor, spreadsheet, and database programs), Works Suite 2000 includes a personal schedule management program—well, let's just call it a *calendar*. Works Calendar looks and acts like a regular calendar, except that you schedule your appointments and events electronically on your computer screen. Because your entire schedule is electronic, you can configure the program to automatically issue *reminders*, so you won't forget anything important coming up. And if you *must* have a copy of your schedule on paper, Works Calendar can print out your schedule in one of several different views (day, week, or month).

With Works Calendar, it's *easy* to manage your schedule!

Opening—and Closing—Works Calendar

The easiest way to launch Works Calendar is from the Task Launcher. Select the Programs tab and then select Works Calendar from the Programs list. Although you can pick a task from the task list, you might as well go right into Calendar by selecting Start the Calendar.

You can also start Works Calendar from within Windows. Just click the Windows Start button, select Programs, select the Microsoft Works folder (*not* the Microsoft Works program icon!), and then select Microsoft Works Calendar.

When you're done using Works Calendar, you close the program by pulling down the File menu and selecting Exit.

Finding Your Way Around the Calendar

Works Calendar looks different from other Works Suite 2000 applications—it looks like a calendar!

Pick a View

Depending on which view you choose, Works Calendar can display either a daily, weekly, or monthly calendar.

When you click the View Day button on the toolbar, you switch to Calendar's Day View, shown in Figure 7.1. In Day View you see the schedule for an entire day, broken out by hours and half hours. You use the scroll bars to view earlier or later in the day; click the Previous Day and Next Day arrows to back or forward through the week.

Figure 7.1

View your daily schedule hour-by-hour...

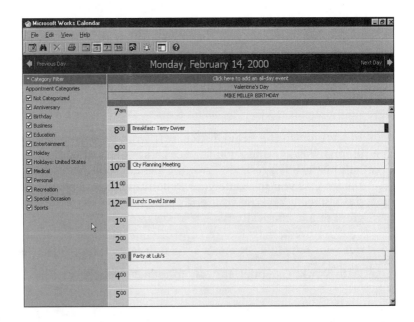

There's a secondary Day View that most users aren't aware of. When you pull down the View menu and uncheck Show Days in Hours, Day View switches to the display shown in Figure 7.2, breaking the day out into larger chunks (morning, afternoon, and evening—instead of hours).

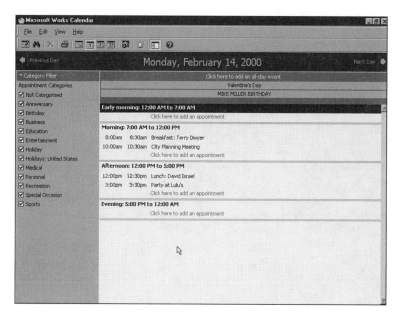

Figure 7.2

...or by block of time.

The Today Show

In any of Calendar's views, you can jump immediately to today's schedule by clicking the Go To Today button on the toolbar.

When you click the Week View button, you switch to Calendar's Week View, shown in Figure 7.3. In Week View you see each day of the current week, with any appointment or events highlighted on the selected day. Click the Previous Week and Next Week arrows to move back and forth one week at a time.

When you click the Month View button, you switch to a view of a traditional monthly calendar, shown in Figure 7.4. Appointments and events are listed on specific days, and you can click the Previous Month and Next Month arrows to move back and forth through the year.

Figure 7.3

Use Weekly View to display all your appointments for the week.

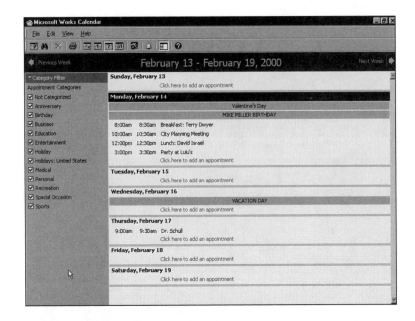

Figure 7.4

It's a monthly calendar—with all your appointments listed.

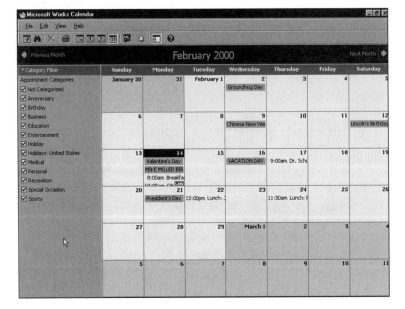

Pick a Day (or Week or Month)

To quickly jump to a specific day, week, or month, you can click the Day, Week, or Month title on your calendar to pull down a calendar or (in the Month View) list of months. Click the day or month you want to jump to, and the calendar displays the day, week, or month you selected.

Use the Toolbar

Most anything you can do with Works Calendar you can do from the toolbar. Figure 7.5 shows the buttons on the Works Calendar toolbar.

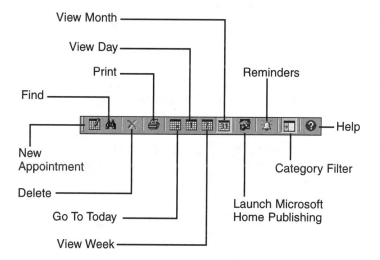

Figure 7.5

Click a toolbar button to make an appointment or change a view.

Get Organized!

Works Calendar lets you schedule both *appointments* (that have a specific starting and ending time) and *events* (that last an entire day). You can also choose to display recurring holidays and birthdays, as well as configure Calendar to remind you of any or all upcoming items on your schedule.

Make an Appointment

There are three ways to make an appointment in Works Calendar:

➤ Click the New Appointment button on the toolbar.

➤ Pull down the File menu and select New Appointment.

➤ In any of the calendar views, double-click on the day or time for your appointment.

Schedule from the Task Launcher

You can also schedule an appointment directly from the Works Task Launcher. On the Programs tab, select Works Calendar, Calendar, Set Appointment. Or you can go to the Tasks tab and select Household Management, Calendar, Set Appointment.

Whichever appointment-setting method you choose, you display the New Appointment dialog box, shown in Figure 7.6. Follow these steps to complete your appointment:

Figure 7.6

Use the New Appointment dialog box to schedule new appointments and events.

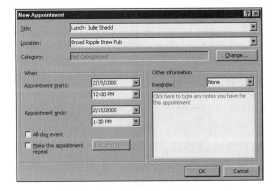

1. Enter the key appointment information in the Title box. (Previous types of appointments are available from the pull-down list at the right of the box.)

2. Enter a location for your appointment in the Location box. (Previous locations are available from the pull-down list at the right of the box.)

3. If you want to assign a category for this appointment, click the Change button and select a category from the Choose Categories dialog box.

4. Select the starting date and time from the Appointment Starts controls. (If you opened the New Appointment dialog box by clicking on a date or time in a calendar view, this information is already selected—although you can change it.)

5. Select the ending date and time from the Appointment Ends controls.

6. If the appointment is an all-day thing, check the All-Day Event option; otherwise, uncheck this option. (Note that checking this option makes the Appointment Ends area unavailable.)

7. If this is a recurring appointment, check the Make This Appointment Repeat option and click the Recurrence button. This displays the Recurrence Options dialog box; select how often the appointment recurs and for how long it will repeat, and then click OK.

8. If you want your computer to display a reminder message before your appointment, pull down the Reminder list and select how long before the appointment you want to be reminded.

9. If you have any notes to add to this appointment, add them in the Notes box.

10. Click OK to add the appointment to your schedule.

Most Information Is Optional

You don't need to enter *all* the information in the New Appointment dialog box. The only essential items are the Title and Appointment Starts fields. You can leave the rest blank, if you want.

Schedule an Event

An event is simply an all-day appointment. To make an appointment an event, check the All-Day Event option in the New Appointment dialog box.

Celebrate Holidays

You can have Calendar automatically add major holidays to your calendar. (You could also enter holidays manually, but why go through all that trouble when the program can do it automatically!)

It's in the Book

To learn how to add information to the Works Address Book, turn to Chapter 8, "Keep Track of Friends and Family with Address Book."

All you have to do is pull down the Edit menu and select Add Holidays. When the Add Holidays to Calendar dialog box appears, select those holidays you want to add, and then click OK.

Look Out for Birthdays

If you've entered birthdays for your friends and families into their contact information in the Address Book, you can automatically import those dates into Calendar. Just pull down the Edit menu and select Birthdays; Calendar will do the rest of the work and let you know when all the birthdays have been added.

Managing Your Calendar

No one's schedule is static—if you're like me, you're constantly canceling and changing appointments as new obligations pop up. Fortunately, Works Calendar is easy to edit—to better manage your fluid schedule.

Edit Your Schedule

Deleting an appointment is easy. Just select the appointment in any calendar view, and then click the Delete button on the toolbar.

You can move an appointment in one of two ways. The easiest is to use your mouse to drag the appointment to a different time or date. If you'd rather edit the appointment information manually, double-click on the appointment to display the Edit Appointment dialog box, enter the new information, and then click OK.

Search for Information

If you're not sure when a certain appointment takes place, you can use Calendar's Find command to search for the appointment. When you click the Find button on the toolbar, you display the Find dialog box. Select the Keyword tab to search for words in the appointment title; select the Time tab to find appointments within a specific time period; or select the Category tab to list all appointments assigned to a particular category. Click Find Now to display a list of appointments that match your query.

Print Your Calendar

Printing a calendar is a little different from printing a document in other Works Suite applications. Follow these steps:

1. Pull down the File menu and select Print.

2. When the Print dialog box appears, select a specific calendar Style: Day by Appointments, Day by Hour, Day List, Day List by Sections, Week, Month (Portrait orientation), or Month (Landscape orientation).

3. Select the range of dates or times you want to display on your calendar.

4. Select to include either All Appointments or only those Appointments Currently Selected in the Category Filter.

5. Click OK to print.

Filter Your Appointments

You can select to view or print only those appointments that are assigned to a specific category. To use the Category Filter, pull down the View Menu and select Category Filter. This splits the Calendar window and adds a Category Filter pane. Check those categories you want to display or print; uncheck those you want to hide.

The Least You Need to Know

➤ Works Calendar lets you schedule appointments, events, holidays, and birthdays.

➤ You can choose to display a reminder in advance of any appointment.

➤ You have the option of viewing and printing your schedule by day, week, or month.

Chapter 8

Keep Track of Friends and Family with Address Book

In This Chapter

➤ Learn how to store names and addresses in the Works Address Book

➤ Discover how to create group lists for mass mailings and emails

➤ Find out how to use Address Book to send emails and make phone calls

Works Suite 2000 includes a contact manager application, called *Address Book*, that you can use to store information about your friends, family, and business associates. You can store individual names, addresses, phone numbers, email addresses, birthdays, and other important information—and then import your contacts into Outlook Express (to send email), Works Calendar (to remind you of birthdays), and Word 2000 (to personalize letters and address envelopes and labels).

Opening and Closing Address Book

To launch Address Book from the Task Launcher, select the Programs tab, select Address Book from the Programs list, and then select Start the Address Book. To start Address Book from Windows, click the Start button, select Programs, select the Microsoft Works folder (*not* the Microsoft Works program icon!), and then select Address Book.

When you're done using Address Book, close the program by pulling down the File menu and selecting Exit.

Adding Names and Addresses

Address Book is like a specialized database, filled with records for each of your designated contacts. Adding a new contact is no more difficult that adding a new record to a database.

Create a New Contact

To add a new contact to your Address Book, follow these steps:

1. From the Address Book toolbar, click the New button; when the pull-down menu appears, select New Contact.

2. When the Properties dialog box appears, as shown in Figure 8.1, select the Name tab. Enter the contact's name (first, middle, last), title, display name (how you want to list the name in the Address Book), nickname, and email address.

Plain Is OK

If this contact cannot receive HTML email, check the Send E-mail Using Plain Text Only option. (See Chapter 14, "Send and Receive Email with Outlook Express," for more information.)

Figure 8.1

Enter as much information as you can (or want!) when you create a new contact.

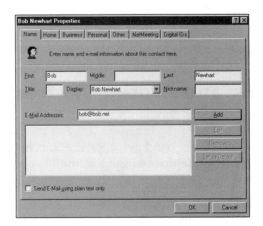

138

3. Select the Home tab and enter the contact's home address, phone, fax, and other information.

4. Select the Business tab and enter the contact's company, title, business address, phone, fax, and other work-related information.

5. Select the Personal tab and enter the contact's birthday, anniversary, and gender, and the names of his or her spouse and children.

6. Select the Other tab and enter any additional notes about this person.

7. If the contact is connected to Microsoft NetMeeting (and he probably isn't), select the NetMeeting tab and enter the appropriate information.

Background Work

What's This Stuff?

NetMeeting and Digital Ids are two things you probably don't need to bother with. NetMeeting is a real-time audio/video conferencing program that lets Internet users communicate with one another with microphones and cameras and all sorts of high-tech gadgets, and isn't included as part of Microsoft Works Suite 2000. A Digital ID is a kind of electronic certificate of authenticity used when sending encrypted email messages; most normal users don't engage in this level of top-security.

8. If the contact has a Digital ID certificate (and he probably doesn't), select the Digital IDs tab and enter the appropriate information.

9. From any tab, click OK to enter the new contact info.

You don't have to enter all this information, of course. If all you know is a last name and email address, you can still create a contact for that person. Just enter as much information as you know, and work from that.

Importing and Exporting Names

If you have similar address books in other programs, you can import names from those address books into the Works Address Book. Just pull down the File menu, select Import, and then select Other Address Book. When the Address Book Import Tool appears, select what kind of address book you want to import, and then click Import.

Conversely, you can *export* contacts from the Works Address Book to other address books and programs. Pull down the File menu, select Export, and then select Other Address Book. When the Address Book Export Tool appears, select the output file type, and then click Export.

Edit an Existing Contact

If you want to edit information for an existing contact, just select the contact name in the main Address Book list, and then click the Properties button. This displays the familiar Properties dialog box for that contact; change whatever information you want, and then click OK.

Create a New Group or Folder

Address Book lets you store multiple contacts in a *group*. This is expedient if you often send mailings or emailings to the same list of people; instead of entering each contact address separately, you can select the group and have the same message sent to all contacts on the list.

To create a group, follow these steps:

1. Click the New button and select New Group.
2. When the New Group dialog box appears, select the Group tab.
3. Enter a name for the group in the Group Name box.
4. To add names to the group list, click the Select Members button. When the Select Group Members dialog box appears, select contacts from your Address Book and click the Select button to add them to your list. Click OK when done.
5. To create a new contact to add to your list, click the New Contact button; when the Properties dialog box appears, enter the information for the new contact, and then click OK.

6. If you want to enter additional information about the group, select the Group Details tab.

7. Click OK to create the group.

Looking at Your Contacts

All your contacts are listed in the main Address Book window, shown in Figure 8.2. Only selected information (name, email address, company, and business phone) is shown for each contact.

Name	E-Mail Address	Company	Business Phone
Abby Adams	johna@congress.gov	Housewife	555-1777
Alec Hauser	alec@nephew.net	Pokemon Inc.	555-1123
Audrey Landers	audrey@com.net	Blondes, Inc.	555-7777
Barbara Gordon	oracle@gotham.net	Gotham City Library	555-2222
Barry Allen	flash@jla.org	Central City Police Dept.	555-5559
Ben Hauser	ben@nephew.net	Pokemon Inc.	555-1122
Benjamin Franklin	statesman@congress.gov	United States Congress	555-1776
Betty Boop	boop@bedoop.com	Fleischer Studios	555-0000
Bob Newhart	bob@bob.net	Bob, Inc.	555-bob1
Bruce Wayne	bats@gotham.net	Wayne Corp	555-5555
Burt Bacharach	alfie@hits.com	Bacharach/David Inc.	555-4789
Clark Kent	supes@metropolis.net	The Daily Planet	555-6666
Dashiell Hammett	op@continental.net	Continental Detective Agency	555-0000
Dick Grayson	nightwing@gotham.net	Haley Bros. Circus	555-1111
Dinah Lance	canary@bird.com	Lance Florists	555-9898
Ebeneezer Scrooge	scrooge@dickens.net	Scrooge & Marley	None
Ed Sullivan	really@bigshow.com	Ed Sullivan Show Inc.	555-9999
Fran Tarkington	fran@nfl.com	NFL Veterans Association	555-4455

27 items

Figure 8.2

View all your contacts in a single list.

Sorting Your Contact List

By default, your Address Book list is sorted by contact name. You can sort your list by any of the other columns by clicking that column head. Click the head twice to sort in the reverse order.

Finding That Special Person

If you have a *lot* of people in your Address Book, you might have trouble finding any single person. To search your Address Book, click the Find People button on the toolbar. When the Find People dialog box appears, enter either the name, email, address, or phone number of the person you're looking for, and then click Find Now. Address Book will return a list of contacts matching your query.

See It All

If any column is too narrow to view the entire contents, position your cursor at the right edge of the column head. You can either use your mouse to drag the edge of the column to a new size, or double-click on the edge to automatically size the column to the widest item.

141

Look on the Internet

If you're connected to the Internet, you can use the Find People command to search for people online. Just pull down the Look In box and select a specific people search site, and then continue your search as normal. Find People will go to the selected site, and look for that person in that particular directory.

Contacting Your Contacts

You can use Address Book to contact your contacts directly—either by email or by phone.

Send an Email

To send an email to one of your contacts, click the Action button and select Send Mail. This opens an Outlook Express New Message window; enter the subject and text of your message, and then click Send to send this message via the Internet, using Outlook Express.

Use Address Book with Other Programs

You can use Address Book with several other Works Suite 2000 applications. To learn how to use Address Book with Outlook Express, see Chapter 14, "Send and Receive Email with Outlook Express." To learn how to use Address Book with Works Calendar, see Chapter 7, "Manage Your Schedule with Works Calendar." To learn how to use Address Book with Microsoft Word to create merged mailings, see Chapter 16, "Create Envelopes and Labels," and Chapter 17, "Create a Large Mailing."

Place a Phone Call

If you have your PC hooked up to a telephone line, you can use Address Book to automatically dial anyone in your Address Book. Just click the Action button and select Dial; when the New Call dialog box appears, make sure the correct phone number is selected, and then click Call. Your computer now dials the number, automatically. (Of course, when the other person answers you'll have to pick up your phone to talk to him or her—your PC can only do so much by itself!)

The Least You Need to Know

➤ Use Address Book to store all important contact information—names, addresses, email addresses, business information, and personal information.

➤ Create a *group* of names for when you send the same message to a large list of people.

➤ Use Address Book either on its own or with Outlook Express to send email messages to people on your contact list.

Chapter 9

Manage Your Finances with Money

In This Chapter

➤ Learn how to set up your accounts for use with Microsoft's Money

➤ Discover how to write checks, pay bills, and enter other transactions

➤ Find out how to pay your bills electronically and manage your bank accounts while you're on the road

Microsoft includes a special version (called the *Standard Edition*) of Microsoft Money 2000 in Works Suite 2000. Microsoft Money is a program that lets you manage all your personal finances—from your checking and savings accounts to your stocks and other investments.

Standard or Pro?

The version of Money included with Works Suite 2000—Money 2000 Standard Edition—is just one of three different versions of Money published by Microsoft. To learn more about the features of—and upgrading to—Money 2000 Deluxe or Money 2000 Business and Personal, go to Microsoft's Money 2000 site at www.microsoft.com/money/.

Getting Started with Money

You can launch Money from either the Works Task Launcher or from Windows. To use the Task Launcher, select the Programs tab, select Money from the Programs list, and then either select Start Microsoft Money or select one of the Money-related tasks. To start Money from Windows, click the Start menu, select Programs, and then select Microsoft Money. (If Money installed an icon on the Windows desktop, you can also start the program by clicking this icon.)

Be Prepared

Before you set up Money—whether you use the Setup Assistant or do it manually—you need to gather all your important financial records. You'll be asked to input account numbers and balances, so make sure you have this information handy—for every checking account, savings account, credit card, bill payee, money market fund, and stock investment.

First-Time Setup with the Setup Assistant

The first time you start Money you're presented with the Setup Assistant. (Actually, this assistant runs any time you create a new Money file—by pulling down the File menu, selecting New, and then selecting New File.) This assistant walks you step-by-step through setting up your Money accounts. You don't have to use the assistant to set up Money—the next section of this book shows you how to do this manually—but things go a lot faster if you use the Setup Assistant.

Here's what you'll need to know to complete the Setup Assistant:

➤ **Your financial plans and interests.** These questions help Money determine how to set up your accounts.

➤ **Your Internet connection.** These questions help configure Money's online features.

➤ **Your account details.** Money will track the following types of accounts: checking, savings, credit card, retirement, brokerage/investment, and money market. For each account you have, you'll need to enter the bank or broker name, the account number, and your current or starting balance.

➤ **Your paycheck details.** Money can be configured to enter your paycheck on a recurring basis. You'll need to know your employer, your take-home pay, and how often you're paid.

➤ **Your bills.** You'll need to enter all the different types of bills that you pay regularly—and, for each bill, the payee, estimated amount, and frequency.

After you're finished with the Setup Assistant you can start using Money normally—or you can go back and edit your account information.

Setting Up Your Accounts

If you need to add a new account, delete an unused account, or just edit any specific account information, follow these steps:

1. From the Money Home Page, select the Accounts tab.
2. When the Pick an Account to Use page appears, go to the Common Tasks list and click Set Up Accounts.
3. When the Set Up Your Accounts in Money page appears, select the appropriate action.
4. To create a new account, click Add a New Account.
5. To close an existing account, click Close or Reopen Accounts.
6. To delete an account from your system, click Delete an Account Permanently.
7. To edit an existing account, click any account listed in the Change an Account You've Already Created list.

After you've made your selection, follow the onscreen instructions to complete your action.

Setting Up Your Categories

You can assign specific expense or income categories to each of your transactions. Money comes with a preselected list of categories; you can also add, delete, and modify categories. Just follow these steps:

1. Pull down the More list and select Categories & Payees.
2. Select the Categories view.
3. When the Set Up Your Categories page appears, examine the existing categories.
4. To add a category, click the New button and complete the New Category Wizard.

5. To delete an existing category, select the category and click Delete.

6. To edit an existing category, select the category and click Modify; when the Modify Category dialog box appears, make your changes and click OK.

Reconfiguring Money

Money offers a large number of program configuration options—too many to cover in this small space. To access all these options, pull down the Tools menu and select Options. This displays the Options dialog box, which includes the following tabs:

➤ **General.** Options for the Money display, color scheme, calendar display, and sounds.

➤ **Home Page.** Select which elements to display on the Money Home Page.

➤ **Backup.** Settings for how often to back up your Money data file.

➤ **Online Services.** Select how and how often Money downloads your financial statements.

➤ **Connection.** Settings for connecting to and downloading information from the Internet.

➤ **Editing.** Data entry and confirmation options.

➤ **Investments.** Determine how to handle various investment options (LIFO versus FIFO, and so on), how to display your portfolio, how to categorize your investments, and how to handle employee stock options and capital gains.

➤ **Planner.** Options for your debt-reduction plan (if one exists).

➤ **Currencies.** Select what currency (dollars, krona, pesos, and so on) you want to use.

➤ **Bills and Deposits.** Set notification and reminder options for your general banking transactions.

➤ **Categories.** Options for how you use Money's categories.

➤ **Print Checks.** Determine how you print checks from Money.

Navigating Money

Microsoft Money looks and feels a little like a Web page. In fact, the main Money screen is called the Money Home Page—and different tabs take you to different task-related "pages" for Money's various financial centers.

Home Sweet Home

The Money Home Page, shown in Figure 9.1, is your "home base" for all your Money-related transactions. From the home page are various links to different activities; you click a link to access that activity.

Access common tasks.

Tab to a specific financial center.

Click to a specific financial center.

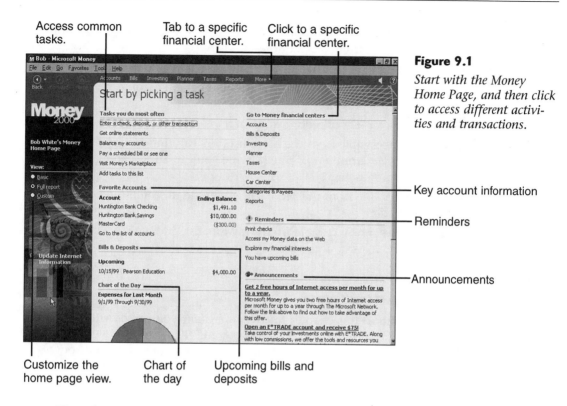

Figure 9.1

Start with the Money Home Page, and then click to access different activities and transactions.

Key account information

Reminders

Announcements

Customize the home page view.

Chart of the day

Upcoming bills and deposits

These links are organized into several sections; which sections you see depend on how you customize your version of the Money Home Page. (You customize your home page from the View options at the left of the page.) If you select the Basic View, you see only the Tasks You Do Most Often, Favorite Accounts, Go To Money Financial Centers, and Reminders sections. If you select the Full Report view, you see all available sections.

If you want to display only selected sections, click the Custom View option; when the Options dialog box appears, check those sections you want to display, and in what order you want them displayed. (From this dialog box you can also configure your Advisor FYI alerts, select articles from specific publisher to display on the home page, and choose which charts are displayed in the Chart of the Day section.)

Money's Financial Centers

Across the top of the Money Home Page are tabs for Money's other financial centers. These pages organize tasks and information by specific type of activity, including:

➤ **Accounts.** View account balances, add new accounts, manage existing accounts, and link directly to each account's register.

➤ **Bills.** Set up new payees and pay bills.

➤ **Investing.** View and edit your portfolio, record new investment transactions, and go online to get current stock quotes.

➤ **Planner.** Create a budget, create a debt-reduction plan, and plan your 401(k).

➤ **Taxes.** Estimate your taxes, see tax-related spending and income, and export data to a separate tax program.

➤ **Reports.** Create a variety of reports and charts.

➤ **House Center.** Accessible from the More list, you can find a home, calculate the cost of a loan, determine how much home you can afford, and go online to look for other home resources.

➤ **Car Center.** Accessible from the More list, go online to search for, purchase, and insure a new car.

➤ **Categories & Payees.** Accessible from the More list, add, delete, and modify the categories used in your accounts.

Daily Money Management

There isn't enough room in this chapter to cover *everything* you can do with Money; to learn everything there is to know about Money could fill up another whole book! There are, however, some tasks common to almost all users—and we'll go through those tasks in the next several sections.

Entering Banking Transactions

Money makes it easy to enter transactions into your checking and savings accounts. You should have set up your accounts when you ran the Setup Assistant; if you need to add or modify your accounts, select the Accounts tab and add or modify accounts there.

After your accounts are created, you need to manage inflow and outflow. The easiest way to do this is from your account register, such as the one shown in Figure 9.2. You open your register by selecting the Accounts tab and clicking on a specific account.

Money lets you enter one of three different types of transactions: withdrawals, deposits, and transfers. To enter a transaction, follow these steps:

1. From the account register, click the appropriate transaction tab (Withdrawal, Deposit, or Transfer) at the bottom of the workspace.

2. To register a withdrawal, select the payee from the Pay To list, select a transaction category from the Category list, enter any memo text for this transaction, select a numbering option from the Number list, enter the Date of the transaction, and then enter the Amount of the withdrawal. Click Enter to register the transaction.

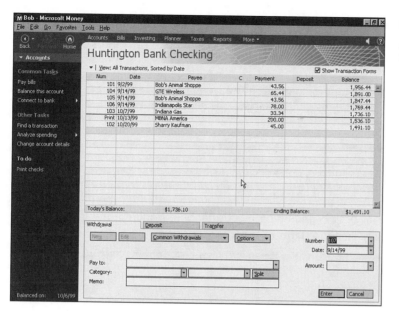

Figure 9.2

Enter transactions directly into an account register.

Pick a Transaction

If you're entering a common transaction—something planned for or recurring—you don't have to enter all the information manually. Instead, you can click the Common (Withdrawals, Deposits, or Transfers) button and select an option from the pull-down list; Money will then enter the appropriate information automatically.

3. To register a deposit, select the payer from the From list, select a transaction category from the Category list, enter any memo text for this transaction, select a numbering option from the Number list, enter the Date of the transaction, and then enter the Amount of the deposit. Click Enter to register the transaction.

4. To register a transfer between accounts, select the appropriate accounts from the From and To lists, enter any memo text for this transaction, select a numbering option from the Number list, enter the Date of the transaction, and then enter the Amount of the transfer. Click Enter to register the transaction.

To edit a previous transaction, select the transaction in the register and then edit the information in the tab below. Click the Options button to display a drop-down menu of various editing options—including the Delete command.

Transact Online

To execute transactions online—including electronic bill payments—see the "Pay Your Bills Electronically" section, later in this chapter.

Paying Your Bills

If you've set up a checkbook account in Money, it's easy to set up a list of payees and use Money for all your bill payments.

If you want to write checks manually and then enter those withdrawals into your Money register, here's what you do:

1. Select the Bills tab.
2. When the Pay Bills page appears as shown in Figure 9.3, select the bill you want to pay.

Figure 9.3

Select which bills to pay, and how you want to pay them.

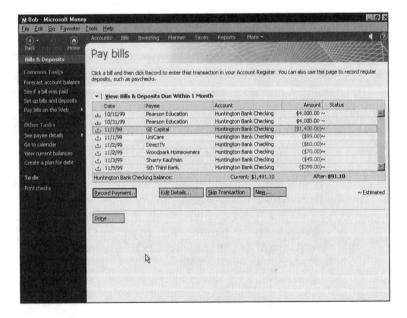

3. Click the Record Payment button.

4. When the Record Payment dialog box appears, enter or modify any payment details, and then click Record Payment.

Set Up a Payment

To add new payees and scheduled payments to your list, go to the Bills tab and click the New button. When the Create New Scheduled Transaction Wizard appears, follow the onscreen instructions to create the new payment.

Writing Checks

To have Money create and print checks (on your computer's printer), all you have to do is change one little option in the Record Payment dialog box. When you pull down the Number list and select Print This Transaction, you tell Money that you want to print a check for this particular payment.

Buy the Forms

You can't print checks on plain white laser paper; you have to purchase special check forms to use with your specific banking accounts. For more information on ordering Money-compatible check forms, call 800-432-1285.

The first time you choose to print a check to a specific payee, Money displays the Print Address dialog box. Enter the appropriate information here, and then click OK. (You'll also be asked if you'll always want to print checks to this payee; if you answer Yes, the Number field will automatically change to Print for all future transactions.)

After you enter a printable transaction, that transaction goes into Money's "to do" list, where it is held until you manually choose to print all waiting checks. To print all waiting checks, select the Bills tab and then select Print Checks on the Bills and Deposit pane. When the Print Checks dialog box appears, select what checks you want to print (all or selected), what type of check forms you're using, the number of the first check form in your printer, and how many checks are on the first page. Click Print to print the selected check(s).

Printing Problems?

If the printing on your checks doesn't line up properly, click the Options button in the Print Checks dialog box. When the Options dialog box appears, you can reset the printing alignment for your printer. You also might want to test how your checks print before you waste a page of forms; click the Print Test button in the Print Checks dialog box to print a test page.

Balancing Your Checkbook

When you receive your monthly statement from your bank, you know it's time for that painful process of balancing your bank accounts. This, fortunately, is one of the things that Money takes the pain out of.

To have Money balance a specific account, follow these steps:

1. Select the Accounts tab.
2. When the Pick an Account to Use page appears, click Balance an Account from the Common Tasks list.
3. When the Which Account Do You Want to Balance? page appears, select an account.
4. When the Balance Wizard appears, enter the following information from your monthly statement: statement date, starting balance, ending balance, service charges (if any), and interest earned (if any). Click Next to proceed.
5. Money now displays a balance page for the selected account. Compare the transactions in the Money register with the transactions on your monthly statement. Click the C column to clear each matching transaction. If a transaction doesn't match, click the transaction and edit it accordingly. If you're missing any transactions (the primary cause of accounts not balancing), click the New button to enter them as new.

6. When you're done comparing transactions, click the Next button to finish the activity.

Tracking Your Investments

Money makes it easy to create and track multiple portfolios. All investment-related activities are accessed from the Investing tab.

I recommend managing your portfolio from the Your Portfolio page, which is displayed when you click the View My Entire Portfolio link, as shown in Figure 9.4. From here you can perform the following tasks:

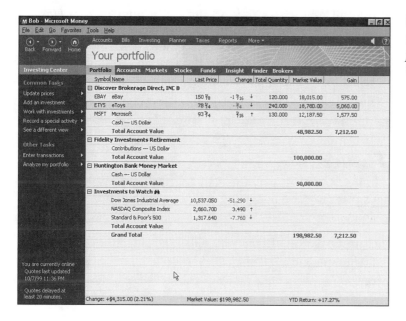

Figure 9.4

Use the Your Portfolio page to manage all your investments.

➤ **Update prices.** Click Update Prices in the Common Tasks list, and then select whether you want to update manually or online. If you select to update online, Money will connect to the Internet and download the latest quotes.

➤ **Add an investment.** To add an investment within any portfolio, click the Add an Investment link. When the New Investment Wizard appears, enter account and investment information—including shares purchased, price paid (per share), and commission. When you complete the wizard, your new investment will appear in your portfolio.

➤ **Buy and sell stocks.** To buy and sell stocks, mutual funds, and other securities, click the Enter Transactions link and then select either Record a Buy or Record a Sell. When the Edit Transaction dialog box appears, select the investment account, the specific investment, the activity (buy, sell, dividend, and so on), the quantity, the price, and the commission, and then click OK. This registers the new transaction and updates your portfolio balance.

➤ **Record a split.** To record a stock split, click the Record a Special Activity link and select Record a Split. When the Split Shares dialog box appears, enter the split information, and then click OK—Money does the rest of the work for you.

Change Your View

Money offers various views of your portfolio. Click the See a Different View link to select from Performance View, Valuation View, Holdings View, and others. You can also generate various investment reports by clicking the Analyze My Portfolio link and selecting Other Investment Reports. When the Pick an Investment Report page appears, select from various performance, value, history, and capital gains reports.

Planning for the Future

When you select the Planner tab, you display the Plan Your Finances page. From here you can engage in various planning and budgeting activities, including:

➤ Creating a budget

➤ Forecasting your account balances after paying bills

➤ Creating a debt reduction plan

➤ Planning your 401(k)

Build a Budget—Step-by-Step

For step-by-step instructions on using Money to create your home budget, see Chapter 21, "Create a Home Budget."

Managing Your Taxes

When you click the Taxes tab, you display the Get Ready for Taxes page. Although Money is not a tax preparation program (for that, check out programs such as TaxCut, TurboTax or TaxSaver), it does offer some tax planning functions, including how to

➤ Estimate your yearly taxes

➤ Display tax-related spending and income

➤ View tax reports and charts

➤ Set up Money to match your personal tax situation

➤ Export your Money data to TaxSaver or other tax preparation software program

➤ File your tax forms with a tax preparation service, by hand, or via the Web

Generating Reports

Money can create a rich library of reports to help you better understand your personal finances. All the reports from the Pick a Report or Chart page are displayed when you select the Reports tab.

Here's how to create a Money report:

1. From the Pick a Report or Chart page, select a category from the Reports list on the left side of the page.

2. Select which accounts you want to analyze from the Accounts list at the bottom of the page.

3. Double-click the specific report you want to create.

4. When the report displays (on a new page), select the date range for the report from the Date Range list at the bottom of the page.

5. If you want to customize this report in any other way, click the Customize icon to display and use the Customize Report dialog box.

6. To view this report in another chart or graph format, select a new format from the icons on the bottom-left of the page.

7. To print this report, pull down the File menu and select Print.

Perhaps the most useful single report in Money is the Monthly Report, shown in Figure 9.5. This report combines several different reports into a single (long) page, including Monthly Expenses Compared, Top 5 Expense Categories, Your Net Worth, and Performance of Your Investments—plus all sorts of alerts, reminders, and comments. If you generate just one report, this should be the one!

Figure 9.5

Use the Monthly Report to track all your important activities.

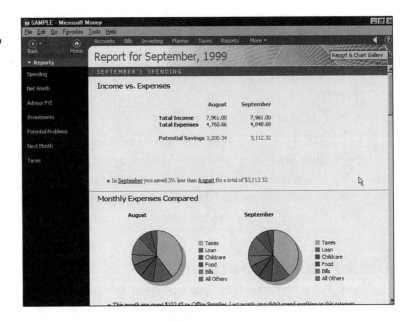

The Best Reports

Although you're sure to discover particular reports that are useful to you personally, I find the more useful Money Reports to be Account Balances, Net Worth, Where the Money Goes, Income vs. Spending, Performance by Investment Account, and the Money Monthly Report.

Fast Money with Money Express

Every time you start up your computer, Money launches a program called *Money Express*. This little pop-up program, shown in Figure 9.6, sits on your desktop and alerts you to any upcoming events—and allows you to make rapid transactions without loading the Money itself.

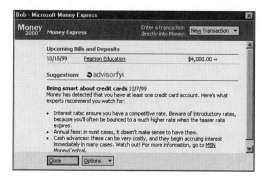

Figure 9.6

Use Money Express for rapid transactions and account alerts.

Stay Alert

When Money Express starts up, it displays a list of recent alerts and messages, including Account FYI Alerts, Bill Alerts, reminders, and announcements. To access more information about a specific alert, click the alert link.

Making a Rapid Transaction

You can use Money Express to make three types of transactions directly from your desktop, without launching Microsoft Money itself. When you click the New Transaction button, you can choose to make a new withdrawal, deposit, or transfer.

When you select a transaction, Money Express displays a Rapid Transaction Dialog box. From here you enter key information about your transaction (account, payee, category, amount, and so on) and click OK. The transaction is automatically registered in your Money account—and you'll see it listed the next time you start Money.

Configuring Money Express

When you click the Options button, the pull-down menu offers you three different configuration options:

➤ **Configure Money Express.** This option lets you determine whether Money Express should prompt you with a password, whether Money Express should run automatically whenever you start your computer, whether the Events List

New Alerts, All the Time

If you leave Money Express running in the background, any new alerts—such as those generated by stock price changes—will cause the Money Express icon in the Windows taskbar tray to blink.

Use the Express Lane

Using Money Express is faster than starting Money when you just have a transaction or two to enter.

should be displayed on startup, and whether Money Express should display your direct deposits and debits. When you click the Advanced button, additional options let you determine how long an alert message should stay visible and how often Money Express should download stock quotes from the Web.

Turn It Off!

If you *don't* want to launch Money Express every time you start your computer, click the Options button and select Configure Money Express. When the Money Express Configuration dialog box appears, *uncheck* the Run Money Express on Startup option, and then click OK. This removes Money Express from Windows' automatic launch list.

➤ **Configure Bill Alerts in Money.** This option lets you enter recurring bills and deposits—which will then appear in the Money Express alerts list and on the Money Home Page.

➤ **Configure Advisor FYI Alerts in Money.** This option lets you determine when Money will alert you about low account balances, high spending in specific categories, important tax-related dates, and when selected securities reach specified prices. All these alerts appear in the Money Express alerts list and on the Money Home Page.

More Money Online

When you connect Money to the Internet, you increase the power and the value of the program. Taking Money online lets you pay bills electronically, manage your accounts when you're on the road, update your stock prices automatically, and access a wide variety of financial help and information not otherwise available.

Sign Up for Electronic Banking

Before you can pay your bills electronically, download your bank statements, and perform online transfers, you have to set up Money to work with your financial institutions. Here's how you do that:

1. Click the Accounts tab.

2. When the Pick an Account to Use page appears, click Set Up Accounts.

3. When the Set Up Your Accounts in Money page appears, click Set Up Online Services.

4. When the Which Account Do You Want to Use Online? page appears, select an account.

5. When the Set Up Online Services page appears, click the Set Up button. (This page informs you of which online services are available from the selected institution; not all banks and financial institutions can be accessed online.)

6. When the Online Services Setup Wizard appears, follow the onscreen instructions.

To activate an account for online use, you'll need to have your Social Security number handy, as well as your online password—which means you probably need to contact your financial institution *first*, tell them you want to activate your account to work with Microsoft Money 2000, and obtain all the necessary information for the setup procedure.

Pay Your Bills Electronically

After you're set up for online operation, you can choose to pay your bills electronically—and never write or print a paper check again!

When you pay a bill electronically, Money calls this an *Epay*. You generate an electronic payment by following these steps:

1. Select the Bills tab.

2. When the Pay Bills page appears, select the bill you want to pay and click the Record Payment button.

3. When the Record Payment dialog box appears, pull down the Numbers list and select Epay.

4. Click the Record Payment button.

No Setup, No Epay

For the Epay option to be available when paying bills, your checking account has to be enabled for online banking. If you haven't yet signed up for electronic banking at this specific financial institution, you won't see the Epay option in the Number field.

The first time you enter an Epay for a payee, Money prompts you for certain details, such as the payee's name, address, and account number. Make sure you enter the correct information (typically available on your most recent bill from that payee), and then click OK.

Any bills you choose to pay electronically will now appear in the To Do list. To send these electronic payments, click the Send Payments link in the To Do list; Money will now connect to the Internet—and to your financial institution—and transmit your electronic bill payments.

Download Electronic Bank Statements

Many banks and financial institutions let you download their monthly statements. If your bank works this way, here's how you do it:

1. Select the Accounts tab.
2. When the Pick an Account to Use page appears, click Get Online Statements from the Common Tasks list.
3. When the Choose Where to Get Online Statements From page appears, click Connect to All.

Money now opens an Internet connection, connects to your financial institution(s), and downloads your latest statement(s).

Use Money on the Road with Money Web Express

Microsoft offers a Web-based version of Money called Money Web Express. With Money Web Express, you can pay bills and keep track of your accounts from any Web browser, anywhere you can find an Internet connection—which is great if you're traveling or you're on the road a lot.

Here's what you can do with Money Web Express:

➤ Pay bills
➤ Enter trip or vacation expenses into your account
➤ Buy, sell, and track stocks and other securities
➤ Check your account balances and transfer money between accounts
➤ Receive Advisor FYI alerts

To sign up for Money Web Express, select Money's Investing tab, and then click Access My Money Data on the Web. When the Roam with Money Web Express screen appears, click the Set Up MoneyCentral Synchronization button. Money will now connect to the Internet and lead you through the online setup procedure.

Even More Online with MoneyCentral

For more financial information and services online, check out Microsoft's MoneyCentral Web site at moneycentral.msn.com. (You can also jump there by clicking the Microsoft MoneyCentral icon Works Suite 2000 installed on your desktop.)

The Least You Need to Know

➤ You set up most of your accounts the first time you launch Money, using the Setup Assistant.

➤ Most Money transactions and operations are accessible from the Money Home Page—which you can customize to display your personal information.

➤ You can add or modify your accounts at any time from the Accounts tab.

➤ You pay your bills—electronically or otherwise—from the Bills tab.

➤ You manage your investment portfolio—and get the latest stock quotes—from the Investing tab.

➤ Before you can pay your bills electronically, you have to obtain online access information from your bank, and set up Money for online operation.

Chapter 10

Make Fun and Useful Projects with Home Publishing

In This Chapter

➤ Learn how to make cards, newsletters, banners, and other projects

➤ Discover how to get started—fast—with predesigned projects

➤ Find out how to personalize your projects in the editing workspace

Microsoft Home Publishing 2000 is an easy-to-use program (included with Works Suite 2000, of course) that lets you create all sorts of crafts and projects—from business cards and newsletters to Christmas cards and gift boxes. When you combine Home Publishing with a good color printer, you have the ingredients to make some great-looking stuff—or just have some creative fun on a rainy day!

Starting and Navigating Home Publishing

Although you can start Home Publishing from the Windows Start menu, it's easier to get started from the Works Task Launcher. When you select the Programs tab and select Home Publishing from the Programs list, you're presented with the option of starting Home Publishing directly (with a blank workspace) or of launching Home Publishing with a particular type of project preloaded.

When you start Home Publishing through one of these tasks, the program automatically takes you to a display of predesigned projects. If you start Home Publishing from the Start Microsoft Home Publishing 2000 link, you're presented with Home Publishing's main screen, shown in Figure 10.1.

Figure 10.1

Click a tab, then select a project to get started.

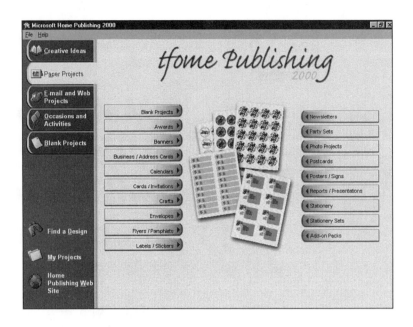

The main screen includes five different tabs—and a few extra options for creating or opening projects. Here's what you'll find on each tab:

➤ **Creative Ideas.** This tab is kind of sort of a mini-Help system or introduction to basic topics. Click any link to read more about that topic.

➤ **Paper Projects.** Use this tab when you want to create a new paper-based project based on a predesigned template. Among the projects you can create from this tab are awards, banners, business/address cards, calendars, cards/invitations, crafts, envelopes, flyers/pamphlets, labels/stickers, newsletters, party sets, photo projects, postcards, posters/signs, reports/presentations, stationery, and stationery sets. Click a category to create that type of project.

➤ **E-mail and Web Projects.** Use this tab to create projects (based on predesigned templates) that you can send via email or post on a Web site. Among the projects you can create from this tab are announcements, greetings, invitations, newsletters, photo projects, postcards, stationery, and Web pages.

➤ **Occasions and Activities.** Use this tab to create cards and other items (based on predesigned templates) to announce or celebrate specific occasions. Among the projects you can create from this tab are baby/pregnancy, birthday, caring, celebrations, Christmas, Father's Day, just because, marriage, Mother's Day, parties, photo projects, romance, Valentine's Day, workplace, other holidays, family activities, kids activities, and school activities.

➤ **Blank Projects.** Use this tab to create blank projects *not* based on predesigned templates. Among the project types you can create from this tab are standard paper, banners, calendars, cards, crafts, envelopes, labels, postcards, posters, Avery labels, Hallmark papers, Kodak papers, and email projects.

Lots of CD Swapping

Home Publishing is a graphics–intensive program, and it stores all those graphics on three different CDs—which means you'll often be asked to insert a new CD when you start a new project.

Three icons on the bottom-left of the main screen provide additional options for starting projects:

➤ **Find a Design.** Enables you to search through all of Home Publishing's pre-designed templates for a specific project.

➤ **My Projects.** Shows you how to reopen projects you created previously.

➤ **Home Publishing Web Site.** Connects you to the Internet and takes you to Microsoft's Home Publishing Web site, which includes product news and enhancements, tips and techniques, and "add-on" packs of new designs and artwork (either free or for purchase).

More on the Web

You can also access the Home Publishing Web site by jumping directly to www.home-publishing.com.

Don't Reinvent the Wheel: Creating Projects from Predesigned Templates

Home Publishing 2000 includes hundreds of ready-to-use predesigned projects. These are great-looking projects that you can use as-is or edit for your own personal use. Using a predesigned project as a template for your own project is the fastest and easiest way to make things happen in Home Publishing.

Creating a New Paper–Based Project

Here's how to create a new paper-based project based on a predesigned template:

1. From the main page, click the Paper Projects tab.

2. Click a specific project type.

3. Depending on the type of project you selected, you may see a screen listing different options for that project type. For example, clicking on Labels/Stickers displays a screen listing different types of Avery labels; clicking on Cards/ Invitations displays a screen listing different occasions for your cards. If you see an interim screen like this, click on the appropriate selection.

4. The next screen, shown in Figure 10.2, displays all the predesigned projects within the category you selected. In some categories projects are grouped by *themes*; if so, select a theme from the Themes list at the top-left corner.

Figure 10.2

Select a theme, and then click the project you want to open.

Read the prewritten message.

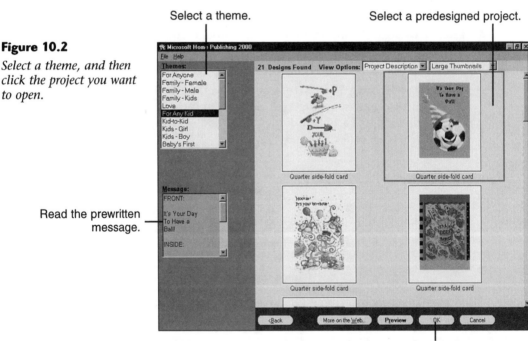

Select a theme.

Select a predesigned project.

Click OK to open the project.

5. Click any project thumbnail. If the project has an accompanying message, that message will be displayed in the left panel of the screen.

6. If you want to preview the design of a specific project, select the project thumbnail and click Preview. This displays the Preview dialog box, where you can see not only the front of the project, but also the inside and back (if this type of project has multiple sides).

7. After you've selected the project you want to open, click OK.

The predesigned project is now opened in the Home Publishing workspace. From here you can print the project as-is, or edit the project, as described in the "Personalize Your Project" section later in this chapter.

Creating a New Email or Web Project

To create a new email or Web-based project, follow these steps:

1. From the main page, click the E-mail and Web Projects tab.
2. Click a specific project type.
3. Depending on the type of project you selected, you may see a screen listing different options for that project type. If so, click the appropriate selection.
4. When the next screen appears, select a theme from the Themes list, and then click the project you want to open.
5. Click OK to open the project.

Pop! Swoosh! Pop!

Many of Home Publishing's email projects include simple animations and accompanying sounds. When you click the Preview button on the editing screen you can experience the full multimedia effect of your selected project.

To send an email project to another user, click the More Options button on the editing screen, and then select Send By Email from the pop-up menu. When the Send by E-mail dialog box appears, select *how* you want to send this message (because you're using Works Suite 2000, you'll probably select Outlook Express) and click OK. An email header will now be added to your project; fill in the To: and Subject: fields as you would any email message, and then click Send to send the message.

If you created a Web page project, you'll need to "publish" your finished project to a Web site. Publishing a Web page involves uploading it to a designated Web server and giving it a specific Web page address, most of which Home Publishing can handle for you. When you're ready to publish your page, click the More Options button and then select Publish to Web Site. When the Publish to Web Wizard appears, fill in the information (most of which should be provided by your Web hosting service) and let Home Publishing save your page to HTML and upload it to your site.

Find a Good Host

To publish a page on the Web, you have to find a site or service that will *host* your pages. Many ISPs offer free hosting services for anyone who signs up. If you haven't yet signed up for any of these services, you can click the Sign Me Up button in the Publish to Web Site dialog box to see the list of hosting services displayed on Microsoft's Home Publishing Web site.

Creating a Project for a Special Occasion

If you have a special event coming up—whether it's a birthday, wedding, or a big holiday—you can use Home Publishing to create greeting cards and other items for the occasion. Just follow these steps:

1. From the main page, click the Occasions and Activities tab.

2. Click a specific occasion or event.

3. When the next screen appears, select a theme from the Themes list, and then click the project you want to open.

4. Click OK to open the project.

You can now personalize the project from the Home Publishing editing screen.

Searching for Projects

Not sure what kind of project you want to create? Then use Home Publishing's Find a Design feature to search for just the right project. When you click the Find a Design icon on the main screen, you're taken to a blank screen (with no designs listed) that contains a search box in the top-left corner. Enter one or more words describing the type of project you want to create then click the Search button. Home Publishing will now display all predesigned projects that match your query. For example, if you search for **superhero**, you'll see eleven different projects that in one way or another have something to do with super-heroes. Pick the project you want and edit it as normal.

Creating a Blank Project from Scratch

You don't have to start with a predesigned project. If you'd rather do all the designing yourself, Home Publishing lets you open and then edit blank projects.

Here's how to create a project from scratch:

1. From the main page, click the Blank Projects tab.

2. Select the type of project you want to create.

3. Home Publishing now displays a selection of blank templates. Pick the template you want to use, and then click OK.

You can now add text and images to your new project, and then print out the final version as you would with a predesigned project.

Opening an Existing Project

To open a project you previously created, click the My Projects icon on the main screen—or pull down the File menu and select Open. When the Open Project dialog box appears, navigate to the project you want to open, select it, and click the Open button.

Personalize Your Project

Whether you start with a blank or predesigned project, you can personalize what you
see onscreen through Home Publishing's various editing options. When a project is
placed in the editing workspace (shown in Figure 10.3), you have the following tools
available to you from the Main Options panel:

Figure 10.3

*Personalize your project
with Home Publishing's
editing tools.*

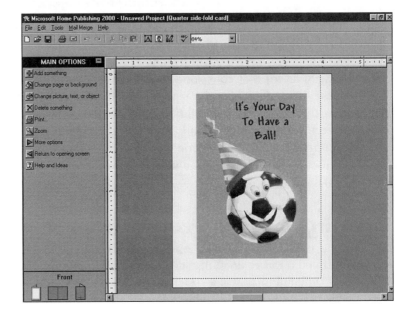

➤ **Add Something.** Click this button to insert text, pictures, shapes, lines, page
backgrounds, page borders, or other elements.

➤ **Change Page or Background.** Select this option to change the page background or border for predesigned projects.

➤ **Change Picture, Text, or Object.** Select this option (then select an object to
edit) to change formatting or to edit objects in predesigned projects.

➤ **Delete Something.** Select this option to delete an element of a predesigned
project.

➤ **Print.** Click this button to display the Print dialog box and print your project.

➤ **Zoom.** Select this option to shrink or enlarge your project onscreen.

➤ **More Options.** Click this button if you want to check spelling, send your project to someone via email, or post your project to a Web site.

➤ **Return to Opening Screen.** Click here to return to Home Publishing's main
screen.

➤ **Help and Ideas.** Click here if you're out of ideas—or just need help!

As you can see, Home Publishing offers a wide variety of editing options for whatever type of project you want to create. Just remember to save your project (pull down the File menu and select Save) when you're done!

The Least You Need to Know

➤ Home Publishing 2000 lets you create all sorts of projects and crafts.

➤ You can start a project from scratch, or by using a predesigned project as a template.

➤ After you select a project, you can personalize it by editing, inserting, and deleting elements in the editing workspace.

Chapter 11

Fix Your Photos with Picture It! Express

In This Chapter

➤ Learn what kind of pictures you can use with Picture It! Express

➤ Find out how to fix red eye and other imperfections in your photographs

➤ Discover how to use your photographs to make picture albums, picture post-cards, and other projects

More and more users are working with digital photos and picture files on their PCs. Whether you're emailing vacation pictures to your family or uploading product photos to a Web page, chances are you're somehow dealing with pictures on your PC.

Picture It! Express 2000 is a program included with Works Suite 2000 that helps you work with your computerized pictures. With Picture It! Express you can touch up imperfect pictures, add special effects, or create photo albums and collages—all with a few clicks of the mouse. This is a very easy program to use, which is great if you're better with a camera than you are with a computer!

Launching and Navigating Picture It! Express

You can start Picture It! Express from either the Windows Start menu (click Start, Programs, Picture It! Express) or from the Works Task Launcher. Just select the Programs tab and then select Picture It! Express from the Programs list; you'll see a number of specific tasks listed, or you can start the program directly by clicking Start Picture It! Express.

When you launch Picture It! Express directly, the program displays the Getting Started dialog box. You can select an option from this dialog box, or click Close to go directly to the program.

Increase Your Resolution

If you're running Windows at a relatively low video color setting (256 colors or fewer), Picture It! Express will display a prompt suggesting that your pictures will look sharper displayed at a higher resolution, such as High Color. If your system can run at a higher resolution, this is a good suggestion; answer Yes to the prompt and, when Windows displays the Display Properties dialog box, select the Settings tab, and select either High Color or (if available) True Color from the Colors list.

Picture It! Express' main page is called the Workbench, which is where you edit and touch up your pictures.

When you select the Projects tab, you can access one of the program's many photo-related projects, including collages, cards, calendars, and mats and frames.

Editing Your Photos

Amateur photographers seldom take perfect photos. Whether you need to correct for bad framing (by cropping the photo's edges) adjust for too much or too little light (by adjusting brightness and contrast), remove scratches from scanned pictures, or remove those red eyes caused by too much flash, you can do it easily from Picture It! Express' Workbench, shown in Figure 11.1.

Get Your Picture

Before you can touch up a picture, you have to put it in the Workbench. To do this, click the Get Picture link, and select from where you want to get the picture. You can Open Pictures from files on your hard disk, Scan Pictures from a scanner, or download pictures from a Digital Camera. Follow the onscreen directions to load your pictures into the Workbench.

Figure 11.1

Use the Workbench to touch up and add effects to your pictures.

After your picture is in the Workbench, it's added to the *Filmstrip* at the bottom of your page. The Filmstrip displays all currently open pictures; click on a specific picture to display it in the main Workbench area.

Touch It Up

If your picture isn't perfect, you can use Picture It! Express' editing tools to touch it up. With your picture loaded into the Workbench, click the Touchup link to display the following options:

➤ **Brightness and Contrast.** When you select this option you see two sliders to interactively adjust your picture's brightness and contrast; move a slider and see your picture change accordingly. If you prefer to let Picture It! fix your picture automatically, click the Smart Task Fix button; the program will attempt to set the optimal brightness and contrast settings for your picture.

➤ **Correct Tint.** With this option you have a couple of different ways to adjust the color of your photo. The automatic method is activated when you click on an area of your picture that should be pure white; Picture It! will then adjust all other colors accordingly. You can also select a color on the color ring to change the overall tint of the picture, and then adjust the slider to adjust the color intensity.

➤ **Fix Red Eye.** Red eye sometimes results when you use flash photography. Picture It! can automatically fix red eye when you click the Smart Task Fix button. If this doesn't do the job, you can click the Select Eyes by Tracing button and manually trace the red areas you want to fix.

➤ **Remove Scratch.** If you've scanned in an old photo, it may be scratched from years of handling and misuse. To eliminate the scratches, select a "ball" to resize your cursor, and then click along the length of the scratch to remove it.

Crop It

Sometimes amateur photographers don't do a good job of framing the subject. Other times, you might want to isolate a person or area within a photo. In any case, you accomplish this "reframing" by *cropping* your photos.

To crop a photo in the Workbench, follow these steps:

1. Select the Size & Position link.
2. Select Crop.
3. When the cropping pane appears, select a shape for your crop.
4. Move your cursor to your picture, and move, resize, or rotate the crop area.
5. Click the Done button to finalize the crop. Figures 11.2 and 11.3 show an image before and after cropping.

Figure 11.2

Yasmine Bleeth before...

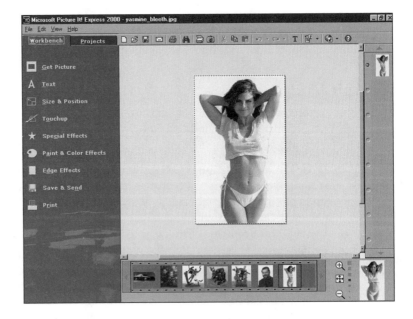

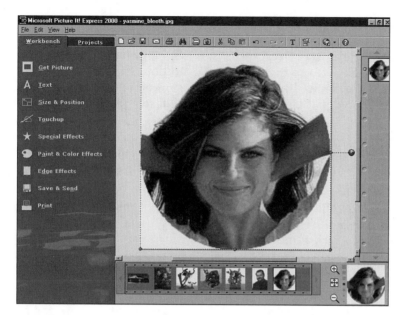

Figure 11.3

...and after cropping.

Other Sizing and Positioning Options

The Sizing and Positioning control includes several other options you can apply to your pictures, including rotating, flipping, and (if you're creating a collage, discussed later in this chapter) moving the picture forward or backward through a stack.

Add Text and Special Effects

Picture It! also lets you add text to your pictures, along with other special effects. Here are some of the options you have available:

➤ **Add text.** To add text on top of your picture, click the Text link and select Add Text. When the Add Text pane appears, type your text, and then select a font, style, and color. Your text appears over the picture in the Workbench; you can use your mouse to move, resize, and rotate the text as desired. Click OK to add the text to your picture.

➤ **Distort your picture.** To add a distorted effect to your picture, click the Special Effects link and select Picture Putty to display the Picture Putty pane. To distort the entire picture, select Distort the Whole Object Automatically; you'll then select a distortion effect and the amount of distortion. To distort part of the picture, select Distort Image by Hand, select a distortion effect, and then use your mouse to select what part of your picture you want to distort.

➤ **Blur or sharpen your image.** You can "soften" a grainy or jagged image—or sharpen an out-of-focus image—with Picture It!'s focus control. Just click the Special Effect link and select Blur or Sharpen Focus. Drag the slider to the right to sharpen the image; drag it to the left to soften (or "blur") the image.

➤ **Paint your picture.** To paint or draw on your pictures and make your photo look like a painting, click the Paint & Color Effects link and then select Freehand Painting. When the Freehand Painting pane appears, select a painting tool, select a paint color, pick a brush size—and then start painting!

➤ **Make it monochrome.** To change a color picture to black and white, click the Paint & Color Effects link and then select Black & White. Click the Make Black & White button to remove all the color from your picture.

➤ **Soften the edges.** Picture It! lets you soften the edges of your picture to add a "framing" effect. Just click the Edge Effects link and select Soft Edges. When the Soft Edges pane appears, adjust the slider until you achieve the desired effect, such as the one shown in Figure 11.4.

Figure 11.4

Soft edges on a cropped picture—nice framing!

Crop and Soften

The Soft Edges effect works best when you've cropped your image to a specific shape. Try cropping to a circle and selecting a value of 100 for edge softness—it's a nice effect!

Producing Picture Projects

Picture It! Express lets you create a variety of projects using your own personal pictures. You access these projects from the Projects tab, using the pictures you've loaded into the Filmstrip. Here are some of the projects you can create:

➤ **Collages.** When you click the Collages link, you have the option of creating a collage with a template, or creating pages for a photo album. The first option creates a "filmstrip" onscreen; you can drag and drop pictures from your Filmstrip onto different frames of the filmstrip collage. The second option presents several predesigned page layouts you can use to create your own photo album, as shown in Figure 11.5.

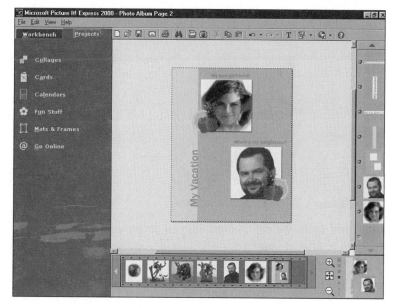

Figure 11.5

Create your own photo album pages.

➤ **Cards.** Click the Cards link to add your photos to predesigned greeting cards, postcards, and sports cards as shown in Figure 11.6.

Figure 11.6

Add your photograph to a picture postcard.

➤ **Calendars.** Click the Calendars link to create a one-month calendar using your own pictures.

➤ **Fun Stuff.** When you click the Fun Stuff link, you can create a fake magazine cover—with your photo on the front!

➤ **Mats & Frames.** The Mats & Frames link lets you add your picture to some fancy frames.

Background Work

There's More in the Store

If you're a little disappointed with the skimpy selection of projects included with Picture It! Express, upgrade to the full version of Picture It!. Go to Microsoft's Picture It! Web site (www.home-publishing.com/PictureIt/) to learn more.

The Least You Need to Know

➤ Picture It! Express can work with picture files, scanned images, and photographs from digital cameras.

➤ Use Picture It! Express to touch up photographs—including adjusting brightness and contrast, taking out red eye, and removing scratches.

➤ Add your own photos to Picture It! projects, including collages, photo albums, postcards, and calendars.

Chapter 12

Get Driving Directions with Expedia Streets & Trips

In This Chapter

➤ Learn how to move around the Streets & Trips map

➤ Find out how to zoom to practically any location

➤ Discover how to create turn-by-turn driving directions for your next trip

---

The next time you're planning a driving vacation, don't worry about getting lost. You can use Expedia Streets and Trips 2000, included with Works Suite 2000, to provide detailed maps and expert driving directions—for wherever you want to go!

Navigating Through Streets & Trips

You launch Streets & Trips from the Works Task Launcher. Just select the Programs tab, Expedia Streets & Trips from the Programs list, and then click Start Expedia Streets & Trips. After you're prompted to insert the Expedia CD, you're presented with a map of the United States—and the Start Screen dialog box.

From this dialog box you can choose to Plan a Route, Find a Place, Find an Address, or Open a Saved Trip or Map. You can make your selections here, or close this dialog box and work from the main Streets & Trips screen.

Streets & Trips has two main screens, each on its own tab. The Map tab displays maps (duh!); the Directions tab displays directions. (This is a pretty easy program to use, truth be told.)

One More Tab

If you're displaying commercial locations on your map, you may see a third tab, labeled Information. This tab presents information about commercial establishments (restaurants, hotels, and the like); if you want even more information, you can click the infoUSA link to jump to a related Web site.

Modifying Your Map

When you click the Map tab, you start out with a giant map of the U.S. You can modify the way this map appears onscreen (see Figure 12.1) in the following ways:

Click to highlight a point.

Click to mark a location with a pushpin.

Click to highlight a line.

Click to move the map.

Show or hide map scale.

Click to select a zoom area.

Find a specific location.   Zoom in or out.

Figure 12.1

Expedia's Map view— zoom in, zoom out, and change the level of detail.

Show or hide drawing tools.

Choose a different map style.

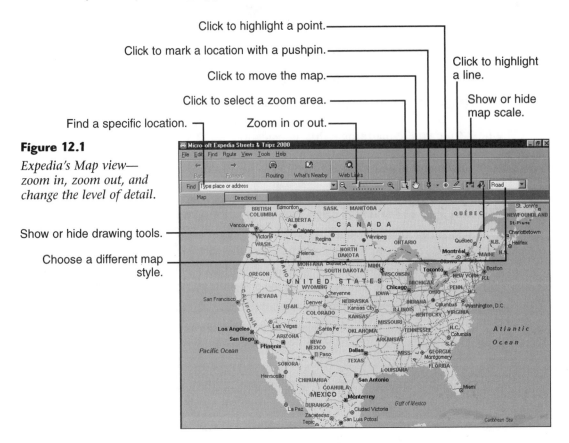

➤ **Change the map style.** By default, Expedia's map is displayed in the Road view, so that all major roads are displayed. But you can pull down the Map Style list and change to either the Terrain (a topographical map) or Political (different colors for different regions) views.

➤ **Zoom in or out.** Use the Zoom slider (or + and - controls) to zoom into a specific area of the map—or zoom out to see more of the country. At maximum zoom, you're literally at street level. Zoom *out* all the way, and you get a global view of things.

➤ **Move around.** Use the Direction control (the little hand icon) to drag your map around the screen—and focus on a different section.

➤ **Mark a location.** If you want to mark a specific location on the map, you have two options. You can add a *pushpin* at a specific location by clicking the Pushpin button and clicking a spot on your map. You can also highlight a location by clicking the Highlight button and clicking a spot on your map. A pushpin is a little more versatile than a highlight, in that you can assign a name (and other descriptive text) to a pushpin, as well as change the pushpin style. After a pushpin is named, you can search for it using the Find box; you can't search for highlights.

➤ **Find what's nearby.** After you've zoomed into a specific location, you can elect to display specific businesses or landmarks on the map. Just click the What's Nearby button to display the What's Nearby pane (shown in Figure 12.2), and then select what types of places you want to display on your map. (You can also select over what range you want to display places, using the controls at the bottom of the What's Nearby pane.)

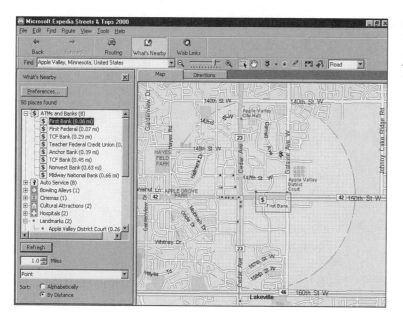

Figure 12.2

Use the What's Nearby pane to find nearby businesses and attractions.

➤ **Show places of interest.** Where the What's Nearby command finds specific landmarks, you can also display *all* landmarks of a specific type on your map. Just pull down the View menu and select Show or Hide Points of Interest. When the Show or Hide dialog box appears, check those items you want to display on your map (and uncheck those you don't want to see). Then click OK. Your map will now be updated with icons for specific types of locations. Click any given icon to see what's there.

➤ **See the big picture.** If you're zoomed into a small part of a city, you can view a larger city overview map by pulling down the Tools menu and selecting Overview Map.

Print a Map

To print the map displayed onscreen, pull down the File menu and select Print. When the Print dialog box appears, check the Current Map View option. If you also want to print an area overview map, check the With Overview Map option. Click OK to print.

Be Precise

You don't want to be *too* vague when searching for a location. For example, if you search for Pizza Hut you'll receive a listing of every Pizza Hut restaurant in the United States!

Find a Place or Address

Although you could zoom in and move around to try to find a location manually, it's easier to use the Streets & Trips Find command to pinpoint specific addresses and locations. Just enter your location in the Find box and press Enter; Expedia will create a list of places that match your query and display them in a Find dialog box. Select which place is the place you were looking for, and then click OK. The map will automatically zoom into the place you selected.

When you're searching for places, you have a lot of leeway as to how you search. You can enter a specific address, a city, a state, a zip code, a place name (such as Times Square), the name of a restaurant or hotel or other business or landmark, or a precise latitude and longitude.

Plan a Trip—Get Directions

You're getting ready to hop in the car and start driving. Do you know how to get to where you want to go?

You can use Streets & Trips to plot your route and present turn-by-turn driving directions. Just follow these steps:

1. Click the Routing button on the Expedia toolbar.

2. When the Routing pane appears (see Figure 12.3), click the Set Start Point button.

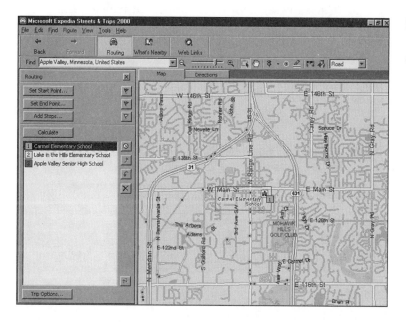

Figure 12.3

Use the Routing pane to set your trip parameters.

3. When the Find a Place to Start dialog box appears, select the Address tab and enter a specific address, or select the Place tab and enter a place or landmark, and then click Find. Expedia presents a list of locations that match your entry. Select the correct entry from the list and click OK.

4. Back in the Routing pane, click the set End Point button.

5. When the Find a Place to End dialog box appears, select the Address tab and enter a specific address, or select the Place tab and enter a place or landmark, and then click Find. Expedia presents a list of locations that match your entry. Select the correct entry from the list and click OK.

6. If you want to schedule specific stops during your trip, click the Add Stops button and enter specific locations.

7. If you want to schedule a specific departure or arrival time for your trip, select either your starting or ending point, and then click the Schedule Times button. When the Edit Time dialog box appears, enter a time and click OK.

8. To select various options for your trip, click the Trip Options button. When the Trip Options dialog box appears, you can select whether you want the quickest route, shortest route, or scenic route; what speeds you typically drive, and when during the day you typically travel; your car's gas consumption and tank capacity; and average fuel price. Select your options, then click OK.

9. When you've entered all the important information, click the Calculate button to create your route and driving instructions.

When your trip has been calculated, Expedia switches to the Directions tab and displays your turn-by-turn directions in the top pane, and an overall route map in the bottom pane (see Figure 12.4). Click any segment in the directions pane to display a more detailed map in the map pane.

Figure 12.4

View your turn-by-turn driving directions—and accompanying maps!

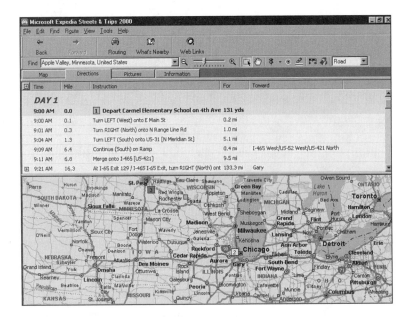

To print your driving directions, pull down the File menu, select Print, and then select Map or Driving Directions. When the Print dialog box appears, check the Driving Directions option, and then one of the following suboptions:

➤ **Directions Only.** Prints your text-based directions only.

➤ **With Turn by Turn Maps.** Prints your directions with small maps for each driving segment.

➤ **With Strip Maps.** Prints your directions with larger maps for long strips of your trip.

➤ **With Complete Trip Map.** Prints one of the first three variations *plus* an overview map of your entire route.

Click OK to print out your custom-made driving directions!

Save Your Trip

Don't want to lose your directions? Then pull down the File menu, select Save As, and use the Save As dialog box to save your directions. You can then reopen the directions for this trip at a future date by pulling down the File menu and selecting Open.

The Least You Need to Know

➤ Streets & Maps can display maps at any zoom level—from global view to street view.

➤ Use the Find box to pinpoint specific locations—including local landmarks, businesses, and specific addresses.

➤ Click the Routing button to enter the starting and ending points for a trip, and Streets & Maps will display turn-by-turn driving directions—complete with accompanying maps.

Chapter 13

Look Up Almost Anything with Encarta Encyclopedia

In This Chapter

➤ Learn how to search for specific information in the Encarta Encyclopedia

➤ Discover how to navigate long articles—and access related articles and Web sites

➤ Find out how to print and copy text from Encarta articles

Works Suite 2000 includes a copy of the most popular electronic encyclopedia available today—Microsoft Encarta Encyclopedia 2000. With Encarta it's easy to look up all sorts of information, whether you're preparing a report for school or just interested in a specific topic!

Launching the Encyclopedia—and Finding Your Way Around

The easiest way to launch Encarta is from the Works Task Launcher. Just select the Programs tab, select Encarta Encyclopedia from the Programs list, and then click Start Encarta Encyclopedia. (You can also start Encarta from the Windows Start menu; click the Start button, select Programs, select Microsoft Encarta, and then select Encarta Encyclopedia 2000.)

When you launch Encarta, you'll be asked to insert the Encarta Encyclopedia disc. This is because Encarta is so large, so comprehensive, it can only be stored on CD-ROM. So insert the CD and get started!

Other Versions

The version of Encarta 2000 included with Works Suite 2000 is kind of the basic version of the encyclopedia. Microsoft also makes other, more fully featured versions of Encarta, including Encarta Encyclopedia Deluxe 2000 and Encarta Reference Suite 2000. These versions include more versatile search options and (in some cases) more reference information. Go to Microsoft's Encarta Web site (www.microsoft.com/encarta/) to learn more about these other versions of the program.

When Encarta launches, it displays the Encarta Home screen, shown in Figure 13.1. From this screen you can:

Enter a query here.

Figure 13.1

Encarta's home page—you can find virtually anything from here!

Limit your search to specific types of entries.

Select a specific article from the Pinpointer list.

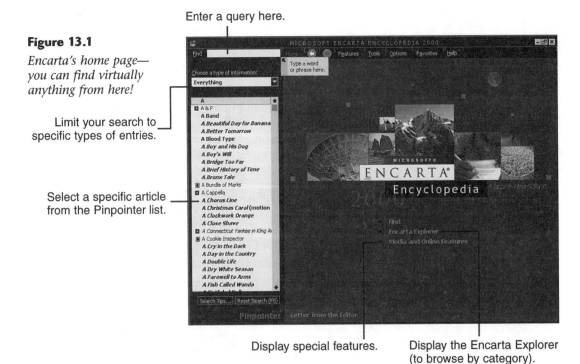

Display special features.

Display the Encarta Explorer (to browse by category).

➤ Use the Find box to search for specific information

➤ Choose from a master list of articles (called the *Pinpointer*)

➤ Use the Encarta Explorer to browse by category of interest

➤ View a list of articles incorporating media and special features

To navigate within Encarta, you use the buttons on the Encarta toolbar, located at the top of the screen. This toolbar is similar to Internet Explorer's toolbar, with navigation buttons to take you back and forward through individual pages. You can also use the pull-down menus to access specific features and tools—and return to Encarta Home at any time by clicking the Home button.

Encarta includes traditional text-based articles, as well as animations, sounds, images, videos, maps, and what Encarta calls *InterActivities*, which are hands-on interactive activities. Some Encarta entries are linked to the Encarta Web site, so you can go online to get additional or updated information. All in all, using Encarta is a rich and rewarding experience—and a fun way to find all sorts of information!

Background Work

Soup Up Your Computer

Some of the multimedia features of Encarta 2000 will only work on computers with audio and video playback functionality. If you're having trouble viewing some of the enhanced articles, you may need to enhance your computer!

Finding What You Want

It's easy to find specific Encarta articles. In fact, you have several different tools available to help you search for specific information.

Choose from the List

All Encarta entries are listed in the Pinpointer, located on the left side of the Encarta Home screen. If you have the patience to scroll through the entire list (ordered alphabetically), you can simply click a title to view the entry.

You can narrow down the entries that Pinpointer displays by making a selection from the Choose a Type of Information list. By default, this list displays everything included with Encarta; you can choose to display only animations, articles, charts and tables, and other types of items.

Limit Your Search

You can use the Choose This Type of Information list to limit your searches to a specific type of Encarta entry.

Use the Find Command

If you don't know what specific article you're looking for (and you probably won't), you can use the Find command to search for all articles that include the word(s) you enter. To use the Find command, simply type a word or phrase into the Find box, and then press Enter.

Encarta now displays the articles that match your query in the Pinpointer list. Click any entry to display it full-screen.

Explore by Category

If you're like me, you will like the serendipity that sometimes results from browsing through a large collection of articles. For browsing purposes, Encarta 2000 offers the Encarta Explorer, which lets you select a category of interest, and then browse through all entries in that category.

To use the Encarta Explorer, click the Encarta Explorer link on the Encarta Home screen. This displays the Explore screen (see Figure 13.2), where you can click one of the following categories:

Figure 13.2

Explore by category with the Encarta Explorer.

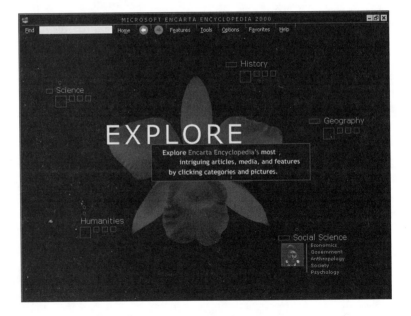

➤ Science
➤ History
➤ Geography
➤ Humanities
➤ Social Science

When you click on one of these major categories, you see a list of subcategories within the category. For example, if you click on Social Science, you see the Economics, Government, Anthropology, Society, and Psychology categories. Click on one of these categories, and you see a list of further subcategories. Click again, and you see even more subcategories. Click enough times and you'll end up at a specific article!

Go Right to the Special Stuff

Encarta 2000 includes a number of special features, all of which are accessible when you click the Media and Online Features link on the Encarta Home screen. These features include:

➤ **Yearbook.** Takes you online to view new and updated Encarta articles.
➤ **Web Links.** Presents a list of interesting and informative links to sites on the Internet.
➤ **World Maps.** Displays a variety of detailed, interactive maps.
➤ **Interactivities.** A series of hands-on interactive activities.
➤ **Mindmaze.** A fun and educational game.

Click on any link to go directly to the contents of the selected feature/section.

Working with Articles

Encarta's articles run the gamut from short text-based entries to long, multi-part dissertations complete with pictures, audio, and video clips.

Navigating Longer Articles

When you encounter a longer article (like the one shown in Figure 13.3), you see a *contents page*. The contents page will often include an outline of the article contents, as well as lists of related articles, multimedia exhibits, relevant Web links and searches, and further reading.

Related articles   Multimedia exhibits

Figure 13.3

Use the Contents page to jump to any point within the article—or to related articles or Web sites.

Outline

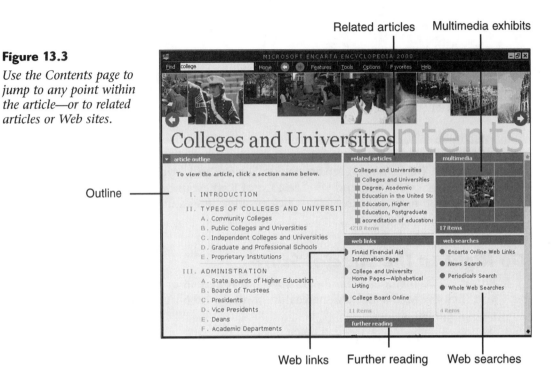

Web links   Further reading   Web searches

To read the article, click on a section of the outline; you'll go directly to that section within the article (like the one in Figure 13.4). After you're in the article, you can scroll through the text using the standard scrollbars, or jump from section to section with the large up and down arrows in the top-right corner. You can redisplay the outline by pulling down the Article Outline list at the top-left corner of the article—and then jump directly to another section in the outline.

Storing Your Favorites

If you find an article you want to keep handy for future reference, you can add it to Encarta's Favorites list. Just pull down the Favorites menu and select Add to Favorites; when the Add to Favorites dialog box appears, select the folder where you want to store the Favorite, and then click OK.

You can jump to any Favorite article at any time by pulling down the Favorites menu. All your Favorites will be listed; click on the article you want, and Encarta takes you there immediately!

Redisplay the outline.   Jump to next section.

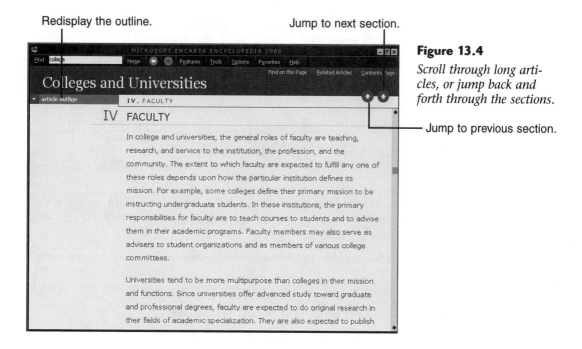

Figure 13.4

Scroll through long articles, or jump back and forth through the sections.

———— Jump to previous section.

Printing Articles

If you'd like to print out a copy of any article, pull down the Options menu and select Print. When the Print dialog box appears, check the Whole Article Text option, and then click Print.

If you only want to print part of an article, use your mouse to select the text you want to print, and then pull down the Options menu and select Print. This time when the Print dialog box appears, check the Selected Text option, and then click Print. Encarta will now print only that part of the article you selected.

Copying Article Text

If you want to use the text of an Encarta article in another document, you can copy the text and then paste it in the other document. Here's how it works:

1. Use your mouse to select the text you want to copy.
2. Pull down the Options menu and select Copy.
3. When the Copy dialog box appears, check the Selected Text option to copy the text you selected, or check the Whole Article Text to copy the text of the entire article.
4. Click Copy to copy the selected text to the Windows Clipboard.
5. Go to your other document (a Word document, for example) and position the insertion point where you want to paste the text.
6. Within that application, pull down the Edit menu and select Paste.

Remember—although you *can* copy Encarta articles, you shouldn't paste text from an Encarta article into a school report and claim it as an original work!

Background Work

It's Copyrighted!

When you copy text or images from an Encarta article, a brief copyright notice is automatically pasted along with the text or image, either under the item, at the bottom of the page, or as a footnote.

The Least You Need to Know

➤ Search for Encarta articles using the Find command.

➤ Browse through categories of interest with the Encarta Explorer.

➤ Print or copy articles using commands found on the Tools menu.

Chapter 14

Send and Receive Email with Outlook Express

In This Chapter

➤ Learn how to use Outlook Express to read and reply to email messages

➤ Discover how to create new email messages—complete with attachments

➤ Find out how to read and post articles in Usenet newsgroups

Outlook Express is the email program included with Works Suite 2000. It's a very versatile email program—so versatile, in fact, that it also handles Usenet newsgroup postings!

Launching and Connecting

You launch Outlook Express from the Works Task Launcher by selecting the Programs tab, selecting Outlook Express from the Programs list, and then clicking Start Outlook Express. You can also launch Outlook Express directly from the Windows Start button or the Windows Quick Launch toolbar.

When Outlook Express launches, it connects automatically to your Internet service provider and checks your ISP for any waiting email. If you have any messages waiting, they're downloaded to Outlook Express' Inbox, and you're notified onscreen of the new messages waiting.

Hook Up Before You Email

Before you can use Outlook Express, you have to have an account with an Internet service provider, and have your PC configured for that account. For more information on connecting to the Internet, see Chapter 2, "Make the Internet Work for You: An Online Primer."

Finding Your Way Around the Outlook Express Workspace

The Outlook Express workspace is divided into three parts (see Figure 14.1):

➤ **Folders list.** This list is where you access the Inbox, Outbox, Usenet news server, and any folders you create to store old messages.

➤ **Message pane.** The top half of the workspace lists all the messages stored in the selected folder (including the Inbox folder).

➤ **Preview pane.** This pane displays the contents of the selected message.

Figure 14.1

Learn the parts of the Outlook Express workspace.

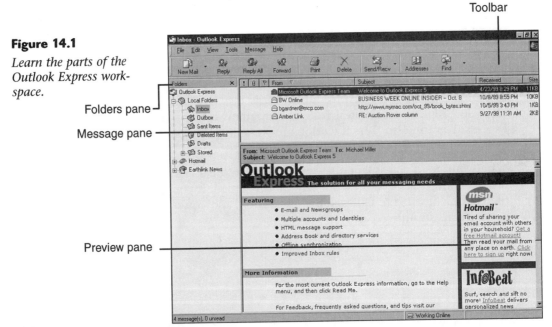

You operate Outlook Express by using the program's toolbar and pull-down menus—and by navigating directly to specific folders in the Folders list.

Managing Mail Messages

Outlook Express makes it easy to read, reply to, and compose new email messages. Each task is as easy as typing a letter and pressing a few buttons!

Reading New Messages

If you've received new email messages, they will be stored in Outlook Express' Inbox. To read a new message, follow these steps:

1. Click the Inbox icon in the Folders list. All waiting messages will now appear in the Message pane.
2. Click the header of the message you want to read; the contents of the selected message appear in the Preview pane.
3. To display the message in a separate window, double-click the message in the Message pane.

View an Attachment

Some email messages have additional files—such as Word documents or graphics files—"attached" to the mail message. To open an attached file, click the paper-clip icon in the Preview pane header and select the file you want to open; to save an attached file to your hard disk, click the paperclip icon and select Save As.

Replying to a Message

Replying to an email message is as easy as clicking a button. Just follow these steps:

1. In the Message pane, click the message header to which you want to reply.
2. Click the Reply button on the toolbar. (Alternatively, you can click the Reply to All button to reply to all recipients of the message, not just the message sender—or you can click on the Forward button to send the message to a completely different recipient.)

3. A Re window appears. The original message sender is now listed in the To box, with the original message's subject referenced in the Subject box. The original message is "quoted" in the text area of the window, with > preceding the original text.

4. Type your reply in the text area above the quoted text.

5. Click the Send button to send this reply to your Outbox.

6. To send the message from your Outbox over the Internet to your recipient's inbox, click the Send/Recv button.

Creating a New Email Message

Creating a new message is like replying to a message, except you have to enter a bit more information. Follow these steps:

1. Click the New Mail button on the Outlook Express toolbar.

2. When the New Message window appears, enter the email address of the recipient(s) in the To field and the address of anyone you want to receive a carbon copy into the Cc box, as shown in Figure 14.2. Separate multiple addresses with a semicolon (;) but no spaces, like this:
   mmiller@molehillgroup.com;gjetson@sprockets.com.

Figure 14.2

Creating a new email message; enter the recipient's address in the To field, the topic of the message in the Subject field, and the text of the message in the big text area.

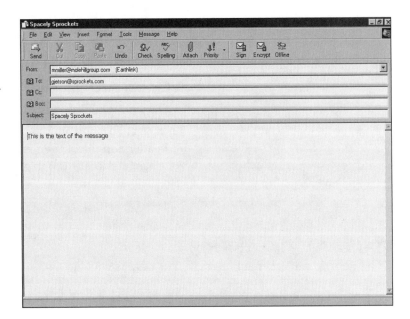

204

3. You can also select names from your Address Book by clicking the To button. When the Select Recipients dialog box appears, select the name(s) of whomever you want to send the message to and click the To button. (You can also select names for carbon copies and blind carbon copies by clicking the Cc and Bcc buttons.) Click OK when done.

4. Enter the subject of the message in the Subject field.

5. Move your cursor to the main message area and type your message.

6. You can choose to send your message in either plain text or HTML format. If you choose to send it in HTML format, you can use the formatting buttons on the toolbar to add boldface, italic, underlined, or aligned text. To select HTML formatting, pull down the Format menu and select Rich Text (HTML); to send without HTML formatting, select Plain Text.

Not Everyone Can Read HTML Email

HTML text formatting in email messages works only when your recipient is using Outlook Express, Microsoft Exchange mail, Netscape Messenger, Eudora Pro, or another HTML-enabled email program. If your recipient is using a nonHTML email program (such as older versions of Lotus cc:Mail, or American Online's email service), all text formatting will be lost.

7. If you're sending the message in HTML format, you can add background colors and graphics. If you simply want to use a background color, pull down the Format menu, select Background, Color, and then pick a color from the color list. If you want to use a background picture, pull down the Format menu and select Background, Picture. When the Background Picture dialog box appears, enter the name of the graphics file you want to use, and then click OK.

8. When your message is complete, send it to the Outbox by clicking the Send button.

9. To send the message from your Outbox over the Internet to your recipient's inbox, click the Send/Recv button.

Tag-Along Files

If you want to send a file to someone over the Internet, the easiest way to do so is to attach that file to an email message. After you've created a new message, click the Attachment button on the toolbar. When the Insert Attachment dialog box appears, locate the file you want to send and click Attach. The attached file now appears as an icon in a new pane under the main text pane of your message, and will be sent along with your normal message when you click the Send button.

Use Usenet with Outlook Express

In addition to being an email program, Outlook Express also functions as a newsreader for Usenet newsgroups. A newsgroup is an electronic gathering place for people with similar interests. Within a newsgroup users post messages (called *articles*) about a variety of topics; other users read these articles and, when so disposed, respond. The result is a kind of on-going, freeform discussion, in which dozens—or hundreds—of users may participate.

Selecting and Subscribing

With Outlook Express you can choose from over 25,000 newsgroups to monitor. You can simply go to selected newsgroups, or you can "subscribe" to selected newsgroups. When you subscribe to a newsgroup, there is no formal registration process; this simply means you've added this newsgroup to a list of your favorites that you can access without searching all 25,000 groups.

Follow these steps to find a specific newsgroup:

1. From within Outlook Express, click the icon in the Folder List for your particular news server. (If you already have the newsreader section of Outlook Express open, just click the Newsgroups button on the toolbar.)

2. If you are not currently subscribed to any newsgroups, you'll be prompted to view a list of all newsgroups. Click Yes and proceed to step 4.

3. If you have already subscribed to one or more newsgroups, you'll now see a list of your subscribed newsgroups. Double-click on a newsgroup to view its contents, or click the Newsgroups button on the toolbar to view a list of all available newsgroups.

4. When the Newsgroups dialog box appears (see Figure 14.3), click the All tab (at the bottom of the dialog box) and select a newsgroup from the main list. You can scroll through the list or search for a specific group by entering key words in the Display Newsgroups Which Contain box.

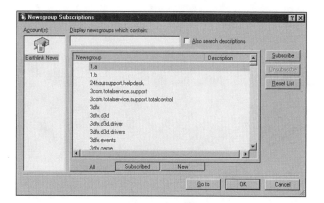

Figure 14.3

Search through more than 25,000 different news-groups for the topic you're interested in.

5. If you want to add this newsgroup to your subscribed list, click the Subscribe button (or double-click the newsgroup item).

6. To choose a newsgroup from your subscribed list, click the Subscribed tab and select the newsgroup you want to read.

7. To go directly to the selected newsgroup, click the Go To button; all the articles from that group appear in the Message pane.

8. Click on a message header to read the contents of the message in the Preview pane.

After you've entered a newsgroup, you can then view articles, respond to articles, and create and post your own articles.

Viewing and Saving Attached Files

Many newsgroups (especially those in the alt.binaries hierarchy) exist to distribute files—generally graphics or sound files. Outlook Express lets you view these graphics files right in the preview pane; you can also save attached files to your hard disk.

To view a graphics attachment, click the article header that includes the attachment. The graphic should automatically display in the preview pane, as shown in Figure 14.4.

Look Out for Dirty Pictures!

Many of the alt.binaries newsgroups contain adult images—particularly those in the alt.binaries.pictures. erotica hierarchy. You should moni-tor your children to make sure they don't access these groups by mis-take—or on purpose!

Figure 14.4

If a newsgroup article includes a picture, it's automatically displayed in the preview pane.

To save an attachment to your hard disk, click the article header that includes the attachment. Pull down the File menu and select Save Attachments, and then select the file you want to save. When the Save Attachment As dialog box appears, select a location for the file and click Save.

Writing and Posting

You can also use Outlook Express to write new newsgroup articles—which you can then *post* to one or more newsgroups. Just follow these steps:

1. From within Outlook Express, click the icon in the Folder List for your particular news server.

2. Click the Newsgroups button and enter the newsgroup to which you wish to post.

3. Click the New Post button. When the New Message window appears, the selected newsgroup is displayed in the Newsgroups field.

4. To post to other newsgroups, click the icon in the newsgroups field. When the Pick Newsgroups dialog box appears, select one or more newsgroups from the list, click the Add button, and then click OK. (To display all newsgroups, uncheck the Show Only Subscribed Newsgroups option.)

5. Enter a subject in the Subject field, and then type the text of your article in the main window.

6. Click the Send button to post this article to the selected newsgroup(s).

Learn a Little Newsgroup Netiquette

Usenet newsgroup users have a strict code of ethics that you don't want to violate. If you are unfamiliar with newsgroups, you may want to just read for a while before you start posting your own messages. When you do decide to participate, remember that advertising can be done only in the context of the topic (if in doubt, don't do it), typing in UPPERCASE is frowned upon, and you shouldn't "spam" multiple newsgroups with identical messages. If you engage in any of these behaviors, you run the risk of being *flamed* by irate users sending you gobs and gobs of hate mail.

The Least You Need to Know

➤ Go to the Outlook Express Inbox to find your newest messages.

➤ Select a message in the Message pane to view its contents in the Preview pane.

➤ Click the New Mail button to create new email messages.

➤ Use Outlook Express to access tens of thousands of Usenet newsgroups.

Chapter 15

Surf the Web with Internet Explorer

In This Chapter

➤ Learn how to use Internet Explorer to go directly to your favorite Web sites

➤ Find out how to manage and use the Favorites and History lists

➤ Discover how to perform more effective Web searches

The World Wide Web is the "cool" part of the Internet. Web pages are colorful and include graphics, sound, and even moving video images. In addition, Web pages are connected via *hyperlinks*; clicking a hyperlink automatically connects you to another linked Web page. There are millions of pages on the Web, covering hundreds of thousands of topics.

You view Web pages with a software program called a *Web browser*. Microsoft's Web browser—included with Works Suite 2000—is called *Internet Explorer*.

Too Many Explorers

Don't confuse *Internet* Explorer, the Web browser, with *Windows* Explorer, the file management utility.

Diving into the Web with Internet Explorer

There's no time to lose—fire up your Internet connection, load up Internet Explorer, and let's go surfing!

Get Connected Before You Surf

Before you can use Internet Explorer to surf the Web, you have to have an account with an Internet service provider, and have your PC configured for that account. For more information on connecting to the Internet, see Chapter 2, "Make the Internet Work for You: An Online Primer."

Getting Loaded

You start Internet Explorer from the Works Task Launcher by selecting the Programs tab, selecting Internet Explorer from the Programs list, and then clicking Start Internet Explorer. In most installations, you can also start Internet Explorer from the Windows Start menu, from the Internet Explorer icon on your desktop, and from the Internet Explorer icon on the Windows Quick Launch toolbar.

Start with a Site

If you select MSN from the Task Launcher Programs tab you see what looks like a list of Works-related tasks. In reality, everything listed here is a Web site—and they're all part of the Microsoft Network (MSN) of sites. When you click one of these MSN tasks, you launch Internet Explorer and jump directly to the MSN Web site related to the chosen task.

Understanding the Internet Explorer Workspace

Internet Explorer functions pretty much like Word or Works Spreadsheet or most other Works Suite 2000 programs, using a series of pull-down menus and toolbar buttons. Because a browser is a bit different from a word processor, however, use Figure 15.1 as a guide to the unique parts of the Internet Explorer interface.

Address Box—enter
Web addresses here.

Links bar

Toolbar

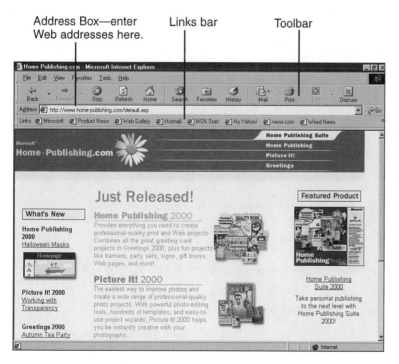

Figure 15.1

Use Internet Explorer to surf the Internet.

Table 15.1 details the buttons on the Internet Explorer toolbar.

Table 15.1   Internet Explorer Toolbar Buttons

Button	Operation
Back	Returns to the previously viewed page
Forward	Views the next page
Stop	Stops loading of current page
Refresh	Reloads the current page
Home	Returns to your designated start page
Search	Displays the Search pane so you can initiate a Web search
Favorites	Displays the Favorites pane so you can jump directly to a Favorite site
History	Displays the History pane so you can see a list of recently viewed pages
Mail	Launches Outlook Express to read email and newsgroup articles
Print	Prints the current Web page
Edit	Displays the HTML code for the current page

Background Work

Learn the Web, by the Book

To learn more about how the World Wide Web works—and how to get connected to the Internet—see Chapter 2, "Make the Internet Work for You: An Online Primer."

Going Surfing

With Internet Explorer, you can quickly and easily browse the World Wide Web—just by clicking your mouse.

Here's what a typical Web session looks like:

1. When you first launch Internet Explorer, it loads your predefined home page.

2. Enter a new Web address in the Address box and press Enter. Internet Explorer will load the new page.

3. Click any link on the current Web page. Internet Explorer will load the new page.

4. To return to the previous page, click the Back button. If you've backed up several pages and want to return to the page you were at last, click the Forward button.

5. To return to your start page, click the Home button.

Get a New Home

To change Internet Explorer's home page, go to the page you want to use as your new home, and then drag the page's icon from Internet Explorer's Address box onto the Home button on the toolbar.

Loading Zone

Sometimes Web pages will take a long time to load—if they contain a lot of graphics, for example. If you get tired of waiting for a Web page to load, you can click the Stop button to stop the process. If you want to reload a partially loaded page, click the Refresh button.

Organizing Your Surfing

After you find a Web site you like, you don't want to type in that confusing URL address every time you want to return to the site. Internet Explorer offers a number of ways to easily revisit the best of the Web.

Saving Your Favorite Sites

When you find a Web page you like, you can add it to a list of Favorites within Internet Explorer. After a site is stored as a Favorite, you can access it (and any other Favorites) just by choosing it from the list (see Figure 15.2).

Figure 15.2

Use the Favorites list to store your favorite Web pages.

Putting Your Favorites in Order

If you add a lot of pages to your Favorites list, it can become over-sized and unwieldy. You can organize the sites in your Favorites list by pulling down the Favorites menu and selecting Organize Favorites. When the Organize Favorites dialog box appears, drag and drop sites from folder to folder to your heart's content. You can also rename links, delete links, and create new Favorites folders.

To store a site in your Favorites list, follow these steps:

1. Go to the page you would like to add to your Favorites list.

2. Click the Favorites button.

3. When the Favorites pane appears, open the folder where you want to save this page.

4. Using your mouse, drag the page's URL icon from the Address box into the open folder in the Favorites pane.

To go to a site in your Favorites list, click the Favorites button to display the Favorites pane, navigate to the folder that contains the Favorite link, and then click the link.

Adding Sites to the Links Bar

Internet Explorer includes a Links bar that can be displayed at the top of Internet Explorer. (To display the Links bar, pull down the View menu, select Toolbars, and then check the Links option.) By default, the Links bar provides one-click access to a variety of Microsoft-related sites. However, you can add any Web site you want to the Links bar—thus adding push-button access to any site you choose.

216

All you have to do is navigate to the page you want to add to the Links bar, and then drag the page's URL icon from the Address box onto the Links bar, in the position you desire. The selected Web page is now displayed on the Links bar. Click the page's button to go directly to that page.

Revisiting Web Pages with the History List

Internet Explorer keeps track of all the Web pages you've visited in the past 20 days; returning to a previously viewed page is as easy as accessing the History list.

To display Internet Explorer's History list, click the History button. The browser window is automatically split into two panes; a list of previously visited sites, organized by day, is displayed in the left pane. Click the folder for the day you want to revisit, and then click the link for any site.

Searching the Web

With millions of pages on the Web, how do you find any single page? You find things on the Web by using *search engines and directories*, special sites designed to catalog and organize pages by topic. Internet Explorer includes a built-in function that lets you access a variety of popular search sites (such as Yahoo!, Excite, Lycos, and AltaVista) with the click of a button—and display the results right in your browser window.

Online Search Secrets Revealed!

If you want to know the real secrets of successful searchers, pick up a copy of my recent book, *The Complete Idiot's Guide to Online Search Secrets*, available wherever computer books are sold.

Searching from the Search Pane

When you click the Search button on the Internet Explorer toolbar, the browser window is automatically split into two panes. From the Search pane, choose a type of search, enter your query in the search box, and then click Search (see Figure 15.3). Your query is sent to the first of several search sites, and the results displayed in the Search pane. To continue your search on the next search site, click the Next button at the top of the search pane.

Figure 15.3

Search faster from Internet Explorer's Search pane.

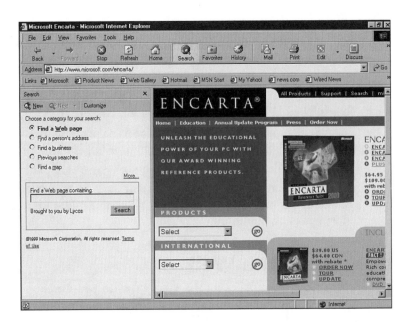

Configure the Search Pane

To choose which search engines are accessed (and in what order) from the Search pane, click the Customize button at the top of the Search pane. This displays the Customize Search Settings dialog box; make your choices here, then click OK.

Searching from the Address Box

Internet Explorer lets you search directly from the Address Box using a technology called *Autosearch*. If you enter one or more words into the Address box (without a www. at the beginning or a .com at the end), Autosearch assumes you're entering a query, and it opens the Search pane and displays a page of results (from the MSN Search service) that matches your query.

If your query actually matches a Web page—if you enter sony, for example—Internet Explorer automatically adds the www. and the .com and jumps to that page.

Searching from a Search Site

The best way to search, however, is to go directly to one of the many search sites on the Internet. Table 15.2 lists what I like to call the Big Six search sites, and the main features of each. Figures 15.4 and 15.5 show two search sites.

Table 15.2 Comparison of the Big Six Search Sites

Site	URL	Pros	Cons	Size
AltaVista	www.altavista.com	Big and fast; powerful search options	Number of matches can be overwhelming; can be difficult to narrow searches	150 million
Excite	www.excite.com	Intelligent Concept Extraction finds related ideas in addition to keywords; very fresh content; good summaries	Limited selection of search commands; can be difficult to narrow searches	125 million
HotBot	www.hotbot.com	Big and fast; wide variety of powerful and easy-to-use search options; includes the user-edited Open Directory	Search options might overwhelm inexperienced searchers	110 million
Lycos	www.lycos.com	MP3 Search for music files; FTP Search for software downloads; includes the user-edited Open Directory	Very limited search commands in basic search; relatively small size	75 million

continues

219

Table 15.2 Continued

Site	URL	Pros	Cons	Size
Northern Light	www. Northernlight. com	Big and fast; on-the-fly organization into Custom Search Folders; proprietary Special Collection provides results when other search engines don't	Searching Special Collection costs $1-$4 per article and requires registration	170 million Web pages plus 4 million full-text articles in the Special Collection
Yahoo!	www.yahoo.com	Very easy to use; well-organized; can either browse categories or search the directory	Very small size; doesn't use Boolean operators	1+ million

Figure 15.4

Yahoo!, the easiest-to-use search site...

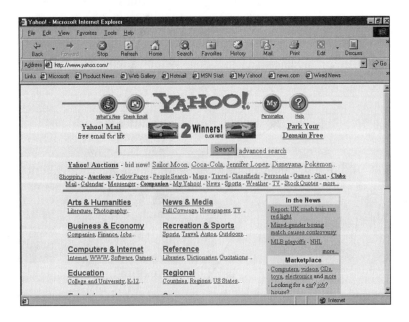

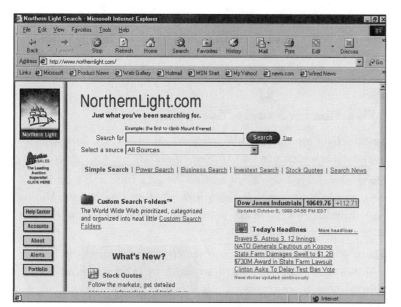

Figure 15.5

...and Northern Light, the biggest search site.

Which search site should you use? Yahoo! is the easiest to use and the best organized, yet has the fewest number of entries. Northern Light and AltaVista have the most sites indexed—and include some powerful search features—but can be intimidating to a beginner. The bottom line: Try a few sites yourself, and see which one fits your personal searching style!

Five Tips for Smarter Searching

To maximize both the effectiveness and the efficiency of your searches, here are five tips you can use no matter which site you choose to search.

1. Start by thinking about what you want to find. What words best describe the information or concept you're looking for? What alternative words might some use instead? Are there any words you can *exclude* from your search to better define your query?

2. Determine *where* you should perform your search. Do you need the power of an AltaVista, HotBot, or Northern Light, or the better-qualified results of a Yahoo!? Are there topic-specific sites you should use instead of these general sites?

3. Construct your query. If at all possible, try to use Boolean expressions (AND, OR, NOT). Use as many keywords as you need—the more the better. If appropriate (and available), use the site's advanced search page or mode.

4. Evaluate the matches on the search results page. If the initial results are not to your liking, refine your query and search again—or switch to a more appropriate search site.

5. Select the matching pages that you want to view, and begin clicking through to those pages. Save the information that best meets your needs.

Just remember to think more *before* you search, and spend more time learning from your results afterwards.

The Least You Need to Know

➤ Internet Explorer is a Web browser; you use it to visit and view sites and pages on the World Wide Web.

➤ You enter the Web site's address (URL) in Internet Explorer's Address box.

➤ Use the Favorites pane to save your favorite sites—and jump back to them with a click of your mouse.

➤ When you click Internet Explorer's Search button, you open the Search pane for fast Internet searches.

Part 3
Get Productive

Now that you know how Works works—and how to work the individual Works programs—you can actually get down to using Works for some actual work! The chapters in this section show you how to create specific types of projects, using the programs included with Works Suite 2000. You'll learn—step-by-step—how to create envelopes and labels, large mailings, newsletters, school reports, home inventories, home budgets, party invitations and favors, personal holiday cards, and sports schedules and stats. So loosen up your typing fingers, make sure your mouse is ready to roll, and fire up your monitor—it's time to get creative!

Chapter 16

Create Envelopes and Labels

In This Chapter

➤ Learn how to address and print envelopes and mailing labels from within Microsoft Word

➤ Find out how to configure Microsoft Word for the specific type of envelope or label you're using

➤ Discover how to attach an automatically addressed envelope to a Word letter for later printing

---

I find it interesting that many computer users aren't aware of all the useful things they can do with their software programs. For example, most of my friends use Microsoft Word to compose all their letters and correspondence, but then *hand address* the envelopes for their letters. Don't they know that Word lets you address envelopes—and mailing labels—for all your letters, with just a few clicks of the mouse?

Well, after you read this chapter, you're going to be smarter than my friends—and you'll be using Word to create envelopes and labels for all your mailing needs!

Single Labels Here, Mass Mailings Next

This chapter covers the printing of *single* envelopes and labels. If you want to create a larger mailing using multiple recipients, turn to Chapter 17, "Create a Large Mailing."

Open Word's Envelopes and Labels Tool

Word includes a handy little tool, found in the Envelopes and Labels dialog box, which performs all your envelope- and label-related operations. You can access this tool in one of two ways.

Starting the Task from Works

You can go directly to the Envelopes and Labels dialog box from the Works Task Launcher. Follow these steps:

1. From the Works Task Launcher, select the Tasks tab.
2. Select Letters & Labels from the Tasks list.
3. If you want to create an envelope, select Envelopes; if you want to create a label, select Mailing Labels.

Don't Choose Decorative

You want to select Envelopes or Mailing Labels, *not* Envelopes, Decorative, or Labels and Stickers, Decorative. The "decorative" tasks launch Home Publisher to create fancy envelope and label *designs*—they're not for addressing envelopes and labels from Word!

4. Click Start.

This launches Microsoft Word with a blank document loaded, and displays the Envelopes and Labels dialog box with either the Envelopes or Labels tab selected.

Starting the Task from Word

If you already have Microsoft Word running, you open the Envelopes and Labels dialog box by pulling down the Tools menu and selecting Envelopes and Labels.

Address an Envelope

After the Envelopes and Labels dialog box is open, follow these steps to choose an envelope size and address the envelope:

1. From the Envelopes and Labels dialog box (see Figure 16.1), select the Envelopes tab.

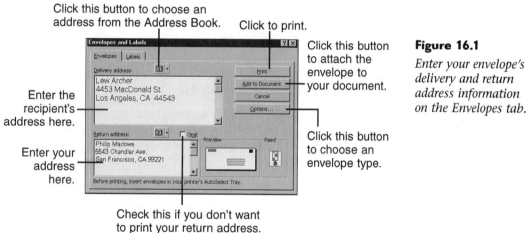

Click this button to choose an
address from the Address Book.

Click to print.

Enter the
recipient's
address here.

Enter your
address
here.

Click this button
to attach the
envelope to
your document.

Click this button
to choose an
envelope type.

Check this if you don't want
to print your return address.

Figure 16.1

Enter your envelope's delivery and return address information on the Envelopes tab.

2. Type the recipient's name and address in the Delivery Address box. Alternatively, you can click the Address Book button to display the Select Names dialog box, and then select a name from your Address Book; when you click OK, the name you selected will be inserted into the Delivery Address box.

Configure Before You Pick

The first time you try to access your Address Book from within Word, you'll see the Inbox Setup Wizard. Follow the onscreen instructions to tell Word about your Internet connection and email account, and to choose the correct location for your Address Book.

Pick a Recent Address

If you've previously used the Envelopes and Labels dialog box to create envelopes or labels, you can click the arrow on the Address Book button to choose from a list of recently used addresses. Click an address to insert it into the Delivery Address box.

3. If you want to print your return address on the envelope, type your return address into the Return Address blank. If you *don't* want to print your return address, check the Omit option.

4. If you haven't yet set an envelope type and size, click the Options button.

5. When the Envelope Options dialog box appears (see Figure 16.2), select the Envelope Options tab, and then pull down the Envelope Size list and select the type of envelope you'll be printing.

6. If you want to print a delivery point barcode on your envelope (and you probably do—the post office likes this), check the Delivery Point Barcode option.

7. To select which font is used for the delivery address, go to the Delivery Address section and click the Font button. When the Font dialog box appears, select a font, style, and font size, and then click OK.

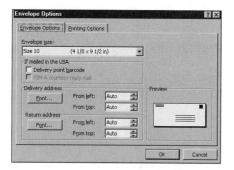

Figure 16.2

Use the Envelope Options dialog box to select an envelope type—and other printing options.

8. To select which font is used for your return address, go to the Return Address section and click the Font button. When the Font dialog box appears, select a font, style, and font size, and then click OK.

9. By default, Word should place your addresses properly on your envelope. If you have trouble with *where* the addresses appear on your envelopes, adjust the From Left and From Top measurements for either the delivery or return addresses.

10. Now you need to determine how your envelopes feed into your printer. You still should be within the Envelopes Option dialog box , so select the Printing Options tab shown in Figure 16.3.

11. Select the Feed Method that best represents how envelopes feed into your printer. Also select whether your envelopes feed in face up or face down, and what tray you're feeding from. (AutoSelect Tray generally works.)

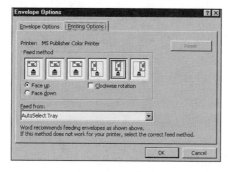

Figure 16.3

Configure how your envelopes feed into your printer from the Printing Options tab.

12. Click OK to close the Envelope Options dialog box and return to the Envelopes and Labels dialog box.

13. Confirm that everything is configured properly, insert a blank envelope into your printer's feed tray, and then click Print to print the envelope.

Your printer should now print a perfectly labeled envelope, ready for mailing. (After you attach a stamp, of course!)

Create a Mailing Label

Creating a mailing label is similar to addressing an envelope—with some different options for label configuration. You can use just about any type of blank labels available in most office supply stores; you can find labels in all different sizes, typically with several labels per sheet.

1. From the Envelopes and Labels dialog box, select the Labels tab (see Figure 16.4).

Check if you want to print a return address instead of a delivery address.

Figure 16.4

Enter your label's delivery information on the Labels tab.

Enter the recipient's address here.

Check to add a delivery point barcode.

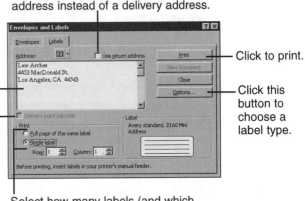

Click to print.

Click this button to choose a label type.

Select how many labels (and which label on a sheet) to print.

Pick a Recent Address

If you've previously used the Envelopes and Labels dialog box to create envelopes or labels, you can click the arrow on the Address Book button to choose from a list of recently used addresses. Click an address to insert it into the Delivery Address box.

2. If you're printing a return address label (or a sheet of return address labels), check the Use Return Address option. If this is a regular delivery label, leave this option unchecked.

3. Type the recipient's name and address in the Address box. Alternatively, you can click the Address Book button to display the Select Names dialog box, and then select a name from your Address Book; when you click OK, the name you selected will be inserted into the Delivery Address box.

4. If you want to print a delivery point barcode on your label, check the Delivery Point Barcode option.

5. If you haven't yet set a label type, click the Options button.

6. When the Label Options dialog box appears, select whether you're using a dot matrix or laser/inkjet printer (see Figure 16.5).

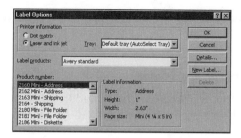

Figure 16.5

Use the Label Options dialog box to select a label type—and other printing options.

7. Select which tray of your printer you'll be using to print your labels.

8. Pull down the Label Products list and select the brand of label you're using.

9. Select the specific label type from the Product Number list.

10. If you want to confirm the information about the label you selected, click the Details button to display the Information dialog box. Change any measurements, if necessary, and then click OK to return to the Label Options dialog box.

Make Your Own!

If the label you're using isn't listed in the Label Options dialog box, you can create a new label template for your label. From within the Label Options dialog box, click New Label. When the New Custom dialog box appears, enter the measurements of your label, give it a name, and then click OK.

11. Click OK to close the Label Options dialog box and return to the Envelopes and Labels dialog box.

12. To set the font used on your label, highlight the entire address and then right-click your mouse. When the pop-up menu appears, select Font. When the Font dialog box appears, select a font, style, and font size, and then click OK.

13. If you want to print a full page of this label, check the Full Page of the Same Label Option. If you want to print a single label, check the Single Label option, and then select which row and column on your label sheet you want to print. (This way you can use a single sheet of labels to print multiple labels over time.)

14. Confirm that everything is configured properly, insert the sheet of labels into your printer's feed tray, and then click Print to print the label(s).

Your printer should now print a perfectly aligned label, ready to be applied to the envelope or package of choice.

Attach an Envelope to a Letter

If you've already composed your letter, it's actually *easier* to address your envelope—and then *attach* your envelope to the letter, for future printing. Just follow these steps:

1. From within your letter, select the recipient's name and address.
2. Pull down the Tools menu and select Envelopes and Labels.
3. When the Envelopes and Labels dialog box appears, select the Envelopes tab. The address you selected in your letter should be automatically inserted into the Delivery Address box.
4. Configure the rest of the envelope information as normal.
5. Click the Add to Document button.

This adds your completed envelope to your current Word document, as shown in Figure 16.6. To print the envelope, make sure the insertion point is somewhere in the envelope part of your document, and then pull down the File menu and select Print. You can now print the envelope (and *only* the envelope—you have to print the letter separately) as normal.

Figure 16.6

Attach an envelope to a letter for future printing.

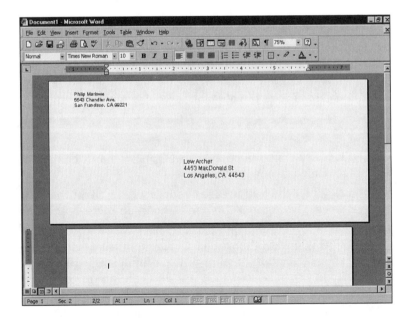

The Least You Need to Know

➤ You configure both envelopes and labels from the Envelopes and Labels dialog box, accessed from Word's Tool menu.

➤ Before you print an envelope or label, you have to configure Word for the specific type of envelope or label you're using.

➤ If you're working on a letter and highlight the recipient's address, you can fill in the envelope address automatically and then attach the envelope to your letter for future printing.

Chapter 17

Create a Large Mailing

In This Chapter

➤ Learn how to use the Works Letter Wizard to create a form letter you can personalize for multiple recipients

➤ Discover how to create personalized envelopes to match your personalized form letters

➤ Find out how to add new merge fields to your merged document

In the last chapter you learned how to use Microsoft Word to create single envelopes and labels. But what if you want to do a larger mailing—say, of a batch of Christmas cards, or of a "personalized" mass-mailing letter?

This chapter shows you how to use various applications with Works Suite 2000 to create and print what Microsoft calls a *mail-merge document.*

Create and Print a Form Letter

With Works Suite 2000 it's easy to create one letter that is then automatically personalized and sent to a large group of people. Just follow these steps:

1. From the Works Task Launcher, select the Tasks tab.
2. Select Letters & Labels from the Tasks list.
3. Select Letters then click Start.
4. When the first screen of the Works Letter Wizard appears, as shown in Figure 17.1, select a style for your letter and click OK.

Figure 17.1

Use the Works Letter Wizard to select a pre-designed letter template and prepare your merged mailing.

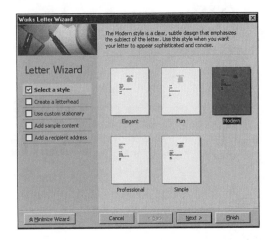

5. When the next screen appears, enter your name and return address information, and then click Next.

6. When the next screen appears, select whether you're using plain paper or custom stationery (and if so, how much margin room you need to leave), and then click Next.

7. When the next screen appears, check the I Want to Write My Own Letter option, and then click Next.

8. When the final screen of the wizard appears, check the Select Entries from the Address Book for a Mail Merge option, and then click the Address Book button.

9. When the Select Names dialog box appears (see Figure 17.2), select the people you want to send this letter to, and then click the Select button to add them to the Merge Recipients list. Click OK when you're done adding recipients.

Figure 17.2

Choose which names you want to merge into your mailing, and then click Select to add them to the Merge Recipients list.

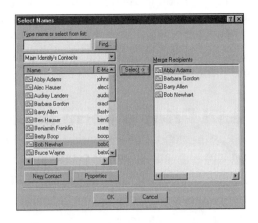

10. When you're returned to the Letter Wizard, click the Finish button.

11. Word now loads a letter template that matches your previous selection; information from the last name in your merge list appears in selected fields. Word also displays a new toolbar—the Mail Merge toolbar, shown in Figure 17.3.

Show the Fields

By default, the *contents* of your document's merge fields are displayed onscreen. If you'd rather see the fields themselves, toggle the View Merged Data button on the Mail Merge toolbar.

Click to view merge fields (and *not* the contents).

Click to display your letter with information from the previous recipient on your list.

Click to display your letter with information from the next recipient on your list.

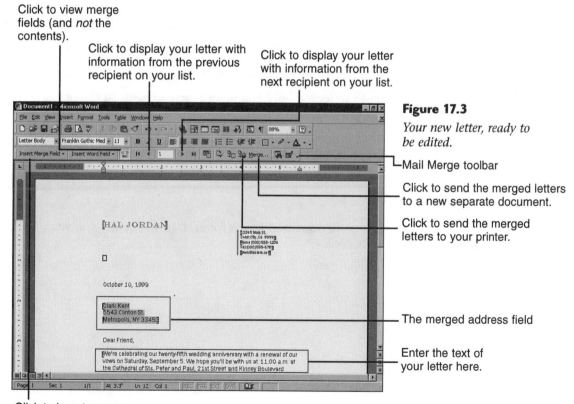

Figure 17.3

Your new letter, ready to be edited.

Mail Merge toolbar

Click to send the merged letters to a new separate document.

Click to send the merged letters to your printer.

The merged address field

Enter the text of your letter here.

Click to insert new merge fields into your letter.

237

12. Let's personalize the greeting line in this letter. Select the word Friend, and then pull down the Insert Merge Field list (on the Mail Merge toolbar) and select First_Name. Now your greeting line should read "Dear Clark" (or Bob or Jane or whatever this recipient's first name is).

13. Move your cursor to the section of the letter labeled "Replace this text with the contents of your letter," delete this text, and enter your own letter text.

14. Move to the bottom of the letter, and replace the word Signature with your name.

15. Review the letter you've just written, check the spelling, and prepare to print. Figure 17.4 shows what your finished document should look like.

16. Click the Merge to Printer button on the Mail Merge toolbar.

17. When the Print dialog box appears, make any necessary adjustments, and then click OK.

Preview Before You Print

A mail merge document can look a little confusing onscreen, with all the merge fields kind of getting in the way. If you want to see what your merged letter looks like with real data (and *without* all the merge fields), click Word's Print Preview button. This view only displays the first letter in your merge list, but it still gives you a good idea how your real printed letter will look.

Word will now print separate personalized letters for each of the names you've selected from your Address Book.

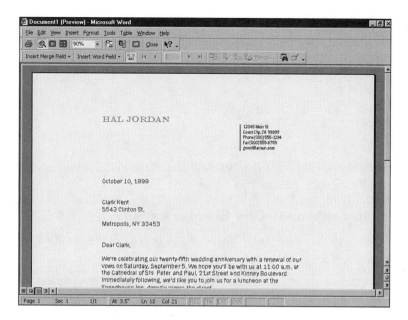

Figure 17.4

Your completed merged letter, ready to print.

Create Merged Envelopes

The easiest way to create envelopes for your form letter is to *attach* the envelopes to your documents—using the merge fields for the recipient's address.

1. From within your merge document, select the recipient's name and delivery address.

2. Pull down the Tools menu and select Envelopes and Labels.

3. When the Envelopes and Labels dialog box appears (see Figure 17.5), select the Envelopes tab; the delivery address for the current recipient should appear in the Delivery Address box.

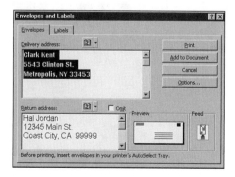

Figure 17.5

Preparing the envelopes for your merged mailing.

4. If it isn't there already, enter your return address in the Return Address box.

5. If you need to select an envelope type, click the Options button and make your selections from the Envelope Options dialog box; click OK to return to the Envelopes and Labels dialog box.

Options Explained—One Chapter Back

To learn more about Word's envelope options—including delivery point barcode—see Chapter 16, "Create Envelopes and Labels."

6. Back in the Envelopes and Labels dialog box, make any necessary configuration changes, and then click the Add to Document button.

Word now attaches an envelope to your document; the delivery address on the envelope is keyed to the merge fields in your form letter (see Figure 17.6). To print your merged envelopes, place your cursor anywhere in the attached envelope, and then click the Merge to Printer button on the Mail Merge toolbar.

Figure 17.6

Your attached envelope—with the current recipient displayed in the merge field.

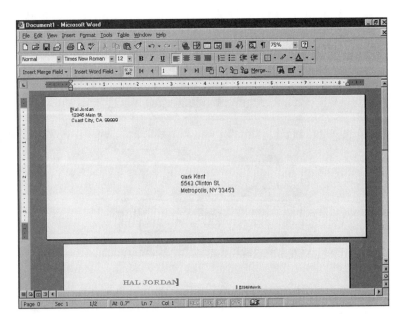

The Least You Need to Know

➤ Use the Works Letter Wizard to create a form letter in Microsoft Word, using merged fields.

➤ Select the recipients of your form letter from your Address Book.

➤ To print personalized envelopes for each intended recipient of your form letter, create an envelope and attach it to your merged document.

➤ Print your personalized letters and envelopes using the Merge to Printer button on the Mail Merge toolbar.

Chapter 18

Create a Newsletter

In This Chapter

➤ Learn how to use Microsoft Word to create professional-looking multiple-column newsletters

➤ Find out how to use Microsoft Home Publishing to create fun and colorful family newsletters

➤ Discover how to modify a newsletter template with your own text and pictures

---

You can use the applications within Works Suite 2000 to create two different types of newsletters. Microsoft Word is great for producing sophisticated, text-heavy newsletters, whereas Microsoft Home Publishing is a better choice if you want a shorter, more graphically appealing newsletter. You can access both these types of newsletters from the Works Task Launcher.

Make a Text-Based Newsletter with Word

Microsoft Word is ideal for making professional-looking newsletters of any length. You can choose from single-column or multiple-column designs, insert graphics and text boxes, and just generally make a very sophisticated newsletter product.

1. From the Works Task Launcher, select the Tasks tab.
2. Select Newsletters from the Tasks list.

3. Select Newsletters (*not* Newsletters, Fancy—that option creates a Home Publishing-based newsletter!), and then click Start.

4. When the Works Newsletters Wizard appears, as shown in Figure 18.1, select a style for your newsletter, and then click Finish.

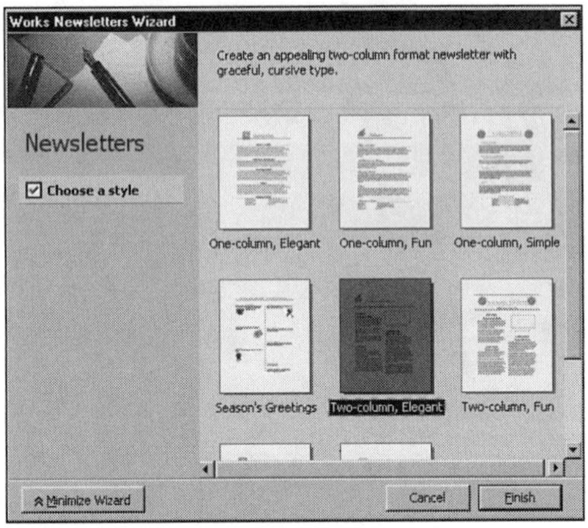

Figure 18.1

Use the Works Newsletters Wizard to select a newsletter style.

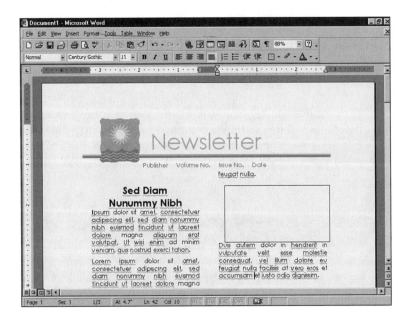

5. Word now launches, with a dummy newsletter in the style you selected pre-loaded (see Figure 18.2).

Figure 18.2

Start with this dummy newsletter—then edit with your own text and pictures.

6. Replace the "dummy" text with your own text.

Make a New Article

To add a heading for a new article, type the heading text and then pull down the *Style* list and apply whichever *Heading* style appeals to you. (This template includes a large variety of different types of headings.)

7. If you want, delete the dummy pictures and replace them with your own pictures or graphics. (To insert a graphic, pull down Word's Insert menu and select Picture; you can then select to insert Word clip art, a picture from a file, or other shapes, drawings, and objects. Make sure you resize any picture you add to fit within the newsletter's column grid—and format the picture's text wrapping so that text flows around the picture.)

8. If you want to change the column layout of your newsletter, pull down the Format menu and select Columns. When the Columns dialog box appears, select a different column layout, and then click OK.

9. Add articles *outside* the standard column layout by drawing a text box across column boundaries and entering text within the text box. If you do this, make sure you double-click the text box to display the Format Text Box dialog box, select the Layout tab, and select the Square wrapping style. If you want your text box to remain in a specified position—that is, to *not* flow with changes in the rest of your document—click the Advanced button on the Layout tab and then *uncheck* the Move with Text option.

When you're done replacing and editing text, remember to save your work, and then pull down the File menu and select Print to send the newsletter to your printer. With a little work on your part, you can turn the default template into something unique—and very professional looking!

Work from a Blank Newsletter

If you prefer to work from a blank newsletter template in Word, skip the Works Newsletter Wizard and go directly to Microsoft Word. With a new blank document in the workspace, insert a text box at the very start of the document (going from margin to margin) to hold your newsletter masthead, and then use the Columns dialog box to change the entire document to either a two- or a three-column design. (The masthead needs to be in a separate box to span multiple columns.) Use the Heading styles for your article heads and subheads, and the Normal style for the newsletter's body text. The articles will automatically flow from one column to another, separated by the article heads. (You should also feel free to tweak the Heading and Normal styles, as appropriate.) It won't be fancy (until you start adding pictures and other elements, that is), but it will be a quick and easy multiple-column newsletter, completely from scratch.

Make a Graphic Newsletter with Home Publishing

Where Microsoft Word is good for longer, text-heavy newsletters, you might prefer to use Home Publishing if you want to make a shorter, more graphically appealing (re: "fun") newsletter.

1. From the Works Task Launcher, select the Tasks tab.
2. Select Newsletters from the Tasks list.
3. Select Newsletters, Fancy (*not* Newsletters—that option creates a Word-based newsletter!), and then click Start.
4. When Home Publishing launches, you're presented with a variety of different newsletter designs, as shown in Figure 18.3. Before you pick a design, select the type of newsletter you want (Family News, Seasonal, Travel/Vacation, and so on) from the Themes list.
5. Click the design you want, and then click OK.
6. Home Publishing now loads a dummy newsletter into the project workspace, as shown in Figure 18.4.

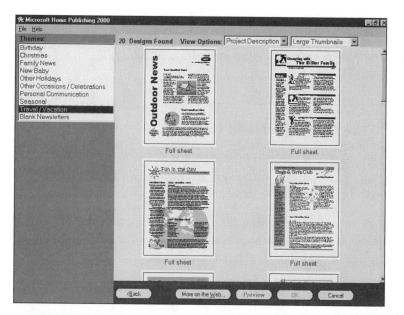

Figure 18.3

Choose a theme, and then select a newsletter design.

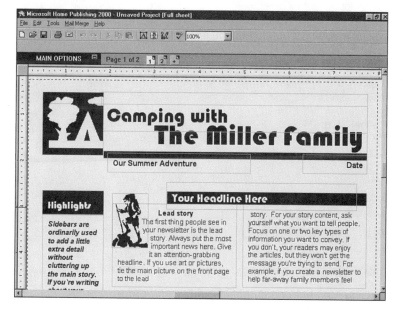

Figure 18.4

Edit this newsletter template to create your own personal newsletter.

7. Replace the dummy text with your own text.

8. If you want, delete the dummy graphics and replace them with different graphics. (To replace a graphic, select the graphic in the newsletter and then click the Replace Picture button in Home Publishing's Picture Options frame; you can then choose from a variety of graphics on the separate art CD.)

When you're done modifying the predesigned newsletter, remember to save your work, and then click the Print button on the Main Options panel to send the newsletter to your printer. As you can see, Home Publishing makes it easy to create a fun and personalized newsletter!

The Least You Need to Know

➤ Use Microsoft Word to create professional-looking text-based newsletters.

➤ Use Microsoft Home Publishing to create more colorful—and more fun!—newsletters.

➤ Whichever program you use, start with a predesigned template and then replace the "dummy" text with your own text.

Chapter 19

Create a School Report

You can use Works Suite 2000 to create just about any type of school report, from start (using the Encarta Encyclopedia for research) to finish (using either Microsoft Word or Microsoft Home Publishing to create the actual report). Read on to learn how to do what you need to do!

Research with Encarta

Just as you and I used to use hardbound encyclopedias for research when we were in school (back in the "old days," before they invented the Internet, videogames, and gasoline-powered automobiles), your children can now use electronic encyclopedias for their primary research. Because you're a proud owner of Works Suite 2000, it's time to rev up the Encarta Encyclopedia!

1. From the Works Task Launcher, select the Tasks tab.
2. From the Tasks list, select Research and Education.
3. Choose Encarta Encyclopedia, Search, and then click Start.

Browse Instead of Search

If you prefer to browse through a category instead of searching for a topic, select Encarta Encyclopedia, Browse to use the Encarta Explorer.

4. When Encarta launches, enter the topic of your report in the Find box and press Enter.

5. When the list of articles appears in the Pinpointer list, click the name of the article you want to read.

6. If you want to copy text from an article, select the text with your mouse, pull down the Options menu, and select Copy. When the Copy dialog box appears, check the Selected Text option, and then click Copy. You can now paste the selected text into your Word or Home Publishing report.

Research on the Internet

If you don't get enough information from Encarta Encyclopedia, you can go online with Internet Explorer to search for more information. There are a number of places to search for information online, including:

➤ **Encarta Online.** When you select Encarta Online, Search from the Research and Education task list, you launch Internet Explorer and jump to the Encarta Online Web site. From here you can search more than 16,000 Web-based articles, as well as link to a large number of related online resources (see Figure 19.1).

➤ **Web links.** On the contents page of most major Encarta articles is a list of Web sites related to the article's topic. Click any of these links to launch Internet Explorer and jump to the related site.

➤ **Web searches.** Also on most article's contents page is a list of Web searches. These are search queries preselected by the Encarta editors to find related information on the Web, using the search engine at the Encarta Web site.

➤ **Web search sites.** You can also use Internet Explorer to go directly to any Web search site, and then enter a query related to the topic of your report. Among the best search sites for homework and school reports are About.com Homework Help (homeworkhelp.about.com), Homework Central (www.homeworkcentral.com), Homework Helper (www.homeworkhelper.com), infoplease Homework Center (kids.infoplease.com/homework/), and StudyWEB (www.studyweb.com). The major search sites—such as Yahoo! (www.yahoo.com) and Northern Light (www.northernlight.com) are also good for finding general information that you can then incorporate into your report.

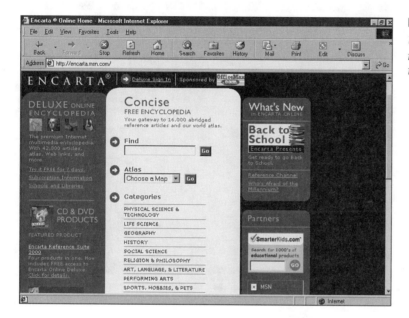

Figure 19.1

Use Encarta Online to research your report on the Internet.

Background Work

Do You Yahoo!?

If you want to learn more about searching the Web with Yahoo!, check out my latest book, *The Complete Idiot's Guide to Yahoo!*, available wherever computer books are sold.

Create Simple Reports with Home Publishing

After you've done your research, it's time to write the report. Perhaps the easiest way to create a great-looking report—especially for younger children—is to use Home Publishing's predesigned report templates.

1. From the Works Task Launcher, select the Tasks tab.
2. From the Tasks list, select Research and Education.
3. Select Reports and Presentations (*not* School Reports—this option creates Word-based reports!), and then click Start.

4. When Home Publishing launches, select Full Page Reports from the Themes list (see Figure 19.2).

Figure 19.2

Create great-looking reports with Home Publishing's predesigned templates.

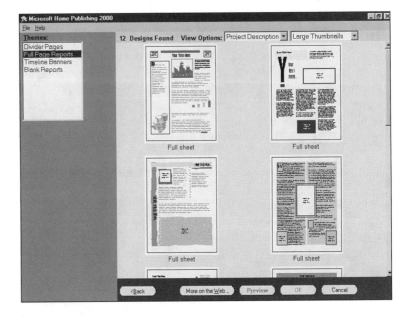

5. Select the report you want, and then click OK.

6. Home Publishing now loads a dummy report, based on the design you selected, into the project workspace (see Figure 19.3).

Figure 19.3

Replace the dummy text with your own writing to create your own personal report.

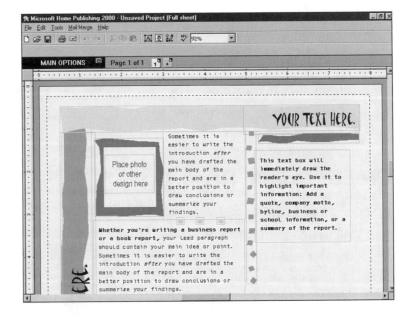

7. Replace the dummy text with your own text.

8. To paste text copied from Encarta Encyclopedia (or from a Web site), place the insertion point where you want to paste the text, and then pull down the Edit menu and select Paste.

9. To insert a picture into your text, click the Insert Something button on the Main Options pane, select Picture from Another Source, and then select My Computer. When the Select Picture File dialog box appears, navigate to the picture file you want to add, and then click Open.

When you're done, make sure to check your report for spelling (click the Check Spelling on the toolbar), and then save and print it—and you're ready for school!

Create Longer Reports with Microsoft Word

If your child is in an upper grade, he or she might need to create a more sophisticated report than is possible with Home Publishing. If this is the case, it's time to turn to Microsoft Word:

1. From the Works Task Launcher, select the Tasks tab.

2. From the Tasks list, select Research and Education.

3. Select School Reports (*not* Reports and Presentations—this option creates Home Publishing-based reports!), and then click Start.

4. When The Works School Reports Wizard appears, select from one of the six report templates (Book Report, Essay, Modern Report, Professional Report, Simple Report, or Term Paper), and then click Finish (see Figure 19.4).

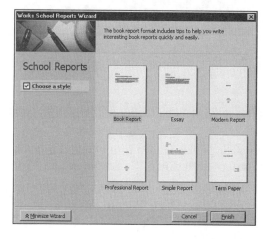

Figure 19.4

Use the Works School Reports Wizard to pick a template for your Word-based report.

Pick a Template

If you're writing a shorter report, I recommend the Simple Report template. If you're writing a longer, multiple-section report, I recommend the Term Paper template.

5. Word now launches and loads a dummy report based on the template you selected, as shown in Figure 19.5.

Figure 19.5

Edit and format the dummy report to create your own personalized report.

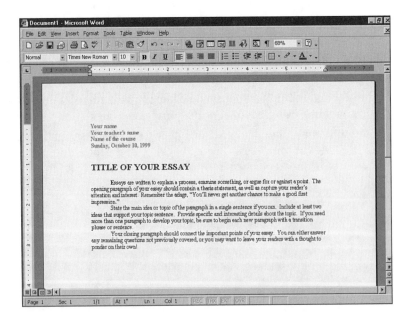

6. Replace the dummy text with your own text. (To insert pasted text from Encarta Encyclopedia—or any other source—pull down the Edit menu and select Paste.)

7. To add a footnote at the insertion point, pull down the Insert menu and select Footnote. When the Footnote and Endnote dialog box appears, check Footnote, check AutoNumber, and then click OK. This adds a footnote at the bottom of the current page, to which you add your footnote text.

8. To add a table of contents to your report, move your insertion point to where you want to add the TOC (normally right after your title page, and then pull down the Insert menu and select Index and Tables. When the Index and Tables dialog box appears, select the Table of Contents tab, make the appropriate selections, and click OK.

9. Add any other elements as necessary, and apply any personalized formatting to your liking.

Remember to run Word's spell checker and grammar checker, and then save and print your report. Because you can use any of the fancy formatting discussed back in Chapter 4, "Write Letters and Other Documents with Microsoft Word," you can create really sophisticated reports—complete with footnotes and tables of contents!

The Least You Need to Know

➤ Use Encarta Encyclopedia to begin the basic research for your report.

➤ Supplement your initial researching by using Internet Explorer to search the Internet.

➤ Use Microsoft Home Publishing to create simple but attractive reports for younger students.

➤ Use Microsoft Word to create sophisticated reports for older students.

Chapter 20

Create a Home Inventory

In This Chapter

➤ Learn how to create a database to track all your household belongings

➤ Find out how to print a report detailing your household inventory—and its current value

---

You have lots of stuff in your house—furniture, appliances, electronics, CDs, video-tapes, jewelry, collectibles, odds and ends, you name it. The question is—*can* you name it? In the event of a fire or robbery or other undesirable event, can you name everything you had in your house—and its value?

Taking inventory of your possessions is not only good protection against future loss, but it's also necessary to help you determine the proper level of insurance needed. (Most homeowners are underinsured for their homes' contents.) Taking stock of every-thing you own—and then keeping that inventory updated—should be an essential part of your home management.

Microsoft Works Database makes it easy to create a database of your possessions. Make the time to create and complete the initial database, and then take the time to period-ically update the information (when you buy new stuff), and you'll be covered in case of any emergency.

Safe Storage

For an extra level of security, make a copy of your Home Inventory database on a removable disk and store that copy offsite—someplace other than your home. In the event your home is destroyed (by fire or other circumstance), you'll still have a copy of your inventory, for insurance purposes.

Create an Inventory Database

Works Suite 2000 comes with a predesigned Home Inventory database. Readying this database to catalog your household belongings is as easy as clicking your mouse a few times.

1. From the Works Task Launcher, select the Tasks tab.

2. From the Tasks list, select Household Management.

3. Select Home Inventory Worksheets and click Start.

4. When the Works Home Inventory Wizard appears, select Home Inventory and click Finish.

Make a Backup

You can have Works automatically make a backup copy of this database by checking the Create Backup Copy option in the Save As dialog box.

5. The Home Inventory database now appears onscreen (see Figure 20.1). It contains fields for each item's description, category, location, manufacturer, model number, serial number, purchase date, purchase price, current value, warranty information, and repair history.

6. If you want to delete an existing field or add a new field, click the List View button to switch to the spreadsheet-like List view, shown in Figure 20.2. Then add or delete columns as necessary.

7. Before you start entering data, you should save the database by pulling down the File menu and selecting Save As. When the Save As dialog box appears, assign a filename and location, and then click Save.

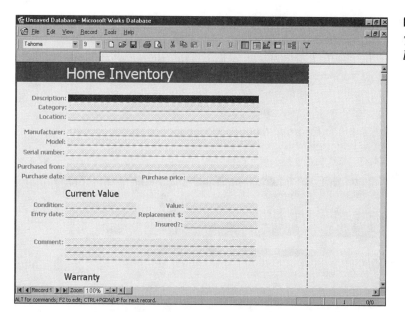

Figure 20.1

The Home Inventory database, ready for use.

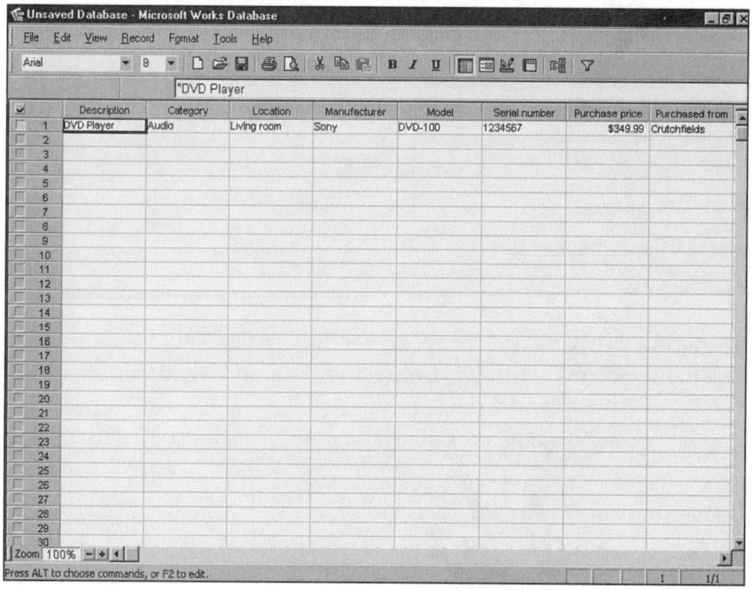

Figure 20.2

Switch to List view to edit the fields in your database.

Enter and Edit Information

Now that your database is created, it's time to fill it up with data. You do this one field at a time, one record at a time. Remember to create a separate record for each individual item in your inventory, and to fill in as many fields as possible. (You don't have to fill in all the fields if you're missing some information or the specific field doesn't apply to all your household items.)

1. Start with the first empty record displayed onscreen; make sure you're using Works Database in Form view (click the Form View button on the toolbar).

2. Position the cursor in the first field (Description), and use your keyboard to enter a description of your first item (see Figure 20.3). (The description could be as simple as "chair.")

3. Use the Tab key to move to the next field, and fill it in.

4. Continue using the Tab key to move from field to field; to move *up* a field, press Alt+Tab.

Figure 20.3

A database record, completely filled in.

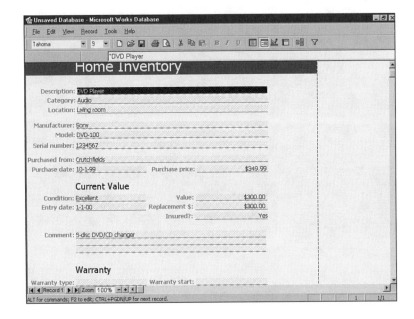

5. When you reach the end of this record, press either Tab or Ctrl+PgDn to advance to the next blank record—and start entering data all over again.

Don't Fill in Total Cost!

The very last field in the Home Inventory database is a *calculated* field—meaning that you don't enter data into it because it's calculated automatically from the values you enter into other fields.

You don't have to enter all your data in one sitting; you can always come back and add more records later. Just remember to save your work periodically by clicking the Save button on the Works Database toolbar.

Print a Home Inventory Report

Microsoft has predesigned a Home Inventory report to accompany the Home Inventory database. This report lists your inventory items, sorted by category, complete with their current value and replacement cost.

1. After you've completed entering data, click the Report View button.

2. The Report view shows the fields in the current report, as shown in Figure 20.4. The report can be printed as-is, or edited for your specific needs.

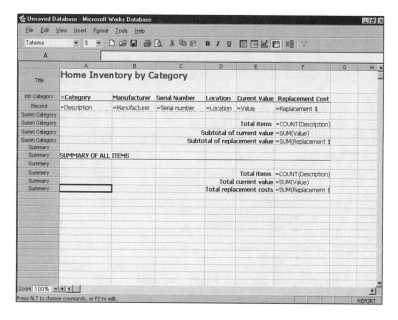

Figure 20.4

The makings of the Home Inventory report.

3. To change the way the report is sorted, grouped, or filtered, pull down the Format menu and select Report Settings. When the Report Settings dialog box appears, change the appropriate settings and click OK.

4. To preview your report before you print it (see Figure 20.5), click the Print Preview button on the toolbar. Click Cancel to close the Print Preview mode.

5. To print the report, make sure you're in Report view, pull down the File menu, and click Print. When the Print dialog box appears, make any configuration changes as necessary, and then click OK.

Figure 20.5

Previewing the Home Inventory report.

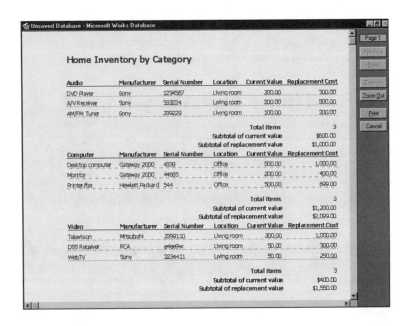

Store a copy of the Home Inventory report in your records, and put another copy in your safe deposit box or in the hands of a trusted friend.

Other Databases for Your Stuff

Works includes three other predesigned databases you can use to catalog your possessions, all accessible from the Works Home Inventory Wizard—Books, CDs and Tapes, and Videos.

The Least You Need to Know

➤ Use the Works Home Inventory Wizard to load a predesigned Home Inventory database.

➤ Complete one record in the database for each important item in your house.

➤ Print a copy of the Home Inventory report to have a record of your home's contents—and their current values.

Chapter 21

Create a Home Budget

In This Chapter

➤ Learn how to create a detailed budget of your income and expenses

➤ Discover how Money starts with your schedule of transactions—and then adds to that data with information you enter via the Budget Planner

➤ Find out how to view a forecast of your budget for the next 12 months

You make a good salary. You try to manage your inflow and outflow. Yet, somehow, at the end of the month you never seem to have any money left over.

Where does the money go?

The best way to manage your money is by creating a budget—and then sticking to it. With a well planned-out budget, you can plan for savings, vacations, and college tuition—and make sure you don't let any overspending throw you off your goals.

Microsoft Money 2000 includes a Budget Planner that leads you step-by-step through creating a budget. All you have to do is follow the onscreen instructions—and then stick to the budget you create!

Before You Budget

Money bases its budget on your predefined categories and scheduled transactions. If you haven't yet set up all your categories or scheduled all your inflows and out-flows, do it now, before you start into the budgeting process. See Chapter 9, "Manage Your Finances with Money," for more information.

Putting Together Your Budget

Money makes it easy to put together a household or personal budget. Each screen in the Budget Planner focuses on a particular budgeting task; complete all the screens to complete your budget.

1. From the Works Task Launcher, select the Tasks tab.
2. Select Money Management from the Tasks list.
3. Select Budget Status and click Start.

The Budget Planner now leads you step-by-step through nine screens of information.

Getting Started

The first screen in the Budget Planner provides an overview of the process. If you want to, click a link to watch a video about creating a budget.

When you're ready to start creating your budget, click the Next button in the top-right corner of the screen.

Income

Use the Income screen, shown in Figure 21.1, to answer the question, *Where does your income come from?*

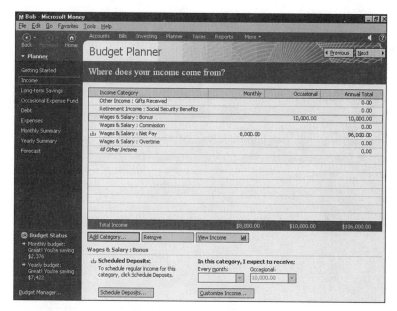

Figure 21.1

Enter all your income items on the Income screen.

Your scheduled deposits should automatically appear on this list. You can change or add to this information in the following ways:

➤ To edit a scheduled deposit, select the deposit and click the Edit Deposits button. When the Edit Deposits dialog box appears, modify the information for this particular scheduled transaction.

➤ To add a scheduled deposit, select the income category and click the Schedule Deposits button. When the Edit Deposits dialog box appears, click New Deposit and enter the appropriate information. Alternatively, you can enter a "gross" number for a particular category (without adding individual scheduled deposits) by filling in the In This Category I Expect To Receive fields at the bottom of the screen.

➤ To add a new income category, click the Add Category button and follow the step-by-step instructions in the Add Category to Budget Wizard.

➤ To remove an income category, select the category and click the Remove button.

➤ To view a graph of your income, click the View Income button.

Click Next to proceed to the next screen.

Long-Term Savings

Use the Long-term Savings screen, shown in Figure 21.2, to answer the question, *"What do you want to put into long-term savings?"*

Figure 21.2

Enter your savings goals on the Long-term Savings screen.

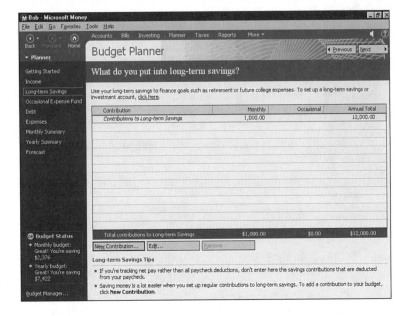

For most people, this is a simple screen. Just select the Contributions to Long-term Savings item and click the Edit button. When the Customize Contribution dialog box appears, enter the target amount you want to save, either on a monthly or an occasional basis.

Click Next to proceed to the next screen.

Occasional Expense Fund

Use the Occasional Expense Fund screen, shown in Figure 21.3, to answer the question, *"What do you set aside for occasional expenses?"*

Think of this screen as an emergency or rainy-day fund. These are moneys to be used for non-regular expenses, such as car repairs or vacations.

You can enter all your occasional expenses under the generic Contributions to Occasional Expense Fund item (click Edit to change the contribution amount), or create separate items by clicking the New Contribution button and completing the Create New Scheduled Transaction Wizard.

Click Next to proceed to the next screen.

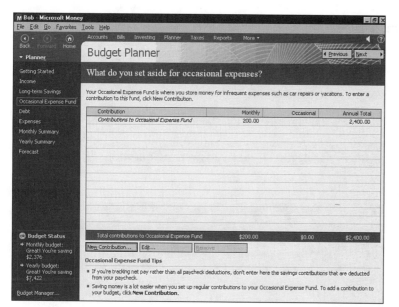

Figure 21.3

Enter the amount you want to save for nonrecurring expenses on the Occasional Expense Fund screen.

Debt

Use the Debt screen, shown in Figure 21.4, to review your debt and loans.

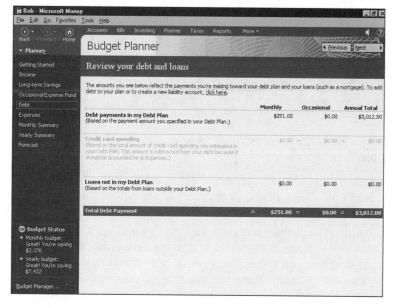

Figure 21.4

Enter the amount you spend on credit cards, loans, and other debt payments on the Debt screen.

This screen reflects the information you entered in the Debt Reduction Planner. If you haven't yet filled out the Debt Reduction Planner, click the Debt Reduction Planner link. Follow the onscreen instructions there to move debt accounts into your debt plan or to add new accounts to your debt plan.

Click Next to proceed to the next screen.

Expenses

Use the Expenses screen, shown in Figure 21.5, to answer the question, *"How do you spend your money?"*

Figure 21.5

Enter or edit your recurring expense transactions on the Expenses screen.

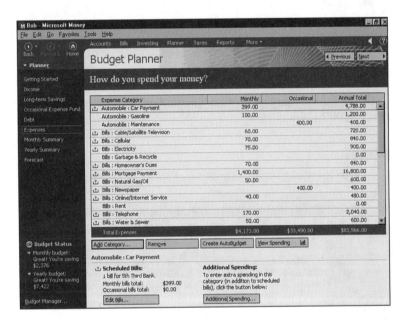

All your scheduled expenses should automatically appear on this list. You can change or add to this information in the following ways:

➤ To edit a scheduled transaction, select the transaction and click the Edit Bills button. When the Edit Bills dialog box appears, modify the information for this particular scheduled transaction.

➤ To add a scheduled transaction, select the income category and click the Schedule Bills button. When the Edit Bills dialog box appears, click New Bill and enter the appropriate information. Alternatively, you can enter a "gross" number for a particular category (without adding individual scheduled deposits) by filling in the For This Category I Expect To Spend fields at the bottom of the screen.

➤ To add a new expense category, click the Add Category button and follow the step-by-step instructions in the Add Category to Budget Wizard.

➤ To add a new expense category *based on your past spending*, click the Create AutoBudget button. Money will analyze your past expenditures and recommend new categories and budgets accordingly.

➤ To remove an expense category, select the category and click the Remove button.

➤ To view a graph of your spending, click the View Spending button.

Click Next to proceed to the next screen.

Monthly Summary

Use the Monthly Summary screen to review your income and expenses on a monthly basis. This screen, shown in Figure 21.6, displays:

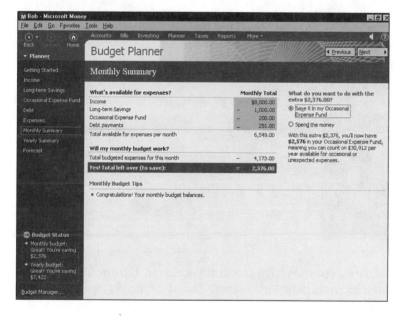

Figure 21.6

Review your monthly income and expenses on the Monthly Summary screen.

➤ **What's Available for Expenses?** This section takes your income and sub-tracts long-term savings, your occasional expense fund payment, and your debt-reduction payments; what's left over can be used to pay your monthly expenses.

➤ **Will My Monthly Budget Work?** This section takes the leftover from the first section and subtracts your scheduled monthly expenses. If the number is positive, you earn more than you spend each month—congratulations!

➤ **What do you want to do with the extra?** Assuming you have some extra left over, you can choose to save it in your Occasional Expense Fund (recom-mended if you scheduled a lot of non-time-specific occasional expenses) or you can choose to spend it. Check the appropriate option.

This screen does *not* display any occasional expenses you entered that were not assigned to a specific month. (These non-time-specific occasional expenses will factor into the Yearly Summary, shown on the next screen.)

Click Next to proceed to the Yearly Summary.

Yearly Summary

This is the big one—where you find out if your budget really works or not. This screen, shown in Figure 21.7, displays:

Figure 21.7

Review your total yearly budget on the Yearly Summary screen.

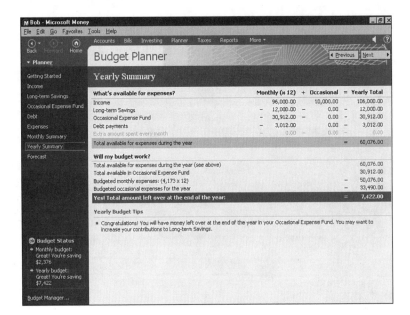

➤ **What's available for expenses?** This section takes your income and subtracts long-term savings, your occasional expense fund payment, and your debt-reduction payments, for both monthly and occasional expenses.

➤ **Will my budget work?** This section takes the leftover from the first section and adds it to the amount in your Occasional Expense Fund, and then subtracts your scheduled monthly expenses and your budgeted occasional expenses. If the balance is positive, you've earned more than you spent; if the balance is negative, you've overspent your budget—which means you should go back and *rebudget* your expenses!

Click Next to proceed to the next screen.

Forecast

This final screen shows a graph of your forecasted income and expenses per month for the next 12 months, as shown in Figure 21.8. Monitor this graph going forward to track your progress against your budget.

Reports and Warnings

If you want to include this forecast in your monthly report, check the Include Forecast in the Monthly Report option; if you want to be warned when your forecast goes negative, check the Warn me when my forecast dips below zero option.

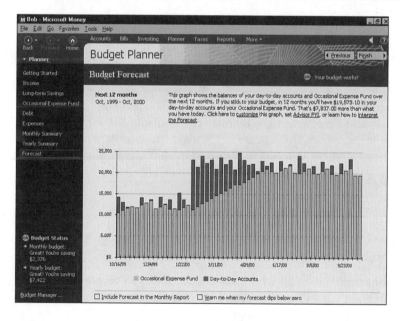

Figure 21.8

View your forecasted income and expenses for the next 12 months.

Save, View, and Update Your Budget

At any time in the process you can save the budget you've created. Just click the Budget Manager link at the bottom-left corner of the screen to display the Budget Manager dialog box. Click the Save Current Budget button to display the Save Current Budget dialog box, enter a name for your budget, and click OK.

To view a report of your saved budget, click the Budget Manager link and when the Budget Manager dialog box appears, select your saved budget and click the View Budget Report button. This displays the My Budget report, shown in Figure 21.9, with all your income and expense items displayed by category. To print this report, pull down the File menu and select Print.

Figure 21.9

View or print your personal My Budget report.

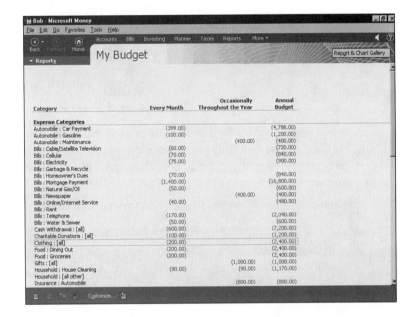

To update your budget at any time, select the Planner tab to display Money's Plan Your Finances page. From here, click the Update My Budget link and you'll be taken to the Budget Planner—from where you can modify any budget item accordingly.

The Least You Need to Know

➤ Microsoft Money's Budget Planner leads you step-by-step through the budget creation process.

➤ The Budget Planner starts with all scheduled transactions you've previously entered; you can then expand on this data by scheduling new transactions or entering "gross" category inflow or outflow.

➤ Save your budget by clicking the Budget Manager link and selecting Save Current Budget.

Chapter 22

Create Party Invitations and Favors

In This Chapter

➤ Learn how to plan for all the activities related to your upcoming party

➤ Discover how to create all the party items you need—including invitations, napkin holders, and place cards—using a similar theme and deign

➤ Find out how to track the gifts you receive—so you can easily send out thank you notes

---

If you're planning a party, you can use the applications in Works Suite 2000 to add pizzazz from start to finish. You can create party invitations, party favors, and all the other elements to make a party great—and make sure all your items utilize a common theme! You can even use Microsoft Word to keep track of all the pieces and parts you have to manage!

Plan Your Party in Advance

Before you start making all your party pieces, it helps to know *what* you have to make—and when you have to have them done! The easiest way to manage your party elements is to use Microsoft Word's Party Planner.

1. From the Works Task Launcher, select the Tasks tab.
2. Select Cards & Crafts from the Tasks list.
3. Select Party Planner, and then click Start.
4. When the Works Party Planner Wizard appears, select Event Planner and click Finish.

5. Word now launches and loads a special Party Planner document, shown in Figure 22.1. Print out this document for your continuing use.

Figure 22.1

Use the Party Planner document to help you plan and manage your party-related activities.

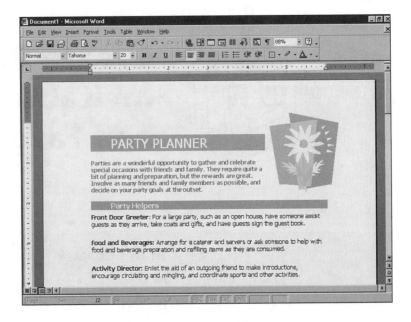

Read and follow the tips and advice presented in the Party Planner to help you better plan all aspects of your upcoming party—then use the accompanying To Do Checklist to manage all your party activities!

Create Everything You Need with a Party Set

Microsoft Home Publishing includes a group of projects called *party sets* that you can use to create pretty much everything you need for your party. Party sets let you make invitations, place cards, party hats, banners, and more—all with a common theme and design.

1. From the Works Task Launcher, select the Tasks tab.
2. Select Cards & Crafts from the Tasks list.
3. Select Party Sets, and then click Start.
4. Home Publishing now launches with a list of occasions (Birthdays, Holidays, General Entertaining, and Life Events). Click the button appropriate to your upcoming party.
5. Now you'll see a list of projects for this occasion, as shown in Figure 22.2. Before you make a selection, choose one of the themes in the Themes list.

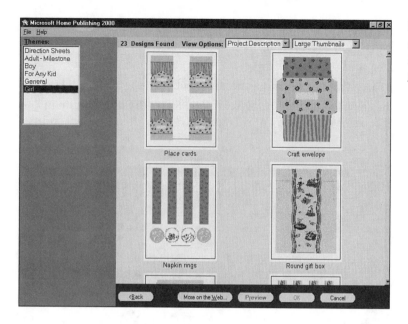

Figure 22.2

Choose from Home Publishing's selection of predesigned party projects.

6. You now see a more-focused list of party-related projects. One-by-one, open the projects you want to complete, and then edit, save, and print those projects.

If you selected a girl's birthday as your occasion and theme, you'll have the following projects to choose from:

➤ Craft envelopes

➤ Invitation cards

➤ Labels

➤ Napkin rings

➤ Party hats

➤ Place cards

➤ Round gift boxes

➤ Thank you cards

You'll have to edit each project separately with the details for your particular party, but if you choose from a "family" of projects, you'll be able to maintain a similar look and feel for all your party items.

After the Party—Tally Up the Loot!

If you received a lot of gifts at your party, you probably want to keep track of who gave what, so you can follow-up with thank you notes. Microsoft Word includes a special *gift log* to help you with this task.

1. From the Works Task Launcher, select the Tasks tab.

2. Select Cards & Crafts from the Tasks list.

3. Select Party Planner, and then click Start.

4. When the Works Party Planner Wizard appears, select Gift Log and click Finish.

5. Word now launches and loads the gift log template. Enter the appropriate information for each gift received, as shown in Figure 22.3, and then save and print the log.

Figure 22.3

Use Word's Gift Log to track all the gifts you receive—and then send out your thank you notes!

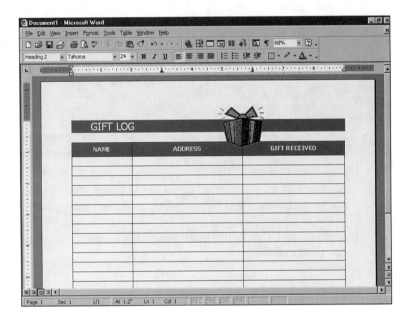

After you've logged all the gifts you received, it's only polite to send thank you notes to all your guests. Use the thank you cards you created in your Home Publishing party set to put the finishing touches on a perfectly planned party!

The Least You Need to Know

➤ Print and use Word's Party Planner and To Do List to pre-plan all your party-related activities.

➤ Use Home Publishing's party sets to create invitations, party hats, place cards, napkin rings, and thank you cards.

➤ Track the gifts you receive with Word's predesigned Gift Log.

Chapter 23

Create Personalized Holiday Cards

In This Chapter

➤ Learn how to turn a predesigned holiday card into a personalized family greeting

➤ Discover how to use Picture It! Express and Home Publishing together to accomplish this task

---

Tired of the same old Christmas and holiday cards? Now you can make your own personalized holiday cards—complete with pictures of your family!

Touch Up Your Photos in Picture It! Express

Before you create your holiday card, you may want to do a little touch up on your family photo. For this, you want to use Picture It! Express.

We'll assume you already have your photograph in digital format, as a computer file in a common graphics format (.JPG, .TIF, .GIF, .PCX, or a similar file format), stored on your hard disk. Now you can load your photo into Picture It! Express, touch it up, and even add some simple special effects!

1. From the Works Task Launcher, select the Programs tab.
2. Select Picture It! Express from the Programs list.
3. Click Start Picture It! Express.
4. When Picture It! Express launches, select the Workbench tab.
5. Click the Get Picture link and select Open Pictures.

6. When the Open Pictures pane appears, navigate to the folder holding your picture file, and then select the file and click Open. The picture will appear, as shown in Figure 23.1.

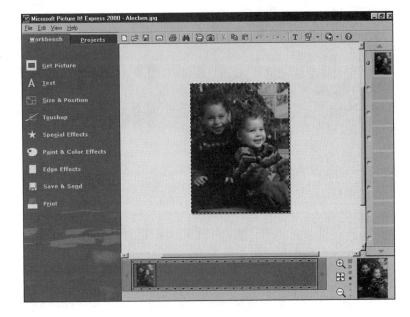

7. Your picture is now loaded into the Workbench. If you need to touch up any picture defects—such as red eye or scratches—click the Touchup link and select the necessary action. Follow the onscreen instructions to perform the selected operation.

8. If you need to crop your photo—to tighten the focus, or eliminate a disliked relative from the shot—click the Size & Position link, and select Crop. When the Crop panel appears, select a crop shape, size the crop area, and click Done.

9. For effect, you might want to soften the edges of your picture. If so, click the Edge Effects link and select Soft Edges; when the Soft Edges panel appears, move the slider to the right as appropriate, and then click Done. You'll see the result as shown in Figure 23.2.

10. When you're finished touching up and modifying your picture, pull down the File menu and select Save As. Assign your picture a name and location, and click Save.

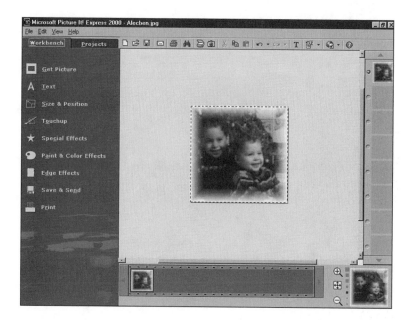

Figure 23.2

Your picture after cropping and edge softening.

Add Your Family Photo to a Holiday Card

Now that your picture is cleaned up and cropped, it's time to add it to your greeting card—and then customize your card with your own personal message.

1. From the Works Task Launcher, select the Tasks tab.

2. Select Cards & Crafts from the Tasks list.

3. Select Cards and Invitations, Fancy (*not* Card, Photo—this option reopens Picture It! Express, which has a *very* limited selection of predesigned cards!) and click Start.

4. When Home Publishing launches, select the occasion for your card. (For this example, select Christmas.)

5. Select the card you want (focus more on the design and message, because you'll be replacing the existing picture with your picture) and click OK.

6. When the card loads in the workspace, as shown in Figure 23.3, select the card's main graphics and then click the Delete button in the Picture Options panel.

7. In the main options panel, click Add Something and select Picture From Another Source. Then select My Computer.

8. When the Select Picture File dialog box appears, select the picture you saved in Picture It! Express.

9. After your picture is added to your card, as shown in Figure 23.4, reposition and resize it as necessary.

Figure 23.3

The Home Publishing card you selected—now select the graphic and delete it!

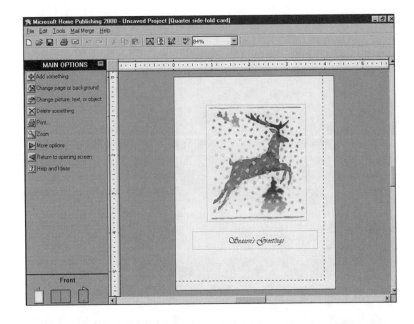

Figure 23.4

The Home Publishing card with your picture added—the perfect personalized greeting!

10. Make any other changes to the card's text or design as necessary.

You now have a perfect personalized Christmas card! Remember to save your card, and then fire up your printer and get ready to print!

The Least You Need to Know

➤ Use Picture It! Express to touch up and modify your family's photo.

➤ Pick one of Home Publishing's predesigned holiday cards.

➤ Replace the existing graphic with your family photo.

Chapter 24

Create Sports Schedules and Statistics

In This Chapter

➤ Discover the many spreadsheets you can use to track your team's roster, schedule, and performance

➤ Learn about the spreadsheets you can use to track your favorite pro sports teams and players—or use to manage your fantasy sports teams

If you have kids, chances are they play sports. In fact, they probably play more than one sport—and if you have more than one child, the challenge of tracking schedules and team performance can quickly become overwhelming.

Fortunately, you can use the predesigned templates in Works Spreadsheet to simplify the tracking of any sports team. Just click a few buttons, enter some key data—and you'll look like a statistical and logistical wizard!

Tracking Your Kids' Sports

Works Spreadsheet features a Works Sports Team Records Wizard that lets you create six different spreadsheets to track your kids' sports. Here's how you open one of the six spreadsheet templates:

1. From the Works Task Launcher, select the Tasks tab.
2. Select Sports & Fitness from the Tasks list.
3. Select Sports Team Records and click Start.
4. When the Works Sports Team Records Wizard appears, select one of the six templates, as shown in Figure 24.1, and click Finish.

Figure 24.1

Use the Works Sports Team Records Wizard to pick a template to track your children's sports activities.

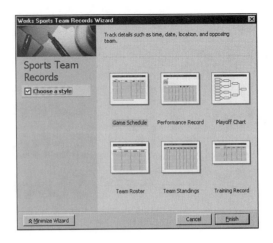

Table 24.1 details the six different templates available.

Table 24.1 Sports Team Records Templates

Template	Description
Game Schedule	Use to create a master schedule of your team's games
Performance Record	Use to chart performance in various track and field events
Playoff Chart	Use to track your league's playoff pairings, as shown in Figure 24.2
Team Roster	Use to create a master list of your team's players, parents, and phone numbers
Team Standings	Use to track team's win/loss records and league standings
Training Record	Use to track training milestones

You can edit any of these templates to insert your team's name, the league name, and information specific to your situation. Just modify any existing text, or add or delete columns as necessary. When you're done editing, save and print the spreadsheet—so you can distribute copies to the entire team!

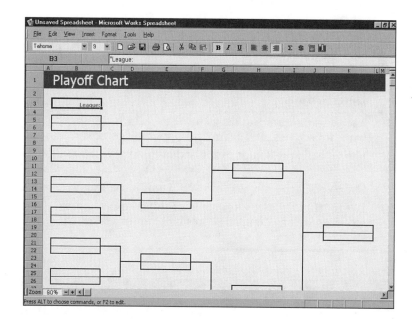

Figure 24.2

Fill in the boxes in the Playoff Chart spreadsheet to display your league's playoff pairings—and track your team's march to the championships!

Track the Pros

If you want to track the performance of professional teams or players—or teams or players in a fantasy league—use the templates presented in the Works Sports Tracking Wizard. Here's how you open one of these four templates:

1. From the Works Task Launcher, select the Tasks tab.
2. Select Sports & Fitness from the Tasks list.
3. Select Sports Tracking and click Start.
4. When the Works Sports Tracking Wizard appears, select one of the four templates, as shown in Figure 24.3, and click Finish.

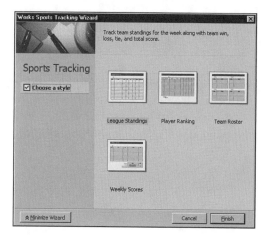

Figure 24.3

Use the Works Sports Tracking Wizard to pick a template to track pro and fantasy sports teams and players.

Table 24.2 details the four different templates available.

Table 24.2   Sports Team Records Templates

Template	Description
League Standings	Use to track team standings for the week (including wins, losses, ties, and team and opponents scores)
Player Ranking and team	Use to track the scores of individual players by owner
Team Roster	Use to track the players for each team in the league
Weekly Scores	Use to display both summaries of this week's team scores as well as detailed scores by team or player, as shown in Figure 24.4

Figure 24.4

Track each team in your league on a weekly basis with the Weekly Scores spreadsheet.

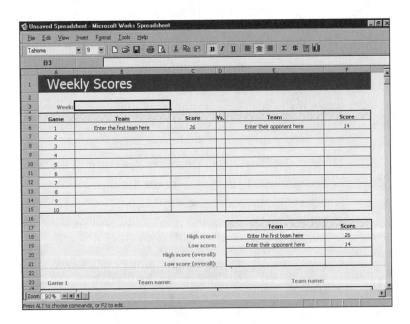

As with any Works spreadsheet, you can edit the rows, columns, and individual cells to better match the needs of your particular league. Remember to save each spreadsheet when you're done, and then print copies for all your friends!

286

The Least You Need to Know

➤ Works Spreadsheet offers a variety of spreadsheet templates for tracking amateur, fantasy, and professional team rosters and performances.

➤ Use the Sports Team Records Wizard to track your kids' sports, or the Sports Tracking Wizard to track pro and fantasy sports.

➤ Pick a template from one of the wizards, enter your specific team information, and then save and print the spreadsheet to circulate to others.

The Complete Idiot's Glossary of Terms

address   The pointer to a particular Web page (also known as a *URL*). Also the specific identifier for a person's email inbox.

Address Book   The Microsoft application that stores names, addresses, email addresses, and other contact information. Interfaces with Outlook Express and other Microsoft applications; included as part of Works Suite 2000.

application   Another word for a computer software program.

Boolean logic or **Boolean algebra** or **Boolean query** or **Boolean search**   A system of operators (AND, OR, NOT, NEAR, and so on) that work with words in much the same way that arithmetic operators (addition, subtraction, and so on) work with numbers.

browser   A software program, such as Microsoft Internet Explorer or Netscape Navigator, that lets a computer or other device access HTML pages on the World Wide Web. Microsoft's Internet Explorer is the Web browser included with Works Suite 2000.

button   A raised object in a dialog box or on a toolbar that can be "pressed" (by clicking it with a mouse) to perform certain operations.

byte   A measurement of space (on-disk or in memory); one byte is pretty much equal to one character. One thousand bytes is called a *kilobyte* (KB), one million bytes is called a *megabyte* (MB), and one thousand megabytes is called a *gigabyte* (GB).

CD-ROM   Compact disc–read-only memory. CD-ROM discs contain large volumes of information and are read by lasers; most software programs (including Works Suite 2000) come on CD-ROM discs.

chat   Text-based real-time Internet communication, typically consisting of short one-line messages back and forth between two or more users. Users gather to "talk" in chat rooms or channels.

click   The process of selecting an item onscreen; what you do with a mouse button.

copy   To place data in a different location, without deleting the original data.

cursor   The highlighted area or pointer that tracks with the movement of your mouse or arrow keys onscreen.

cut   To erase data from a location while still keeping it in Windows memory (called the Clipboard) for pasting into a different location.

database   A computer program that stores and manipulates any type of data in *records* composed of multiple *fields*.

delete   Erase. Kill. Zap. Get rid of.

desktop   The entire screen area on which you display all of your computer work. The Windows desktop can contain icons, a taskbar, menus, and individual application windows.

dialog box   An onscreen window that either displays a message or asks for user input.

directory   (1) An index for files you store on your disk. Also known as a *folder*. (2) A search site that collects and indexes Web pages manually, either by user submission or editorial selection. Yahoo! is the Web's most popular directory.

disk   A device that stores data in magnetic format.

diskette   A portable or removable disk.

document   A piece of information in a computer file.

domain   The name of a site on the Internet. Domains are hierarchical, and lower-level domains often refer to particular Web sites within a top-level domain. Examples of domains are .com, .edu, .gov, and .org.

DOS   The pre-Windows operating system for IBM-compatible computers. Probably not something you need to worry about these days.

double-click   Clicking a mouse button twice in rapid succession.

download   The process of receiving information or data from a server on the Internet.

drag   The movement of a file or object by clicking it with the mouse and then moving it to a new location while holding down the mouse button.

drop   The insertion of a file or object into a new location after dragging, by releasing the mouse button.

DVD   A new optical storage medium, similar to CD-ROM but with much higher storage capacity. (The acronym DVD actually doesn't stand for anything anymore; at one time it stood for Digital Versatile Disk, and at another Digital Video Disk.)

email   Electronic mail, a means of corresponding to other computer users over the Internet through digital messages.

Encarta Encyclopedia   Microsoft's CD-based multimedia encyclopedia, included as part of Works Suite 2000.

Expedia Streets & Trips   Microsoft's mapping and trip routing software, included as part of Works Suite 2000.

field   An area within a database record where specific data is stored.

file   A collection of data, with its own unique name and location; files can be documents or executable programs.

file type   A specific type of file, associated with a specific application.

filename   The formal name assigned to a file; in Windows 95 and Windows 98 a filename can be up to 256 characters long.

floppy disk   Another term for *diskette*.

folder   A way to group files on a disk; each folder can contain multiple files or other folders (called subfolders).

frames   An HTML technique for combining two or more separate HTML documents within a single Web page.

FTP   File Transfer Protocol, an older, non–Web-based convention that enables files to be downloaded from other computers on the Internet.

function key   One of the special keys labeled F1 to F12, located at the top of your computer keyboard. In certain programs (such as Microsoft Word), function keys are preprogrammed to execute a specific operation when pressed.

graphical user interface   The look and feel of an operating system that uses graphical elements instead of character-based elements. Also known as the GUI (pronounced "gooey").

graphics   Picture files. (Pictures, photographs, and clip art are all commonly referred to as graphics.)

hard disk   A piece of hardware that stores large amounts of data for future access.

hardware   A piece of electronic equipment that you can actually touch. Your personal computer and all its peripherals are hardware; the operations of your PC are controlled by *software* (which you *can't* touch).

home page   The initial page screen of a Web site.

Home Publishing   Microsoft's software for creating projects and crafts, included as part of Works Suite 2000.

host   An Internet server that houses a Web site.

hosting service   An Internet site created to host personal Web pages from Internet users. Geocities, Tripod, and Acme City all offer hosting services, as do many ISPs (including America Online).

hover   In Windows 98, the act of selecting an item by placing your cursor over an icon *without clicking*.

HTML   HyperText Markup Language, the scripting language used to create Web pages.

hyperlink   Special text or graphics on a Web page that, when clicked, automatically transfers the user to another Web page.

icon   A graphical representation of an object onscreen. Typically, you *click* an icon to initiate a function.

idiot   Something you're not—even though you may feel like it when confronted by frustrating computer programs!

Inbox   The virtual container where unread email is stored.

insertion point   The point in a document where new text will be added, sometimes shown as a blinking cursor.

install   How you get software from its box to your hard disk.

instant messaging   Text-based real-time one-on-one communication over the Internet. Not to be confused with *chat*, which can accommodate multiple users, instant messaging (IM) typically is limited to just two users.

Internet   The global "network of networks" that connects millions of computers and other devices around the world. The World Wide Web and Usenet are both parts of the Internet.

Internet Explorer   Microsoft's PC-based Web browser software, included as part of Works Suite 2000.

Internet service provider (ISP)   A company that connects individual users (calling in via traditional phone lines) to the Internet. Some Internet service providers—such as America Online—also provide unique content to their subscribers.

keyword   A word which forms all or part of a search engine query.

kilobyte   One thousand bytes, more or less. (Actually, it's 1,024 bytes). Also known as KB, as in 640KB.

launch   To start a program.

link   See *hyperlink*.

megabyte   Approximately one million bytes. Also known as MB.

menu   A selection of items or services. Most applications in Works Suite 2000 organize their commands in a series of pull-down menus on a central menu bar.

microprocessor   The chip inside your system unit that processes all the operations your computer can do.

Microsoft   The company that developed and publishes the Windows operating system and hundreds of other bestselling programs, including Works Suite 2000.

modem   Modulator-demodulator. A hardware device that enables transmission of digital data from one computer to another over common telephone lines via modulating and demodulating.

modifier   A symbol that causes a search engine to do something special with the word directly following the symbol. There are three modifiers used almost universally in the search engine community: +, -, and " ".

Money   Microsoft's personal finance management program. Money 2000 Standard Edition is included as part of Works Suite 2000.

mouse   The hand-held device with a rollerball and buttons you use to navigate through Windows and other graphical applications.

move   To place data in a different location, and delete it from its original location.

MSN   The Microsoft Network, a collection of Microsoft topic-specific Web sites, such as Expedia (travel), MoneyCentral (personal finance), and CarPoint (automobiles).

multimedia   The combination, usually on a computer, of interactive text, graphics, audio, and video.

My Computer   The chief file management utility in Windows, with its own shortcut on the desktop.

network   Two or more computers connected together. The Internet is the largest network in the world.

newsgroup   A special-interest discussion group, hosted on Usenet.

operating system   The core system software that lets you (and your software programs) communicate with your hardware.

Outbox   The virtual container where newly created email is stored until it is sent over the Internet.

Outlook Express   Microsoft's email and newsreader program, included as part of Works Suite 2000.

pane   A distinct part of a window.

paste   To place data cut or copied from another location into a new location.

path   The collection of folders and subfolders (listed in order of hierarchy) that hold a particular file.

personal computer   A multi-function hardware unit that includes a hard disk, memory chips, microprocessor chip, and monitor. Personal computers perform tasks when enabled by *software* entered into memory.

Picture It!   Microsoft's picture and photo editing program. A limited version of this program (Picture It! Express) is included as part of Works Suite 2000.

pop-up menu   The context-sensitive menu that appears when you right-click an object.

printer   The piece of computer hardware that lets you create hard copy printouts of your documents.

pull-down list   A button with a down arrow that, when clicked, displays a list of further options or items.

query   A word, phrase, or group of words, possibly combined with other syntax or operators, used to initiate a search with a search engine or directory.

record   An individual entry in a database; each record can be composed of multiple fields.

Recycle Bin   The "trash can" on the Windows desktop that temporarily holds deleted files.

resolution   The size of the images on a screen; how the quality of screen displays is measured.

right-click   The act of hovering over an item and then clicking your right-mouse button; this often displays a pop-up menu of commands related to the object selected.

root directory   The main directory or folder on a disk.

search   To look for information in an orderly fashion.

Search box   The text box on a search site where you enter your search query.

search engine   A Web server that indexes Web pages, and then makes the index available for user searching. Search engines differ from directories in that the indexes are generated using *spiders,* where directories are assembled manually. Search engine indexes typically include many more Web pages than are found in directories.

search site   Generic term for a Web site that offers either a search engine or directory (or both).

search term   See *query.*

server   A central computer that responds to requests for information from one or more client computers. On the Internet, all Web pages are stored on servers.

setup   How you configure your system (or individual software or hardware).

shortcut   (1) A combination of two keys on your keyboard that, when pressed simultaneously, execute a specific function. (2) An icon on the desktop used to represent an application; click a shortcut to launch an application, or right-click to view and modify its properties.

site   A unified collection of Web pages on the Internet.

snail mail   Traditional U.S. Postal Service (USPS) mail.

software   A digital program that instructs a piece of hardware to perform a specific task.

spam   Email or newsgroup messages that are unsolicited, unwanted, and generally irrelevant.

spamming   The act of sending large numbers of unsolicited email messages.

spreadsheet   A file that stores text and numerical data in rows and columns, and enables algebraic calculations to be performed within and between individual cells.

Start menu   The menu used to start most Windows programs and utilities; visible when the Start button is clicked.

tab   The top of a "page" in a dialog box; many dialog boxes display multiple sets of data on a series of tabs.

table   A collection of data organized into rows and columns.

Task Launcher   The "mission control" screen for launching all programs included in Works Suite 2000.

taskbar   The bar at the bottom of the screen (normally) in Windows; the Start button and temporary buttons for active applications appear on the taskbar.

template   A predesigned set of styles and elements used to create new documents in Microsoft Word and other similar programs.

toolbar   A menu bar, containing icons representing programs or commands, that can be "docked" to the Windows taskbar.

tray   The area of the Windows taskbar that holds icons for "background" utilities, such as the Windows clock.

uninstall   To delete a software application—and all its associated files, drivers, and associations—from a computer system.

upgrade   To add a new or improved peripheral or part to your system hardware. Also to install a newer version of an existing piece of software.

upload   The act of copying a file from a personal computer to a Web site or Internet server.

URL   Uniform Resource Locator; the address of a Web page.

Usenet   A subset of the Internet that contains topic-specific *newsgroups*.

virus   A bad, nasty, evil computer program that can cause untold damage to your data.

Web   See *World Wide Web*.

Web browser   See *browser*.

wildcard   A character that substitutes for one or more characters within a query. For example, the * wildcard typically substitutes for any combination of characters.

Windows   The generic name for all versions of Microsoft's graphical operating system.

Windows 95   The version of Microsoft's Windows operating that was released in 1995.

Windows 98   The latest version of Microsoft's Windows operating system, released in 1998.

Windows 2000   The new name for Microsoft's *Windows NT* operating system; where Windows 95/98 is designed for individual consumer PCs, Windows 2000 is designed for networked PCs in a corporate environment.

Windows Explorer   The dual-paned file management utility in Windows; Windows Explorer is not to be confused with the *Internet Explorer* Web browser.

Windows NT   An operating system from Microsoft designed for networked computers in a corporate environment; the new version of Windows NT is called *Windows 2000*.

wizard   An interactive utility that leads users step-by-step through a specific procedure.

World Wide Web   A subset of the Internet that contains HTML pages.

Word   Microsoft's premiere word processor, included as part of Works Suite 2000.

Works   Microsoft's "combination" program that includes a spreadsheet, database, and calendar program.

Works Calendar   The scheduling component of the Microsoft Works program.

Works Database   The database component of the Microsoft Works program.

Works Spreadsheet   The spreadsheet component of the Microsoft Works program.

Works Suite   A collection of Microsoft software accessed through a single Task Launcher. The latest version of the program is Works Suite 2000, and it includes Microsoft Works 2000 (including Works Spreadsheet, Works Database, and Works Calendar), Microsoft Word 2000, Microsoft Money 2000 Standard Edition, Microsoft Home Publishing 2000, Microsoft Picture It! Express 2000, Microsoft Expedia Streets & Trips 2000, Address Book, Internet Explorer 5, Outlook Express 5, and Microsoft Encarta Encyclopedia 2000.

Index

C

301

G

Y-Z